ACROSS MANY MOUNTAINS

MOUNTAINS

Three Daughters of Tibet

Yangzom Brauen

Across Many Mountains

Three Daughters of Tibet

Translated from German by
Katy Derbyshire

Harvill *Secker*

LONDON

Published by Harvill Secker 2011

First published in Germany as *Eisenvogel* by Wilhelm Heyne Verlag in 2009

2 4 6 8 10 9 7 5 3 1

First published in Great Britain in 2011 by
HARVILL SECKER
Random House
20 Vauxhall Bridge Road
London SW1V 2SA

www.rbooks.co.uk

Addresses for companies within The Random House Group Limited can be found at:
www.randomhouse.co.uk/offices.htm

The Random House Group Limited Reg. No. 954009

A CIP catalogue record for this book is available from the British Library

ISBN 9781846553448 (hardback)

ISBN 9781846553455 (trade paperback)

The publisher would like to thank the Brauen family for the use of their photographic archive.
The photograph on page 8 of the picture section is © Tashi Brauen. We are grateful to
Hansjörg Sahli for use of the photograph of Martin Brauen with the Dalai Lama

The Random House Group Limited supports The Forest Stewardship Council (FSC),
the leading international forest certification organisation. All our titles that are printed
on Greenpeace approved FSC certified paper carry the FSC logo. Our paper procurement
policy can be found at www.rbooks.co.uk/environment

Mixed Sources
Product group from well-managed
forests and other controlled sources
www.fsc.org Cert no. TT-COC-2139
© 1996 Forest Stewardship Council

FSC

Typeset in Quadraat by Palimpsest Book Production Limited,
Falkirk, Stirlingshire
Printed and bound in Great Britain by
Clays Ltd, St Ives PLC

For my *pala*, who since his youth has been advocating freedom for the Tibetan people and the preservation of Tibetan culture.

The names of some individuals and towns have been changed to protect those still living in Tibet.

Contents

Prologue

It is late autumn and the wind whistles across the dry, rocky fields and meadows. As I step out of the house, a fierce gust pushes me aside, so strong that I have to tilt my body into its force. Mola stands with her legs planted wide, buttressing herself against the gale. Mola means grandmother in Tibetan. My grandmother is a ninety-one-year-old Buddhist nun. In the tradition of all Buddhist nuns, her hair, now snow-white, is cropped close to her scalp, and she wears only red, orange and yellow. Her floor-length Tibetan chupa billows out like a sail, and she has to concentrate to keep her balance. My grandmother wants to perform kora. For Tibetans, kora means walking around a sacred place absorbed in prayer, a kind of pilgrimage that can encompass hundreds of miles or only a few yards.

There is no Buddhist shrine here on the Greek island of Paros, so Mola has brought her own sacred artefacts with her: a photo of the Dalai Lama, a picture of her guru Dudjom Rinpoche and one of Buddha, all in gold frames, which she has set up in a small niche in the living room of the ancient farmhouse where we are staying. She has laid a few incense sticks in front of them to create an impromptu altar. For Mola, this has become the most sacred place on the island. To perform kora, she must walk once around the house clockwise. But today the wind gets the better of her and she has to move inside.

My parents, my brother, Mola and I have all met here for a short family holiday. Life has scattered us to Berne, Zurich, Los Angeles, New York and Berlin. If Tibet had remained Tibet, we would all be together in Pang, a remote mountain village in the south-east of the country, where Mola, along with my grandfather, a Buddhist monk, lived in a monastery. But my grandparents fled Tibet in the winter of 1959 when Chinese soldiers were destroying monastery after monastery, looting their treasures, leaving only rubble. Fifty years on, the country still suffers under the Chinese occupation. Every member of my family feels the pain of this.

Later in the day, when the wind has calmed and the bright red sun is sinking, Mola sits in front of her farmhouse altar and begins to sing. My brother and I often listened to her songs as children but we haven't heard them for a long time now. In a voice that sounds a little shaky, but is still clear and mild, she sings to us of a long-gone, faraway world. Mola sings as she sang as a young girl, and as a nun, when she lived the life of a hermit in a hut high in the Tibetan mountains.

Back then, she would meditate at the first light of day. Now, towards the end of her long life, she meditates with the last rays of sunlight. She is free from pain, free from melancholy and sorrow. She is entirely here, in the present, entirely with us. She knows she will be leaving us one day soon, but the thought does not scare her. She is calm and composed; she does not cling to earthly existence. My mother – my amala – worships in a different way. As Mola sits by her altar, her butter lamps lit, my mother climbs to the small whitewashed Greek Orthodox chapel at the top of the hill above our house. She loves to go there at the end of the day, to light a candle, leave an offering and pray. Often she is the only one there, but sometimes she is joined by a few villagers, who pray to their Greek Orthodox God as she prays in Tibetan to her deities. Mola would never think of praying in another religion's chapel. She must bring her own altar with her, no matter where she is. Meanwhile,

I read books, lazing in the garden hammock, listening to the chickens and crickets and to the sound of Mola's prayers emanating from the house. How different we three generations are . . .

When my mother has made her way back from the chapel on the hill, and Mola has finished her prayers, the three of us stand outside together to watch the sun set behind the mountains. This landscape of stone and sky looks almost like Tibet. That is why my family loves this place. Mola, Amala and I fall silent as the last glow of the sun fades in the sky. I am moved almost to tears. I feel as if we are nearing the end of a long journey, a journey I want to tell you about in this book.

1

Trapped

For fear of Chinese soldiers, they only dared walk through the freezing nights, with no light to guide them but the stars. The mountains were black towers before the dark sky. The group, numbering a dozen or so, had set out shortly before the Tibetan New Year festival, which, like the beginning of the Chinese calendar, usually falls on the second new moon after the winter solstice. New Year was deemed the best time to escape. The high passes were covered in snow, and icy winds whistled across them, but the snow was frozen hard at night and was sometimes even stable by day, in contrast to the warm season, when trekkers sank knee or navel-deep into a mixture of snow, ice, water, mud and scree. It was common knowledge that the Chinese border guards preferred to keep warm in their barracks during the winter rather than go on patrol in the biting cold. Everybody agreed that the soldiers would sooner spend the New Year festival, the most important Chinese holiday, celebrating, drinking and playing cards than doing their actual duties.

My mother Sonam's heart beat wildly as she struggled to keep up with the adults. She was only six years old.

5

Soon they caught sight of danger looming in the distance. In the valley far below their path, they saw large, brightly lit buildings. They could only be housing Chinese soldiers; Tibetans had no such huge and uniformly built houses as these, with such bright lights. Shouting voices, crashes of music, laughter, sometimes terrifying screams emanated from the buildings, echoing off the mountain. The Chinese soldiers loved *chang*, Tibetan beer made from barley, and they presumably had plentiful supplies. The sounds Sonam heard were blood-curdling, like a herd of wild beasts gathering in the distance. But her mother whispered to soothe her. 'It's good that they're celebrating,' she said. 'They won't come up here if they're cosy and warm and drunk.'

The refugees' path was narrow and stony and barely visible in the darkness. Often the group had to pick their way through thorny scrub and fields of scree, and then carry on between low trees. The roots of the trees protruded from the ground, tripping them up, and the dry branches scraped their hands and faces. All of them were covered in scratches, their feet bleeding and their clothes torn. The higher they climbed, the more often they had to cross snowfields.

It was the winter of 1959, the same year the Dalai Lama went into exile and a prophecy made by Padmasambhava, the founder of Tibetan Buddhism, was being fulfilled in a terrible way. This ostensibly 1,200-year-old prophecy says: 'When the iron bird flies and horses run on wheels, the Tibetan people will be scattered like ants across the face of the earth and Buddhist teachings will reach the land of the red man.' The iron birds, or Chinese planes, were flying over our land, and the horses on wheels, or Chinese trains, had brought troops to the border forcing my mother and grandparents to set out on a perilous journey.

Although the Chinese had invaded and occupied our land in

1950, it was not until years later that they dropped their initial false friendliness and began systematically arresting, torturing and imprisoning Tibetans, especially Buddhist monks and nuns, and aristocrats. As my grandmother was a nun and my grandfather a monk, they were in great danger. Their monastery was attacked and pillaged by Chinese soldiers. The Chinese ran riot in the village below the monastery. They dragged aristocrats across the village square by their hair and beat them, made them clean latrines, destroyed their houses, stole their sacred statues and gave their land to the peasants. They stole livestock, hurled insults at venerable lamas and trampled on centuries-old village traditions. It was this barbarism that made my grandmother Kunsang Wangmo and my grandfather Tsering Dhondup decide to flee to India with my mother Sonam Dolma and her four-year-old sister. They planned to cross the Himalayas on foot, with little money and no idea of the trials and tribulations they would meet along the way. They were equipped with nothing but home-made leather shoes, woollen blankets, a large sack of *tsampa* – ground-up roasted barley – and the certainty that escaping to the country that had taken in the Dalai Lama was their sole chance of survival. This conviction was based solely on their unshakeable faith. My grandparents couldn't speak any Indian language, they knew not a single person on the Indian subcontinent and they hadn't the slightest idea of what awaited them – apart from the knowledge that the Dalai Lama, whom they had never seen in their lives but who for them was the supreme authority, had been granted asylum there.

My mother's shoes were hardly adequate footwear for climbing mountains in the winter. The smooth leather soles slid across the snow, sending her slipping or falling to the ground every few feet. The snow gradually soaked through the roughly sewn seams, making the hay she had stuffed into her shoes in place of socks

7

cold and slimy. She wanted only to sit down and cry, but she had to concentrate all her willpower on placing her feet, one step at a time, into the footprints left by the adults ahead of her. Just don't get left behind, she repeated to herself. She knew it would be the end of her.

It became harder and harder for Sonam to continue. The water in her shoes had long since frozen. Her feet felt like big, heavy clumps of ice that she had to drag along with her. Her little sister was much better off: although she could walk, she would never have been able to keep up with the trek, so Kunsang carried her younger daughter, fastened to her back like a rucksack, tightly wrapped in blankets to keep her warm. The little girl never cried or screamed. She sometimes reached a hand out of her blankets to stroke her mother's head as she walked, whispering a soothing '*ela oh*' in her ear, meaning something like 'oh, I'm sorry' in the language of Kongpo. It was as if she wanted to apologize to her mother for adding to her burden. Sonam sent yearning looks up to the warm bundle on her mother's back. How envious she was of her little sister!

When another joyless morning dawned after a long night's trek, the group sought shelter under a rocky outcrop, beneath which a narrow cave opened up, just high enough for a small child to stand. At least the wind wasn't blowing in their faces, and nobody could spot them here. Yet it was bitterly cold in the small space between the smooth walls of the cave. My mother's feet were completely numb, although she couldn't tell whether the numbness was from the pain or the ice and the cold. Cautiously Kunsang freed Sonam's feet from the ice-caked leather, now more like tattered spats or gaiters than shoes. With even more care she plucked the frozen, crushed straw from Sonam's blue-tinged soles and placed her feet deep into the warming folds of her own dress, on to the bare skin between her breasts. What a shock those freezing feet must have been for my poor grandmother, and what an indescribable relief for my young mother. I can vividly picture her as a small child from the many stories she has told of this escape.

That was the only pleasant part of the short rest the group granted themselves. Nobody was allowed to light a fire, so they were unable to melt snow for drinking water, and they were running low on food, since nobody had expected to be on the road for weeks.

The only way to quench their burning thirst and soothe their chapped lips was to gather water in their cupped hands at an ice-free spot where a rivulet ran across the rock, or to shove snow into their mouths. This allayed their thirst but left a terrible icy feeling in their throats and chests, and later their stomachs.

Rocks and ice and snow were not the only obstacles nature had placed in their way. Every few hours, a stream, a foaming waterfall or a wild river shot out from between vertical rock faces on the flanks of the mountains. Most of these rivers were only partially frozen and gave an impertinent display of their strength. Wading through them and continuing onwards with their clothes soaked up to their hips was a miserable experience. Walking on the pebbles frozen on to the thin soles of their shoes made every step a hellish torture.

A few hours after they left the cave, they heard the distant rushing of a raging stream, which grew louder and louder as they approached. The torrent sliced though the rocks, leaving a deep ravine with a rope bridge suspended above it. Their immediate feeling was relief – until they saw the condition of the bridge. Four ropes were stretched across the canyon, tied together at the bottom with thinner ropes intended as rungs. These were far apart from each other, and through the large gaps you could see spray and foam and the rocky ravine below. My mother was terrified, certain

9

that she would lose her grip and plummet from this phantom of a bridge into the bottomless depths below.

Kunsang left her daughter no time for thoughts like that. With a jerk, she pushed her towards the precipice, then led the way, clinging firmly to the ropes but always leaving one hand free for Sonam. The bridge began to sway terrifyingly, the water roaring so loudly that even Kunsang, directly in front of my mother, could barely hear her piercing screams. She grabbed her daughter as she slipped, holding her up on the ropes and pulling her along, struggling to keep her own balance and trembling with fear. Step by step, they made it to the other side of the ravine.

Once they had crossed the swaying makeshift bridge, the familiar tortures began anew for my mother, tramping one foot after the other through the ever snowier and ever icier mountain wasteland with no destination in sight. She could see nothing else. She had seen nothing else for days. To make matters worse, it was growing colder and the wind was becoming more biting. On and on the group climbed, to the frozen heights of the Himalayas.

Suddenly the ground opened under Sonam's feet and she slid into a crevasse. She bounced off an icy wall and fell six feet on to hard-packed snow. Panicking, she saw that the crevasse dropped away next to her, becoming even deeper. And she saw too how far it was to get back up. Everything was white – the snow, and the cold, indifferent sky suspended above the mountains. Nobody had noticed her fall; she had been bringing up the rear. She waited, listening breathlessly, but heard only the whistling of the wind. She cried. She didn't scream, because she was afraid to. Whatever happens, don't call out, don't cry, don't scream, the adults had instructed her dozens of times. No fire, no noise, no shouting; the Chinese could be anywhere. Seized by panic, she clawed at the icy

10

sides, yet her smooth, wet, snow-caked shoes slipped down the walls of her prison. Was this how her escape would end? Was she never to see her parents again? Was she to be imprisoned for ever in this dark hole in the ice?

2

A Land Far From Time

My grandmother, Kunsang Wangmo, may well have been the youngest nun in Tibet. When I was a child, and she would tell me stories of her own childhood, I found it hard to imagine that at an age when I was still playing with toys, my mola was dedicated to a religious life. 'But I always wanted to be a nun, even when I was very small,' she would say. 'I loved to watch the nuns who spent their days in the temple at the Ahne nunnery, praying, singing and meditating. I wanted so much to be like those women. I wanted to shave my head like they did and wear the same red and yellow robes; I wanted to be as dignified and calm and holy as they were.'

The Ahne nunnery was in the easternmost corner of Tibet, in the province of Kham. It was high in the mountains, a good three hours' climb from the village. On the other side of the valley were the gilded parapets and spires of the monastery, where the monks lived. At that altitude, little grew but grass and herbs and wild flowers – ox-eye daisies, orchids, gentians and edelweiss, by turns swaying in the summer winds or buried under a layer of snow by the winter storms. The apricot and nut trees, willows and water lilies and small vegetable gardens that thrived in the village could not survive at this elevation. Here, the only trees were the tall wooden masts constructed by the monks and nuns with the brightly coloured prayer flags strung between them. As the flags fluttered in the wind, they scattered the prayers printed upon them in all directions.

On the steep slopes about half an hour's walk above the nunnery were the crooked huts and tiny houses where the hermit nuns lived. Some of the huts were provisional structures made of dry branches and leaves tied together with long grasses; others were built of wood or bark. The villagers attended the temple in town for religious festivals, and sometimes visited the monasteries to bring offerings to the monks and nuns and ask for special prayers and rituals. They rarely climbed the extra distance to the hermit nuns' huts, out of their great respect for the women who spent most of their time in silent contemplation. The hermit nuns did not speak to strangers and barely talked among themselves. They did not receive visitors, and only ventured down to the village to collect food. When they did descend to the valley, they prayed outside the houses with their eyes cast to the ground, accompanied by the steady *dram-drum* rhythm of the wooden hourglass drums they twisted in their right hands. The nuns set an example of the Buddhist ideals of humility and poverty, and showed the villagers their devotion by praying for them. The villagers, who reaped rich spiritual rewards from the nuns' prayers, paid them back in food. They gave the nuns *tsampa*, cheese, tea and butter.

My grandmother was the youngest of four children; both her brothers, five and seven years older than she, were monks, and her sister, ten years older, was a nun. Kunsang was the only child still living at home. 'I learned at an early age that clinging to earthly possessions only causes suffering,' she would tell me. 'I wanted to

13

achieve my own freedom and peace, unhampered by worldly objects.' Though it was common for a young boy to be interested in becoming a monk, it was unusual for a girl, especially such a young girl, to want to be a nun. When she was only five or six, Kunsang went to the temple in the village and had her head shaved. Other girls wanted to do the same, but they didn't like the results and soon let their hair grow back. For Tibetans, long hair is a very important part of being a woman. My grandmother has kept her hair close-cropped her entire life.

My grandmother does not know her exact age. Nor does she know what date her birthday is according to the Gregorian calendar. It does not interest her. What matters for Tibetans is the animal symbol of their year of birth and the associated element. My grandmother knows she was born in an iron-bird year. Age is measured in relation to the New Year, which falls on the second new moon after the winter solstice. My mother, for example, was born in a snake-water year, five days before the Tibetan New Year. That made her one year old at New Year, even though she had only been alive for five days. Had she been born a week later, she wouldn't have counted as one year old until 360 days later.

When she was much older, my grandmother had her birth documents made up based on estimated dates. I don't think she has ever taken a single look at these documents. Although the authorities demand them, to her they are unimportant. There were no identity documents in old Tibet, just as there were no birth registers, birth certificates or registry offices. Children were not born in hospitals; there were no hospitals in the entire country. Women gave birth at home, in huts, in nomadic tents, in farmhouses in the villages or in the stately town houses of the rich families.

It is said that every fifth man in Tibet at that time was a monk living in a monastery or a hermitage. The country then encompassed twice as much territory as today's 'Tibet Autonomous Region', which the Chinese set up in the 1950s after awarding the northern and eastern parts of the Tibetan territory to the Chinese provinces of Qinghai, Gansu, Sichuan and Yunnan. Old Tibet had approximately five million inhabitants, half of them men, meaning that there were some half a million monks. There are no estimates for nuns, but their numbers were much smaller.

Almost every Tibetan village in those years had a monastery. Some were home to more than one monastery or nunnery; a few were populated entirely by monks and nuns. Historians estimate that there were more than 6,000 monasteries and nunneries in Tibet. Some monasteries were occupied by only two or three men, others housed several thousand.

Monks were in charge of the monasteries' estates, goods and workers; they did the bookkeeping, paid wages and gathered taxes and dues. Some monks took care of practising and teaching classical Tibetan medicine, while others taught astrology, which was considered a science. Some copied religious texts, which circulated nearly exclusively among the monks themselves. There were very few schools, most of them privately funded; only the very rich could afford to employ a tutor for their children or send them to school in India. Apart from the noblemen, monks and nuns, most Tibetans were illiterate.

My grandmother came from a respected family, Chökhortsang, from the region of Samanang in the province of Kham. They owned land and large herds of animals, which they drove up to the surrounding mountain pastures in the summer. They were prosperous enough to give generous donations of food to the neighbouring monastery. Kunsang was born in Rege, where her parents had recently moved. In Rege, the family was not so wealthy; they owned only a few fields. Her father made paper out of the branches of a particular bush, which her mother collected. These branches were boiled until they produced a paste, which was then poured into a cloth-covered frame. The mixture dried into a thin layer and became a sheet of paper, which would be traded for other goods. Neither of my great-grandparents could read.

When Kunsang was born, in the early 1920s, there were no roads in Tibet, no railways, in fact no means of transport except animals. Although people were familiar with the wheel, it was a religious symbol for Buddha's teachings and the country's government of monks did not want it desecrated by everyday use. Heavy loads were transported on the backs of yaks, horses, donkeys – and human beings. Buddhism determined every aspect of life. Everyone prayed to the gods, used prayer wheels and prayer beads, consulted prophets and asked monks or nuns to perform rites and rituals for them in times of need. Tibet clung to its traditional view of the world and its spiritual way of life, disregarding many scientific, modern and enlightened ideas. The people left political, social and economic decisions to a small circle of aristocrats, monks and spiritual dignitaries, most of whom came from respected families.

The authorities were a small, close-knit class of worldly aristocrats and high clerics under the personal guidance of a Dalai Lama, or 'ocean teacher' (the literal translation of what was originally a Mongolian title). However there wasn't always an adult Dalai Lama in office. Often the new Dalai Lama wasn't recognized in a young child until years after his predecessor's death, and he had to grow up and complete his education and training before he could take charge. During these long power vacuums, the influential noblemen and clerics of Lhasa made the decisions.

Communication was by word of mouth. News of developments in the capital and more rarely from outside the country trickled down to the villages through stories told by nomads or merchants travelling with horses and yaks. Around hearths fired by yak dung, news, rumour and gossip gave rise to imagination. Runners took what little official post there was from one village to the next – a letter from Lhasa would take several weeks to reach Kham. Life on the roof of the world almost a century ago was one of deep spirituality, peace and self-imposed isolation. The Tibetans were completely unaware of the crises going on outside their country. They herded their yaks, *dris* (yak cows) and sheep as they had done for generations. They planted barley, then roasted and ground it to make what is called *tsampa*, which they mixed with butter and tea as they had always done. The peasants handed over part of their harvests to the monasteries and noblemen from whom they rented the land or for whom they worked as serfs, just as they had for centuries. In return, they lived in a firmly structured society, which gave them security and stability.

Hundreds of thousands of monks and nuns prayed day and night for the blessings of the protective deities, soothing any evil intentions from local spirits, calming dissatisfied gods and winning the favours of placid ones. Many Tibetans made once-in-a-lifetime pilgrimages to cleanse themselves of all sinful deeds and bad karma. The pilgrims would perform *kora*, circling a sacred mountain or monastery making a thousand prostrations – kneeling, sliding along the ground and lying down, before standing up again and continuing.

Of course the Tibetans were perfectly familiar with the scourges of disease, premature death, hardship and deprivation. They had no concept of hygiene; medical care was extremely limited and the average life expectancy short. It was not unusual for children to die at birth or shortly afterwards. Many adults died of diseases that could have been cured with simple medication or operations. Yet they did not feel themselves to be deprived. They knew nothing

17

outside their own lives, lives without depression or neurosis, lives without insecurities or doubts. Their deeply rooted, unshakeable faith kept them upright, however adverse the circumstances might be. Those who had lived honourably had every hope of a good reincarnation, a better life to come. For Tibetans, their current life was merely one link in a long chain of lives. My grandmother was fortunate to have this faith, given the difficulties she was soon to face.

3

Sickness

One morning when Kunsang was about six years old, her *amala* suddenly collapsed. On the previous day, Kunsang's mother and a friend had walked to visit the next village. She returned in the best of moods. She had been offered plenty to eat and drink, including boiled meat; the two women had even brought some of the meat home as a treat for their families. But as soon as they got back, both of them fell ill. They were seized with stomach cramps and vomiting; feverish, alternately sweating and shivering, they seemed close to losing consciousness. Kunsang's mother's friend died the next day. The day after that, her daughter – Kunsang's friend – followed her. The entire village was in a state of alarm and agitation. Fearing the sickness might be contagious, Kunsang's mother left the village, even though she was so ill she was barely capable of standing. With no doctors or medication, self-quarantining was the only solution the villagers had to avoid mass infection.

My great-grandfather was away with his herds, so Kunsang had to help her mother, supporting her weight as they struggled up the mountain towards the nunnery. It took several hours; the two had to pause countless times before they reached a vacant hut, where they collapsed. For two days and two nights the child watched over her mother, falling asleep by her side out of sheer exhaustion. She brought her mother water, dried her brow and prayed. Her mother vomited over and over again, and did not always make it to the door when she needed to relieve herself. Kunsang cleaned up after her as best she could.

On the third day Kunsang went down to the village to fetch food and found that her father had returned. But when he heard the terrible news, he asked his daughter to go up to the hut again. He was scared of catching his wife's disease and leaving his daughter without parents. He made soup, which Kunsang had to carry back up the mountain to her mother. The path to the hut was narrow, steep and treacherous, snaking across mountain pastures and over rocks. Kunsang had no lid for the heavy pot of soup and she spilled much of it. The next day she made the exhausting trip again; no one else dared to get close to her sick mother.

In the meantime, her father went to the monastery and brought the monks offerings so that they would hold ceremonies for his wife. The monks recited the *bartsche lamsum*, a prayer against the spirits that caused difficulties and suffering.

On the fifth afternoon Kunsang was surprised to see her *amala* finally resting peacefully. One moment she had been writhing with cramps, moaning and rolling her eyes; the next she lay still, calmer than she had been for days, with only her eyes twitching. Her pain seemed to have subsided. The hand that had been clutching her daughter's slipped to the floor next to her makeshift bed, as limp as a rag. She seemed to be sleeping, even though her eyes were open.

Evening was drawing in. The mountain shadows were getting darker. When the butter lamps in the hut burned out, Kunsang

20

could no longer see her mother. She was hungry, so she went down the mountain to her father, hoping he might have some soup or tsampa for her.

'How is your mother today?' her father asked.

'She is more peaceful,' Kunsang replied. 'She is sleeping with her eyes half open, and she is quiet, no shivering or sweating.'

Her father was silent. The change Kunsang had found comforting seemed to make him sad. He sat with his head bowed, not moving. 'We'd better go up to her,' he said finally.

Kunsang was surprised that he now wanted to go to his sick wife. He took a piece of kindling with him for light. When they arrived at the hut, Kunsang's father greeted her mother, but she did not reply. Her silhouette danced across the walls in the flickering light of the tiny flame. He touched her hand, but she did not react.

'She's asleep,' said Kunsang.

Her father stood stock still as he looked down at his wife. Tears flowed down his face. 'I had never before seen my father cry,' my grandmother told me. 'Before this moment he had always had something to do, something to say; he could explain almost anything. Now he did nothing, said nothing and knew nothing. We stood there for what seemed an eternity, neither of us moving a muscle. I had never experienced such a deep silence; it was not a good silence, and I was gripped by fear but I didn't dare to interrupt my father's thoughts.'

An age passed before her father said in a quivering voice, 'We have to fetch a lama. He has to perform powa.'

'What's that?' she asked.

'Your mother is dead.'

So that was it. Kunsang had heard adults talking about death, but she didn't know exactly what it was. She had never seen a dead

21

body. She knew that death was important because it was followed by reincarnation, and a new life, which comes after the old one. But she didn't know exactly how the various lives interlinked. It must be something like sleeping, she thought. When her mother woke up again, she would have a new mother.

Her father wanted to set off straight away to fetch the lama, who lived in a hermitage much higher up the slope of the mountain. He had known the lama for many years, and had made several previous visits, taking him food and asking for blessings. He gestured to Kunsang to come with him, but she did not want to leave her mother.

'Let me stay here with Amala,' she said. 'I'll look after her if she wakes up.'

'She won't wake up,' her father answered. 'She's dead now.'

Kunsang still didn't want to go with him. She wanted to stay with her mother. She hadn't yet absorbed the meaning of her death.

'You have to come with me,' said her father. 'It's dark, the moon's not out. My old eyes can't find the way in the darkness.'

Kunsang went with him with no further protest. Tibetan children never disobey their parents, especially not their fathers and especially if they are girls. Elders are always right, their instructions must be followed – tradition and respect for age are very strong in Tibet.

In the darkness, Kunsang and her father climbed the mountain with steady steps. Kunsang walked ahead, her woollen chupa hitched up so it didn't get wet or catch on the stones and scree along the way. Her father carried a long stick to aid him when the climbing got difficult. As the path snaked higher and higher up the mountain, they heard nothing but their own laboured breathing and the wind whistling through the mountaintops.

When they arrived, they found the lama asleep in his sparse

22

quarters, lying on top of a thin mat on the bare floor. Kunsang's father woke him up with great caution, even timidity. With a jerk, the red-robed man sat up as straight as a rod, as if he had not been asleep at all. When he heard what had happened, he began calmly preparing for the powa. He got up, lit the embers beside his bed with a few twigs of kindling, made tea and poured some for his visitors, mixing it with tsampa and butter. He himself ate and drank nothing, simply lit some herbs in a small dish, which burned with much smoke and crackling. As they burned, he knelt, murmured prayers and began swaying his upper body to and fro. With his eyes closed, he recited holy mantras that Kunsang had never heard before and which she did not understand. All she could tell was that his murmured words were very important. Soon, she fell asleep.

It was light again when Kunsang awoke and found herself slumped on the floor. Only when she saw the praying lama still sitting in the same place and inhaled the smoke of the burnt herbs did she remember where she was. What was her mother doing now, all alone and helpless in the hut further down the mountain?

The lama was well advanced in his powa. It was a ceremony that had to be carried out as soon as a person died. Buddhists believe that after death, the consciousness should not be allowed to leave the body through one of the nine 'normal' and impure orifices – the nostrils, the eyes, the ears, the mouth, the anus and the genitals. Instead it should be directed through the top of the head, at the spot where a baby's fontanelle is. This experienced lama could prevent my great-grandmother's consciousness from wandering dangerously and guide it in the right direction, thus enabling her to make a favourable reincarnation. At this point in time her karma, the consequences of her good and bad actions while she was alive, was of secondary importance.

Father and daughter knew my great-grandmother was in good

hands. They saw that there was nothing they could do for the rest of the *powa*, so they took their leave of the lama in the traditional way, bowing deeply and walking backwards. The lama, his mind entirely on the ceremony, turned briefly towards his visitors to say goodbye. Kunsang's father would soon bring *tsampa*, tea, butter, cheese and cured meat in return for the lama's efforts. Without these offerings, the holy man's prayers would have no effect, as it is was in this way that a petitioner proved his sincerity.

4

Forty-Nine Days

My great-grandfather wished for a sky burial for his dead wife, the traditional Tibetan funeral ritual where, after all the required prayers and blessings, the monks expose the corpse to the vultures. In the Tibetan mountains and high plains, digging graves is often all but impossible; the ground is hard, rocky, often frozen. Wood for burning the dead is always difficult to come by. Disposing of a body is far less important to Buddhists than their concern for the deceased's consciousness. Once the soul has left the body, the corpse is merely an empty vessel according to Buddhist belief, and this vessel should be put to the greatest possible use for the benefit of other creatures. We respect birds that feed on carrion just as we respect all living beings.

Sky burials can only take place in very particular places, and are conducted by skilled masters. They have to cut up the corpse in a certain way, then break up and grind down the bones. All this requires someone who knows how to open a skull and how to mix the brain with *tsampa* so that the vultures will eat as much of the remains as possible. Almost nothing should be left after this feast of transience.

To his great regret, Kunsang's father could not afford a sky burial for his wife. The nearest burial site was several days' journey away. It would have been far too complicated and expensive for him to move the body there. So he had to choose a more modest form of burial. Fortunately, there were meadows in the valley where a ditch could be dug as a temporary resting place for the corpse.

'Your mother's consciousness is already on its way to a new body,' Kunsang's father told her. 'She is being accompanied by the lama's prayers.'

Usually burials were accomplished with the help of family, friends and neighbours, and afterwards everyone was served a hearty meal. But their friends and neighbours refused to help, fearing they might catch the deadly disease from the corpse. Kunsang and her father had no close relatives in the village. Kunsang's two brothers were travelling the country as monks, and her older sister was a nun living several difficult days' journey away. None of them yet knew that their mother had died. So the funeral procession to the ditch was not only sad, but lonely and laborious. Before the burial, Kunsang's father had asked an astrologer to calculate the best moment for the body to leave the hut on the mountainside. At the designated time, he fetched his wife's corpse from the hut, dragging it out of the door to a low wall, where Kunsang had to keep it stable while her father stooped to balance it across his shoulders. He lugged the body down the narrow, bumpy path, then pulled and dragged it towards the ditch. Kunsang was horrified; she could see her mother's body already decaying, and the finality of this began to hit her as she helped her father push and tug and lift her poor mother's body so that it would not be scratched to pieces by thorns and sharp stones. At last it landed in the ditch, and they covered it with heavy rocks. As her father stood praying, Kunsang tried to join in, but she was too choked with tears.

Afterwards the two of them went to the monastery, taking the monks a sack of *tsampa*, butter, tea and other food and asking them to pray for the dead woman for forty-nine days. During this period, prayers are said to help the deceased so that they have no fear of what is coming, and to lead the way to rebirth. Each week for these seven weeks my great-grandfather took offerings up to the monastery. Kunsang and her father collected her mother's *chupas*, aprons, blouses, shoes and jewellery and took them to the monastery too. Later the monks exchanged the women's clothing for food and kitchen utensils to meet their own everyday needs.

Many times my grandmother has told me how dead people spend three days reliving their lives down to the tiniest detail. At sunrise on the third day the consciousness returns to the body, not realizing what has happened. Then the dead wander among the living but no one acknowledges them, no one talks to them, looks at them or touches them. They want to be with the living and they do not understand why we ignore them – until a terrible suspicion dawns upon them. To test their fears, they walk across sand, seeing to their horror that they do not leave footprints. They lower themselves into water and see that they make no waves; they try to break off a twig and see that the twig resists as if it did not feel their touch. They try all these things until they realize they are no longer among the living; their consciousness has parted from their body. After these three days, the consciousness of the dead comes across forty-two peaceful and fifty-eight wrathful deities. Anyone who has seen pictures of these terrifying divinities can imagine how disturbing and frightening such encounters must be. Therefore it is important that the dead are accompanied by the monks' prayers, which prepare their souls for these meetings.

The prayers were also intended to explain to my deceased great-grandmother that the gods she saw were not real but merely illusions and there was no need for her to fear them. The monks hung up pictures of the one hundred gods, so that she could get used to the sight of them. They also made a simple drawing of a woman, to represent my great-grandmother, and showed this image little pictures of the individual divinities. Many monks keep a stock of pictures for this purpose.

After the forty-nine days, Kunsang's father fetched his wife's body from the ditch, this time with the help of some monks. 'The ground is not a good place for the dead to remain,' he told Kunsang. The monks burned the now semi-putrefied corpse and carried out a fire ceremony, a ritual that calms and banishes all damaging energies and pacifies the spirits that wish evil upon the dead. Liquid butter is poured into the flames and presented as a gift to the god of fire, along with twelve other substances including rice, flour, grasses and blossoms. The fire god, Tibetan Buddhists believe, takes the essence of these offerings to the other deities.

After the cremation, the ashes were gathered and mixed with clay and water. This mixture was pressed into a mould to make tsa tsa, small, roughly shaped figures of divinities. The ashes could simply have been scattered into the river, but my family has always been very religious, and tsa tsa was a more spiritual choice. My mother still has the heavy, funnel-shaped brass mould used by the family to make tsa tsa for generations. The inside has a finely carved lotus border, below which are 108 small cavities. 108 is a holy number for Tibetans. The mould is used to make a tsa tsa in the form of a small stupa, or shrine, representing the entire universe.

Tsa tsa can be placed in a pure or holy place – any place where no animals graze, no crops grow and no wood is felled. They can be placed on a stupa or under an outcrop of rock high in the mountains, or even on the shores of a river, where the waves will gradually take them to the ocean, an inconceivably long journey for Tibetans.

It was not until much later that Kunsang realized her mother's death must have been caused by the meat she ate. All three people who had eaten it had fallen ill; on arriving back from the neighbouring village, Kunsang's mother's friend had given some to her daughter. It was only because my grandmother had been asleep when her mother came home that she didn't eat any.

Food poisoning was common in those days. The only method Tibetans had for preserving meat was curing, but the process took place either in the open air or above the fireplace, where the meat could easily be contaminated.

Buddhists are not supposed to kill animals. When they built houses, worked in the fields or the garden or simply walked along a path, Tibetans took care not to step on earthworms or other insects. If they found spiders in their houses, they carried them outside rather than killing them. But because little grew in the mountains other than barley, a few types of vegetables, herbs and grass, meat was the only high-calorie, high-protein food source. The only people who did not eat meat were those who could not afford it. In the larger towns, a caste of slaughterers had grown up, often Muslims who did not follow Buddhist religious rules. However, since there were no Muslims living in the villages or among the nomads, many Tibetans had to slaughter their animals themselves. They avoided killing small animals, which meant they did not eat fish, poultry, rabbits or other such creatures. Killing a small animal destroys a life just as much as slaughtering a yak does. But a yak feeds a dozen people, whereas one fish is sometimes not even enough to fill a single stomach. It is better for karma to divide up the guilt of killing among many, keeping the blame as small as possible for each individual.

29

When an animal had to be slaughtered, Tibetans gutted it completely, using almost every part of it: the flesh and the hair, skin or fur, the brain, the intestines, the tendons and the bones. It was unthinkable to throw away part of a creature to which they had caused suffering. For this reason, meat was often kept for too long, even after it started to smell bad – a custom that had tragic consequences for Kunsang's mother.

5

A Young Nun

The years went by. A new world war broke out in Europe, but the prayer wheels at the monastery gates continued to turn, as they had done for centuries. Although Kunsang lived at home with her father, she now spent her days at the nearby nunnery. She worked alongside the nuns, taking part in their rituals, learning to read the holy scriptures and practising the art of Buddhist prayer, which with its self-immersion is more like meditation than Christian prayer. Each day she would repeat the mantra *om mani peme hung* over and over again, once for each of her 108 prayer beads.

Originally from Sanskrit and known across the Buddhist Himalayas, this mantra has accompanied my grandmother throughout her life from morning to night, whether spoken, murmured or simply voiced in her thoughts. It is impossible to translate literally. The Dalai Lama tells us:

the meaning of the six syllables is great and vast. The first, *om*, symbolizes the practitioner's impure body, speech, and mind; it also symbolizes the pure exalted body, speech,

31

and mind of a Buddha. The path is indicated by the next four syllables. *Mani*, meaning jewel, symbolizes the method: the altruistic intention to become enlightened, compassion, and love. The two syllables *peme*, meaning lotus, symbolize wisdom. Purity must be achieved by an indivisible unity of method and wisdom, symbolized by the final syllable *hung*, which indicates indivisibility. Thus the six syllables, *Peme hung*, mean that in dependence on the practice of a path which is an indivisible union of method and wisdom, you can transform your impure body, speech, and mind into the pure exalted body, speech, and mind of a Buddha.

Each of the six syllables stands for one of the six areas of existence into which living beings are reborn, and from which Bodhisattva Avalokiteshvara can redeem the faithful. This bodhisattva embodies universal compassion, and is closely linked with this widespread mantra.

A bodhisattva is an enlightened existence with the ultimate but distant goal of becoming a buddha, a being in a state of perfect enlightenment like Siddhartha Gautama, the historical Buddha from the fifth century BCE. Many people refer to him as 'the' Buddha, but Buddhists believe there have been a number of buddhas and will be more in the future. While bodhisattvas are not complete buddhas, they are no longer mortals either. Instead, they consciously refrain from reaching buddhahood for the time being so that they can help all beings in this world to free themselves from the cycle of suffering. A bodhisattva does not want to attain buddhahood while even a single entity suffers. Once one attains buddhahood, one leaves the wheel of suffering, birth and rebirth. Bodhisttavas concentrate on their own final determination only after they have reached their goal of guiding all living beings to enlightenment.

Most Buddhists know that they will never become a buddha or a bodhisattva; rather they recite the *om mani peme hung* to earn merits and good karma.

Kunsang was growing into a young woman; at her age, probably about thirteen, she was considered almost an adult. Her father's health was deterioraing and he now spent most of his days in bed. He suffered from a liver disease that gave his skin a yellow sheen. A lama had examined him and diagnosed his illness as incurable. There were no doctors in the region, and even if there had been, the only help they would have offered was traditional Tibetan herbal medicines. Though there was no state welfare system, the Tibetans had the best social safety net in the world: the family. Unfortunately, because her father had not married again, Kunsang was the only member of the family left to help him. Every evening when she returned from her day at the nunnery, she collected firewood, raked the fire in the hearth, fetched water, made soup and stirred *tsampa*.

She had seen enough in her life to know that her *pala* might be nearing his end, and she knew too that death might come quickly. She wanted her father to be able to experience something wonderful one last time, so she decided to take him to a performance of *cham* – dances at the monastery. In these ritual dances, monks don magnificent robes to play the role of divinities. They are accompanied by other monks playing music and reciting texts. These performances are a beautiful combination of opera, theatre and religious ceremony.

Kunsang supported her emaciated father's weight on her shoulders as he limped up the path. By the time they had gone less than half the distance, she had to admit to herself that they would never manage to climb the many steps to the monastery, and then the many steps down again into the courtyard. So she improvised by leading him to an earthen wall, from where they had a good view of the spectacle. She laid her exhausted father on a blanket and he watched entranced. Dressed as the deities who appear immediately after death, the monks danced around masts decorated with prayer flags. It was a ghostly and magical scene, re-creating the twilight realm between life and death. After the long performance, Kunsang and her father struggled home again. Her *pala* was exhausted and trembling, but he was calm, almost carefree. Something had been released within him. A few days later he died peacefully in his house with Kunsang by his side.

Once again, *powa* – the ritual accompanying a dead person's soul – was held. This time Kunsang not only watched the ceremony, but provided help and support. She knew how it worked, having seen it performed several times since her mother's death. An old nun led the ritual, and Kunsang assisted her. That was unusual; normally men perform *powa*. In the Buddhist spiritual hierarchy, women are worth less than men. Yet because the flame of deep belief clearly burned within Kunsang, she was allowed to hand the old nun the ritual instruments, light the butter lamps, place the offerings on the altar and remove them again when the time came. She played an important role in the ceremony to accompany her father's wandering soul on its way to its next incarnation.

After her father's death, Kunsang felt very alone. She had no relatives in the village, and she longed to see another member of her family. Her sister, Pema Dolma, had often sent messages inviting her to visit her nunnery, but Kunsang hadn't wanted to leave her father by himself. Now she fervently wanted to make the journey, but could not do so alone. Her sister lived a six-day trek from Rege; Kunsang would have to walk at least twelve hours a day for nearly a week to get to her. Then she heard that a group of nuns and monks who had been staying at the local monastery were heading for her sister's nunnery. She gathered her things, put her wooden food bowl into a fold of her *chupa*, filled a sack with *tsampa*, rolled up her blanket and set off to join them.

It was not unusual to make such a long journey. Monks and nuns often travelled great distances, over several weeks or even months, to receive teachings from lamas or rinpoches. The title 'rinpoche' means something like 'precious one' and is normally used towards an experienced teacher, or lama. Some rinpoches made long pilgrimages to Lhasa and other holy sites, often journeying for years, teaching at monasteries and villages along the way.

Winter had arrived. Snow drove across the bare high plains of Tibet, accumulating in the channels between the rocky precipices that the group had to climb. But Kunsang barely took in her harsh surroundings. She concentrated on moving forward, constantly murmuring *om mani peme hung*. Suddenly she found her path blocked by a man lying on the ground. He was not dead, but asleep in the snow. When Kunsang stepped closer to him, she could smell that he had been drinking *chang*, Tibetan beer. She had no experience with alcohol, but she knew the man would freeze to death if he stayed there on the path. She called out to the others, who had gone on ahead, but they were intent on getting across the mountain pass and finding a nomad's tent or a hut, or at least a sheltered spot from the wind, in which to spend the night.

Kunsang couldn't help thinking of her mother and how she had summoned up the last of her strength to make it to the hut, where she could die in peace. The memory brought tears to her eyes. She grabbed hold of the man and shook him until he woke up. She spoke to him encouragingly as she tugged at him, trying to pull him upright. Reluctantly, he rose and followed her. She was taken aback by how forceful she could be.

The man began to speak, but he was rambling and raving and

Kunsang could not understand what he was saying. She didn't care; all she wanted was to drive him on along the path. The snow was falling harder and darkness was descending. The man slumped down on the ground again, and this time she couldn't persuade him to continue. She looked up at the pass, but there was no one to be seen. She called but no one answered. She tugged at the man again but he would not budge. Suddenly, she was afraid. The icy air stabbed at her lungs, and she was shivering with cold. When she saw that the snow had already covered her footprints, she felt a surge of panic. She pulled at the drunk again but he did not react. Finally she abandoned him and hurried up the mountain. When she reached the top of the pass she caught sight of her group making a camp in a niche in the rock. Miraculously, they had lit a small fire, although there was no wood to be seen for miles and no yak dung either, only ice and snow. They were all relieved to see that Kunsang was safe, but it was with a heavy heart that she huddled towards the fire to warm her almost frostbitten limbs. What had happened to her Buddhist charity? How could she have abandoned another human being? Her toes felt like stones, and as they gradually warmed up, they were so unbearably painful that she screamed in agony.

The first thing she saw when she opened her eyes the next morning was the drunk, sitting like a ghost by the embers of the fire, his face as white as snow. The others tried to give him tea, but the man writhed and bent double, screaming and babbling. There was nothing the monks and nuns could do for him but pray. Still the man did not calm down. He screamed and shouted until he started foaming at the mouth. Clearly he would be unable to make it down the mountain with them, so the group stayed where they were for another day and night. On the third day the man's agony had become even worse and he writhed on the ground. Suddenly he jerked upright and died. The monks and nuns performed the necessary ceremonies and prayed that his spirit might find its way to a good body.

After she arrived at her sister's nunnery, Kunsang's feet became septic. Her sister was the oldest in the family and Kunsang the youngest, and they had never been particularly close, but it hurt her greatly that her sister showed her so little kindness or concern. Unable to take care of herself during this terrible time, and with her sister unwilling to look after her, she fell ill. Her *chupa* was infested with lice, her skin pale and sticky. In the end, she lost two toes. When the stubs of her toes healed over a little, she was able to move around again, but it was two months before she was well enough to return home. She had hoped to enjoy the warmth of a family member, but most of what she remembered about her visit was the pain of her frostbite, made worse by her sister's lack of pity and compassion.

She left the nunnery with a group of nomads who were passing through the village. They had invited her to accompany them in the hope that a young nun's prayers would offer them and their animals protection against disease. She was very happy to accept their offer; she wanted to return home but could not have tackled the dangerous and strenuous journey alone. Now she was to have a comfortable trip, travelling with many yaks and mules and sleeping in the tents the nomads put up every evening. Unfortunately her prayers were not enough to keep evil spirits at bay.

As Kunsang's group travelled, they met other nomads, who warned them that there were Chinese soldiers in the region. Starved of supplies, the Chinese were capturing and killing every herd they came across, attacking herdsmen to get hold of meat; even – it was rumoured – skinning cows alive. Terrified by these reports of cruelty, the nomads and Kunsang hid in a side valley until they heard the soldiers had left the area. They were lucky to arrive home safely. All the other nomads they came across told horror stories about how the Chinese were mercilessly butchering Tibetan soldiers, leaving the dead and injured where they lay.

Twelve hundred years ago, the Tibetans had been a feared military force, marching up to the gates of the Chinese emperor's residence in Chang'an, conquering the city and dictating a humiliating peace treaty. Over the centuries, the Tibetan army had shrunk to an insignificant cavalry troop that was no match for its huge neighbour. A small Chinese force had been enough to overrun Tibet in 1910, advancing all the way to Lhasa. The thirteenth Dalai Lama had been forced to flee to India and could not return to the Potala palace until 1913, when he declared Tibetan independence. Chinese troops had been involved in constant skirmishes with the Tibetans since the early 1930s, particularly in the Tibetan province of Kham under their general and commander Liu Wenhui.

Kunsang was shocked when she saw what the Chinese had done to the neighbouring Dama monastery. The statues of the gods had been smashed into a thousand pieces; the ground between the partly collapsed walls was strewn with old books containing holy Buddhist texts, trampled by the looting soldiers. This was a monstrous sacrilege: Buddhists would never lay their holy scriptures on the ground, let alone place the soles of their feet on them or walk across them. She did not know then how this was just the beginning of events that would dramatically change her life and that of her country.

6

Ape Rinpoche

When Kunsang returned to Rege, she was probably about fourteen years old. She owned little. Her house, which also belonged to her siblings, contained only a few pieces of furniture: a table, two beds and a few rugs, and some pans and dishes in the kitchen. In a little room beside the kitchen was a simple altar on which stood seven silver bowls of water, several goblets filled with butter, which were used as lamps, an ancient *thangka* – a painted banner depicting Buddhist stories – and a small Buddha statue. The *tsa tsa* mould was safely stored away. Kunsang's only personal possessions were her red nun's dress, which she wore every day, her wooden food bowl and her prayer beads. These she usually wore around her neck. She needed nothing more. She felt it was her destiny to focus her existence on developing her spirit, meditating and praying for the well-being of all living creatures, and therefore she decided it was time to commit herself to a holy life of abstinence at the nunnery. She was old enough, and experienced enough in spiritual matters.

Before she could enter the nunnery, she needed to undergo the 'lock of hair' ceremony. This ceremony could be led only by a formally ordained monk. Nuns were on a low rung of the Tibetan hierarchy, well below monks. With very few exceptions they could not attain the same status as Buddhist monks, and therefore it was monks who performed the 'lock of hair' ceremony. One of these exceptions was the nun Jetsün Dolma, but she lived far away so couldn't perform it for Kunsang.

The founder of Buddhism, Buddha Siddhartha Gautama, taught that monks and nuns were equal, but his pioneering approach never took root in Asia's male-dominated societies. Tibet was no exception. That never troubled my grandmother, and still doesn't today. She regards Buddhism as an unchangeable system established by wise divinities and Buddha himself, which is being constantly refined and brought to perfection by the bodhisattvas – the enlightened beings – and the lamas – the spiritual teachers. She would never call into question any of its practices or restrictions. She didn't feel second-class, excluded or discriminated against. She simply wanted to strive for enlightenment according to her own possibilities.

Soon after her lock of hair ceremony, the younger of Kunsang's two brothers, Pema Lodroe, came to her village. He was making a long journey from one guru to another and she decided to join him on the next stage of his strenuous trek, in which he would visit Ape Rinpoche, the highest guru of the neighbouring village, who was well known far beyond the borders of the Kham region and even beyond East Tibet. A rinpoche is a monk of the highest spiritual ranking, commanding great respect and honour. Kunsang was very curious to meet this famous man, and she sensed that the meeting would guide her young life in a new direction. At the same time, she was fearful that she might not be allowed into his presence.

Ape Rinpoche gave both Kunsang and her brother a friendly

reception. They bowed low before him and he blessed them, prayed with them and told them the story of his life. He originated from a rich noble family; his father was a village chief and had powerful forefathers. When he came of age, he was supposed to marry a woman from another rich family. Arranged marriages were very common in Tibet, especially in wealthy families, where they were used to maintain and multiply fortunes, esteem and influence. The young Ape had no desire to live with a woman he didn't even know, and he didn't want his life to be devoted to preserving and expanding power and possessions. To help himself clarify his thoughts, he went on a hunting trip high up in the mountains with two friends, armed only with bows and arrows. The three young men wanted to hunt tschirus, the rare Tibetan highland antelopes. It was the first time Ape had been on a hunt; he knew it was against Buddhist teaching to kill an animal.

As the three men moved higher into the mountains, Ape was overcome by more and more doubts. It was not just the hunt and the killing that worried him; it was also his upcoming wedding. Tired and hungry from the climb, he signalled to his friends to carry on without him and sat down to rest on a stone. After the two young men had disappeared behind a flank of the mountain, Ape looked up at the birds circling high above. He watched the clouds scudding even higher across the deep blue sky, letting his thoughts drift along with them, further and further, until he lost contact with everything that had previously seemed important to him. His family, the bride who had been chosen for him, the estate he would inherit, his beautiful home, his horses, his magnificent robes, his servants: all the luxuries of his youth vanished from his thoughts as if they too were clouds, fleeting structures that dissolved under the brilliant sun of the high Tibetan plateau.

Surfacing refreshed, as if from a deep sleep, Ape had no idea

41

how long he had been sitting there on the stone. He stood up and walked on, but he didn't follow the path his two friends had taken up the side of the mountain. Instead he headed in the other direction, across a wide saddle to the next valley, where there was a monastery. He knew that a well-known lama lived there. Ape wanted to go to him and ask him to teach him. With that, he took his leave from his former life. He was never to see his parents, his family or his home again.

Ape spent many years learning from his 'root guru', as Buddhists call their most important spiritual teacher, before he moved to a hermitage. There he lived alone, prayed and meditated for three years, three months, three weeks and three days. He then returned to the valley and took on pupils of his own, instructing them in matters of faith. He later heard that one of his two sisters, who had been forced to marry a rich nobleman, had fled to a nunnery and become a nun. This news gladdened Ape's heart.

Kunsang and her brother were very impressed by Ape Rinpoche. They returned to their village with new strength. Kunsang lived at the nunnery, and Pema Lodroe moved into the monastery on the other side of the plateau. When they heard that Ape Rinpoche wanted to make a pilgrimage to Ngabö in Kongpo, they decided to join him. It was a unique opportunity to go on a beneficial pilgrimage in the company of a holy man.

The trek to Ngabö would take many months. They packed the few things they wanted to take: a sack of tsampa and a couple of compressed bricks of tea, two blankets, two old jackets and their wooden bowls and prayer beads. But when they reached Ape Rinpoche's monastery, they found he had left a few days previously. Kunsang's brother wanted to go back home, but Kunsang burst into tears of frustration and refused to eat or drink until he promised her they would continue together. It was a brave decision – they had heard that marauders had attacked and robbed travellers along the route they were to take.

It was a long, hard journey. Kunsang and her brother took countless wrong turnings and had to ask nomads to lead them back to the right path. It rained heavily and the wind whipped at their faces. They had to sleep in the open air, huddled together against the cold nights, which can be extreme even in the Tibetan summer. Their *tsampa* almost ran out and they were in constant fear of being robbed of their remaining provisions by bandits who roamed the high plateaus far away from the villages. How they would have loved to sit by a cosy fire and dry their clothes overnight, but for four days they saw not a single house, not one village or monastery, only water, rocks, woods and grass.

The snaking path had led them to a steep pass, above which snow fell and a cruel wind blew. They had almost reached the end of their strength and Kunsang was about to give up. At the top of the pass, she sank to the ground to rest next to one of the route markers typical of much-travelled passes – a pyramid of stones such as Tibetans have built since the dawn of time in worship of local deities. Prayer flags hung suspended from long masts, flapping loudly in the gale. Suddenly her brother shouted out, pointing to a caravan struggling up the other side of the pass. It looked like a group of merchants, their horses loaded with goods. At last there was someone they could ask about the way and whether they had seen the rinpoche.

To their joy, the travellers told them that Ape Rinpoche and his monks were taking a break from their journey in a pasture not far away. If they hurried, they might catch up with them. Kunsang and her brother scrambled down to the valley, waded through an ice-cold river and soon stood before the pilgrims' tents. Ape Rinpoche gave them a warm welcome, plying them with hot tea and sweetened *tsampa* and promising that they could travel with him.

My grandmother so admired Ape Rinpoche's friendliness and goodness that she decided to make him her root guru. She wanted never to leave his side, but for the time being she told no one, entrusting this decision only to her heart.

7

The Hermitage

My grandmother and her brother continued happily on their journey alongside Ape Rinpoche. They travelled for many months, from the Kham region to Kongpo. When they reached the village of Ngabö, the villagers ran to meet them. They recognized the guru and were very excited to have him in their village. He had given his teachings there in the past and offered people medical treatment. He was an expert in basic Tibetan diagnosis methods such as examining urine and the tongue and feeling the pulse. Ngabö Ngawang Jigme, the mayor of Ngabö, immediately welcomed the rinpoche with many reverent bows and good wishes. The mayor was still a young man at that time, a promising politician from a noble family. When the Chinese invaded in 1950, he immediately surrendered, and later headed the Tibetan delegation sent to negotiate in Peking. There he signed the seventeen-point treaty between Tibet and China. This treaty promised the Tibetans regional autonomy, freedom of religion and the right to their own reforms – promises that later turned out to be lies. The Tibetans never received autonomy; rather they continued to be shamelessly oppressed. Ngabö Ngawang Jigme enjoyed a distinguished career in the Chinese administration of Tibet and China.

After the villagers had got over their initial excitement and given Ape Rinpoche their many greetings, the guru and his companions continued to a hermitage a few hours away in the mountains above the village. Even before his arrival, the villagers had begun to build a house there for the holy man, hoping to persuade him to stay; it would be a great blessing for the village if he were to live close by, even for a short while. They knew the rinpoche was planning ultimately to extend his pilgrimage all the way to Lhasa. The building was a sign of how fervently they wanted him to remain with them. The villagers knew that the guru had no interest in worldly comforts and had left material things behind him, so the new building was correspondingly modest. It had two rooms, a bedroom and a shrine room where the rinpoche would pray and set up statues of gods and other holy artefacts.

The hermitage was a collection of huts built by a group of nuns who were eagerly awaiting the rinpoche's teachings. Here was the sign Kunsang had been anticipating for so long. The huts had been built at least fifty yards apart; this was a place of peace and contemplation. The nuns used only plants in their construction, no stones, mortar, earth or clay. As their chosen site was above tree level high in the mountains, they had to carry the building materials on their bent backs from the valley below. First long branches, then flexible poles rather like bamboo, followed by sticks and hard grasses. They planted the branches in the ground in a circle leaning inwards, leaving a small opening at the top so that smoke could escape. This woven tent-like structure was sealed with sticks, grass, roots and bark. The huts were so low that even a small woman could hardly stand up inside, and so cramped that she could barely stretch out on the ground. They warmed up quickly when a small fire of roots, dry sticks or yak dung was lit in the middle, but cooled down just as fast once the fire went out, as the wind and the cold easily penetrated the woven walls. Yet the nuns looked to the winter storms and snow with light hearts; they would warm themselves in the sun of their faith and the wisdom of the rinpoche.

Assisted by some of the older nuns my grandmother began building her own hut, as if it were the most natural thing in the world. There she stayed. Since it was not seemly for a male to live among the nuns, Pema Lodroe settled in the village below, where he later married and started a family.

Almost unnoticed, Kunsang became one of Ape Rinpoche's pupils and embarked upon many years of contemplation and maturation. During this time she achieved her calm, her concentration and the kindness I knew and loved even as a child. It was these years that gave her the inner glow and the strength that have sustained her even in the most difficult times and the most trying circumstances. Meditating on death, a central part of her daily contemplation, gave her the serenity that made everyday problems seem unimportant. She never sees the bad side of people, only the good. For her, problems that trouble people are nothing but their own thoughts projected outside of them.

During her years at the hermitage, she lived each day according to a strict schedule. The day began before dawn, when one nun woke the others with her *kangling* trumpet. Tibetans make these trumpets out of human femurs, drilled at each end. A *kangling* can play an extraordinary range of notes. The nun in charge of the morning call sent her long, lamenting melody out over the white-frosted fields and the rocks behind them, up to the clouds. One after another, the other nuns joined in, until a blanket of sound lay over the mountain pastures, woven from the hollow yet powerful tones. After this, the nuns spent several hours meditating in their huts. Depending on their age and the stage of their training, they practised various techniques and studied various subjects. Then the nun who had heralded the day signalled the end of meditation with her *kangling*, and once again the other nuns chimed in with their bone horns. After that, they all walked through the wet grass to a water boiler to wash their hands and faces.

Next the nuns reignited the embers beneath the ashes in their hearths, which they had piled high before they went to bed the night before. They placed a tripod over the flames to warm the previous evening's tea, filled their wooden bowls with *tsampa* and added one or two flakes of butter and a pinch of *chuship*, grated cheese. They poured hot tea over the mixture to complete their meal.

After breakfast the bone trumpet sounded again, to signal the nuns to withdraw to their huts for more private meditation. Towards noon, at the next trumpet signal, the women knew that it was time for their lunch break. Kunsang supplemented her meagre Buddhist fasting diet with occasional soups, or *ala buk*, the flat, unleavened buckwheat bread eaten in the Kongpo region. When pilgrims brought gifts of food for the nuns, they ate *thugpa*, a thick soup made of dried meat, peas, daikon or wheat, seasoned with chilli or yoghurt if any was available. *Momos*, dumplings filled with meat, vegetables or cheese, were eaten only on special occasions. If they had nothing with which to fill dumplings, the nuns kneaded the dough into *bazamagu*, a kind of noodle that they ate with melted butter.

The days passed in silent meditation, prayer and contemplation, guided by the sound of the *kanglings*. The nuns even meditated through the night, regarding deep sleep as a waste of time that could be put to better use in spiritual contemplation. On particularly holy days they came together in the rinpoche's wooden house

48

to raise their voices in religious song, culminating in an invocation of the lama.

Kunsang wanted to spend three years, three months, three weeks and three days meditating in complete seclusion. But first she had to perform the ngöndrö. This involved several stages. Through prayer she had to take refuge a hundred thousand times in her guru, in Buddha, in the dharma, the teachings of Buddha; and in the sangha, the community of all monks and nuns. To do this, she had to make one hundred thousand prostrations, kneeling, then stretching her body along the ground, only to stand up and begin again. She also had to recite the mantra of Buddha Vajrasattva, a mantra of purification, a hundred thousand times. After that she had to make a hundred thousand offerings of the universe mandala.

To make the mandala offerings, she sprinkled grains of barley on to a round surface at each of seven precisely defined points. On top of these she sprinkled grains directed towards the four points of the compass. When she completed the mandala, she immediately shook the grains off, catching them in a small cloth lying on her lap, and started the ritual anew. Spending weeks making the exact same mandala, watching its repeated formation and disappearance, is thought to lessen one's attachment to the ego. For Buddhists, the ego, the belief that we are solid, separate and permanent, is the root of all suffering. The mandala meditation frees the consciousness from the individual ego, lifting the spirit to a higher level. At the same time these created and instantly destroyed mandalas made of grains, rice or sand are symbols of the transience of all things, even life itself. For Buddhists, making mandalas is an exercise in freeing themselves from the desires and emotions of the earthly world. Kunsang was taught that these mandalas were a symbolic offering of the universe to all buddhas and bodhisattvas. The grains in the hand of the person making the offering symbolize the wealth of the entire universe. Every grain is as valuable as a jewel or a precious stone, as valuable as all the riches of the universe.

Finally, she had to carry out a hundred thousand guru yoga practices honouring her own guru. This practice merges one's mind with the wisdom mind of the guru.

The ngöndrö are known as the five hundred thousand preliminaries. My grandmother took her path to cleansing and preparing herself very seriously. She spent many months accomplishing her rituals. She considered it her vocation to immerse herself in this seemingly never-ending chain of meditations.

Kunsang also practised the ritual called chöd, meaning 'cutting through the ego'. Buddhists feel we take our egos much too seriously: I suffer because I do not achieve a certain thing; I worry because I hate something; I feel sad because others do not praise me. Destroying this egocentricity is the purpose of the chöd ritual. It is one of the few religious practices in Tibet introduced by a woman, the Tibetan holy woman Machig Labdrön, who lived in the eleventh and twelfth centuries and recorded her teachings on the chöd rituals, which are still practised today exactly as they were almost a thousand years ago.

Kunsang imagined she was offering herself and her whole body to the gods. As she did so, she sang beautiful mantras, accompanying herself at regular intervals with the 'dong-dang, dong-dang' of a large hand drum, which joined either the bright chimes of a small bell she rang or the wails of her bone trumpet.

Only after these rituals and the five hundred thousand preliminaries were completed was Kunsang considered mature enough to receive the deeper teachings of her lama. These were mainly concerned with the Buddhist concept of emptiness – the idea that nothing exists of itself; that everything is a product of human thought. In the beginning, she understood little of what Ape

Rinpoche said and couldn't follow his explanations. His reaction to her difficulties was never gruff or impatient; instead, he'd start again from the beginning, over and over. For the guru, these lessons were not only for the purpose of teaching his pupils; they were also an exercise in humility for himself. Ape Rinpoche did not consider himself perfect or enlightened, but saw himself as a simple pilgrim on the long and difficult path to illumination.

Only when the rinpoche felt that Kunsang had absorbed his teachings and was filled with his wisdom like a sponge full of water did he release her for her three years, three months, three weeks and three days of secluded meditation. This was to be her final initiation on the long path to all-embracing wisdom.

Like the other nuns at the hermitage, Kunsang had to interrupt her great meditation at least once a year to replenish her supplies. The villagers rarely climbed the mountain to bring the women and their guru a share of their meagre harvests. The hermitage was a sacred place that was not to be disturbed.

The nuns' annual descent to the valley was the only variation in their lives of meditation. Since nothing grew around their huts but grass and herbs, they had to beg the villagers for the little food they needed, just as my grandmother had seen monks and nuns doing in her own childhood village. Now it was her turn to go from house to house with two other nuns during the harvest season, singing and praying, accompanying themselves on drums. The nuns provided a welcome distraction for the villagers. First they sang the om mani peme hung three times, then one of the nuns unfurled a thangka. The stories on this banner were moral fables, beautifully illustrated in bright colours and designed as both entertainment and religious instruction. Rather like folk epics, they were so popular that people immediately gathered around as soon as they heard that the nuns had come to sing a Buddhist story, a mani.

These presentations were usually made in the evenings, when the farmers had returned home from the fields. The nuns would sit next to the *thangka* hung from a wall, except for the one who stood and sang its story, pointing to the characters with a long stick. The audience followed the pictures in the semi-darkness of their smoke-blackened kitchens, illuminated by the flickering light of burning wood and butter lamps.

The villagers were deeply moved by these recitations and songs. They heard of brave men fighting evil spirits, of the unending kindness of benevolent gods. A mysterious new world was presented to them, so beautiful and rich but so full of desire and sorrow that many of them were moved to tears. They were simple people who knew only their immediate surroundings, their families, their neighbours, their livestock, their fields and pastures. They were familiar with the mountains that surrounded them, if only from a safe distance, and the sky above them. What did they know of distant lands, powerful rulers, buddhas, paradise, tropical gardens and ornate palaces? They had never come across cinema, books, radio or magazines. Except for the *thangkas* the singing nuns brought into their homes, they had never seen any pictures of the world outside their valley.

The villagers rewarded the nuns with everything they could spare. Soon the nuns' sacks were so heavy with barley, butter, cheese and cured meat that they could hardly lift them. In some of the houses lived rich people who owned large herds of livestock and employed workers; in others were poverty-stricken peasants with just enough to survive on, yet they were given donations in every home. The villagers believed that helping these women, who lived simple lives and contributed to the karma of the village as a whole through their prayers, brought blessings upon them all. Everyone knew that the nuns did not hoard food, but only went from one house to the next until they had enough to eat for another year.

Not all nuns had to earn their keep in this way. Some of the young women came from wealthy families who sent them regular deliveries of food. One of these was Ani Pema-la, who became my grandmother's best friend. Her actual name was Pema – *ani* means 'nun' and *la* is a polite form of address.

Ani Pema-la's parents were initially unhappy that their daughter had decided to become a nun. They had chosen a wealthy husband for her and made all the preparations for a wedding befitting her social status. But Pema ran away from home to escape the marriage, and her parents had little choice but to respect their daughter's decision and support her as best they could. They sent an old servant woman to the mountain, where she occupied her own hut a few yards away from Pema's. Unlike the other nuns' accommodation, Pema's hut was made not of branches and twigs, but wooden boards and planks. The maid cooked for her, washed her clothes and cleaned her hut, still modest despite its extra comfort. She also combed Pema's beautiful long hair, which she had not cut off. The lama granted her this extravagance.

Rumours of Ani Pema-la's wealth and privilege must have spread far and wide, for one night two thieves paid a visit to the old servant woman's hut and stole the valuables that she kept for Pema: silver coins, clothing, silver bowls and food. Fortunately, the maid was asleep and unharmed.

Ape Rinpoche was horrified that common criminals had invaded his hermitage devoted to godliness and illumination. He and his pupils immediately began a three-day ceremony to counter the negative energy the thieves had left behind. Many butter lamps were lit, herbs burned and long prayers recited. Like a sign of divine rage, the previously agreeable weather suddenly changed, and a fierce rain storm set in.

News of the theft reached Pema's family, and her concerned

parents sent her brother to her. Once he had made sure she was unharmed, he used his special spiritual abilities for seeing the future and the past. First he asked for a butter lamp. Then, standing in the altar room next to the rinpoche's hut, surrounded by a crowd of curious nuns, he held the lamp as close to his thumb as the heat of the flame allowed. On the tip of his thumb he saw that one of the thieves had been attacked by a bear and ripped to pieces. Two of the nuns could make out the same picture, although my grandmother didn't see anything. Then Pema's brother saw the other thief climbing a tree to escape from the bear, and falling out of it. The nuns were extremely impressed by his divination skills; later, other nuns told them that everything really had happened just as he had reported. The stolen objects were found next to the bear's victim. For my grandmother and the other nuns, the incident was positive confirmation of the power of karma.

Although Pema's servant woman was reassured by the fate of the thieves, she did not serve her mistress much longer. The cold and damp in the hut were doing great damage to her health. After she left, Pema's parents promptly sent a new, younger maid.

Neither Kunsang nor any of the other nuns felt envious of Ani Pema-la's privileges, nor did they bear her any ill-will because of them. Buddhists abhor such emotions, but Kunsang did not need to fight them; she simply did not feel them. It was the most normal thing in the world to her that aristocrats and rich people had different rights and opportunities from common people. For my grandmother, hierarchies were god-given, karmic and fixed. She would never have dreamed of questioning them and she still thinks that way to this day. For her, anyone who has achieved a favourable reincarnation such as an aristocrat, a rinpoche or a wealthy person must have collected so much good karma in their past life and done so many good deeds that they have earned their first-class rebirth.

54

She has always done everything in her power to collect good deeds and avoid bad deeds, hoping for a similarly privileged reincarnation, for which people should envy her just as little as she envies those in that position today.

After her three years, three months, three weeks and three days of meditation, Kunsang entered a new stage of her spiritual journey. She was ready for her first light meditation, which meant looking at the sun with semi-closed eyes and meditating on its blinding light. My grandmother has always been reluctant to talk about the ritual, never giving more than hints or insinuations. 'This type of meditation is secret and I promised my guru not to pass on my knowledge of it,' she says. In Buddhism, very special ideas and practices are not written down, but passed from teacher to pupil. Even the briefest mention that such as thing as meditation on the sun's light exists makes my grandmother feel guilty. Nowadays there is Western literature about light meditation, and even courses for learning it. My grandmother cannot comprehend such a development. 'I can't explain what happens in this meditation,' she says. 'I don't think it's good for it to be explained.'

The most she would ever tell me was that this particular meditation is a preparation for death. Later, I read that it teaches pupils to transform their bodies and every part of their selves into light at the moment when death enters them, in order to achieve what is known as a rainbow body.

The light meditation was not the highest level of contemplation that Kunsang's guru had in store for her and her fellow nuns. Next came another, more difficult exercise, taking the women into even lonelier realms. It involved going up into the mountains to meditate, away from their tsampa sacks and the pot of hot tea always simmering in their huts, far away from the guru who could answer their spiritual questions.

One day Kunsang was sent with a small group of nuns high up the mountain, where there was only rock and scree and the occasional field of snow. Tibetans climb to such heights only when they have to cross a pass to get to the next valley or are on a pilgrimage. They never do so for sport. They regard the high mountains either as sacred, in which case they walk around them, or as dangerous and threatening, in which case they watch the icy giants with dread as the clouds chase past their peaks.

Kunsang had to ascend to this mountain world to meditate in a state of semi-nudity recommended by her guru, concentrating on emptiness. She was to set aside all worldly accoutrements and merely be herself. In the most isolated, distant and snowy side valley, where she was certain to be alone, she was to recognize that everything was an illusion: her ego, her fellow human beings, her surroundings, the entire world. She was to recognize that everything was empty, with no meaning of its own. She was to recognize all things, including her thoughts, as a product of her consciousness: nothing was real, nothing existed, only emptiness, in which there were no words or ideas or objects.

My grandmother has always refused to talk about what happened up there in the mountains. After a while she was so cold, she told me, that she dressed again and went down the mountain, to the hut she had built, where she resumed her everyday meditation practice.

In the mountains of Kongpo, the long days of meditation were interrupted only by the daily teachings, by the sound of the bone trumpets, by the group recitations and singing, and now and again by herdsmen with their yaks passing by at a respectful distance.

During her years with Ape Rinpoche, Kunsang would sometimes go on pilgrimages, and travel to receive teachings and initiations from other important lamas. Her most revered visit was to Dudjom Rinpoche, a *tulku* who was then in residence at Thadul Barchu

Lhakhang in Kongpo. A *tulku* is a wise monk, a spiritual master who has not only achieved wisdom in this life but has been recognized as a reincarnation of an earlier spiritual master. This most high lama was considered a direct reincarnation of Shariputra, Buddha's most important disciple, although the consciousness living within him had since been through many other significant incarnations, including some of the greatest gurus, yogis and scholars, among them Shariputra and Saraha. Whenever he gave teachings in Tibet and India, great teachers came to receive them. Among all the high lamas there were practically none who hadn't received teachings from him.

Close to Dudjom Rinpoche's monastery were the remains of the spiritually important monastery Zangdrok Palri, which had been destroyed by a severe earthquake. Dudjom Rinpoche had made it his task to rebuild the monastery with the aid of religious volunteers. Kunsang went to join them. For two months she stayed at the monastery, helping to calm the earth spirits with rituals and prayers as the rebuilding took place, hoping that the sacred ground might return to peace. She was also engaged in the construction work.

My grandmother remembers her time at Ape Rinpoche's hermitage as the most wonderful years of her life.

8

Tsering Arrives

In the spring of the wood-bird year – 1945 – a young monk named Tsering Dhondup travelled to the collection of modest huts that made up Ape Rinpoche's hermitage. Like many others, he had been drawn by tales of the guru's wisdom and illumination, and also by the rumour that he gave generous teachings. When he finally arrived at the hermitage after a long and arduous journey, the famed rinpoche was not the only person he noticed. He was also struck by Kunsang, now in her mid-twenties, in the full bloom of her young womanhood, and fell in love with her, even though monks were not supposed to allow themselves such feelings.

At first Kunsang was bewildered by Tsering's obvious interest. She had never thought about a man being attracted to her. She was even more bewildered when she realized that she reciprocated his feelings. Never in all her years in the hermitage had she talked to other nuns about men. The subject was as distant from their lives as the moon. They talked about their religion, their meditation, the rinpoche, the nature all around them, the silence, the light and the gods.

Ape Rinpoche, Tsering and Kunsang belonged to the Nyingma school of Buddhism. The Nyingma tradition is often referred to as the 'old school' of Buddhism and is considered the oldest established line of Buddhism in Tibet. The Nyingmapas, as the followers of this school are called, still study the first translations of the holy texts of Vajrayana Buddhism from Sanskrit into Tibetan. There is one important difference that distinguishes the Nyingmapas from the Kagyüs, the Sakyas and the Gelugpas, the most widespread school, to which the Dalai Lama belongs: the Nyingmapas do not have such hard and fast rules about their monks and nuns remaining celibate. Although the Nyingma lineage frowns upon them marrying and having children, the sanctions are less severe.

Kunsang didn't have to fear losing her vocation if she were to become involved with a man, though she did have to expect negative comments from her fellow nuns, and especially from her guru. What worried her most, however, was not other people's opinions but the question of what effect love for a man might have on her spiritual development. Would such a love not lead her further away from her goal of achieving inner emptiness? Would a relationship conflict with her objective of reaching buddhahood? She had spent years meditating, praying and making offerings, but she still felt she was only at the beginning of her journey. She was young; compared with other nuns she had only a few years of contemplation behind her, and there were many writings, meditations and practices she had not yet mastered – and did not even know by name.

These questions troubled her, even though she did not have to make a decision right away. Tsering soon moved on again; it was not fitting for him to stay long in a hermitage where nuns lived. Kunsang was relieved to return to her everyday life. She was content with the companionship of the other nuns, especially Ani Pema-la

59

and her other favourite Puko Ani-la, who had also left a rich, aristocratic family to become a hermit nun. Puko Ani-la and Kunsang were younger than the other nuns at the hermitage and had become close friends, having so much fun giggling and chatting that the guru had been forced to reprimand them, and told Puko Ani-la to build her hut further away from Kunsang's so that they both could better concentrate on their contemplation.

The villagers had recently built a small assembly room next to the guru's hut and altar room. Every month the nuns held a ceremony there in honour of Ape Rinpoche. Kunsang was not the only one to have noticed that her revered master was becoming pale. At that month's ceremony, he sat still as a stone. This was very upsetting for all the nuns; the rinpoche was sixty-one years old, a great age for those times, and they feared that his present life might not last much longer. The nuns were especially concerned because their guru had told them on several occasions that he would die in a wood-bird year.

Wanting to do something for their revered rinpoche, the nuns carried out more ceremonies and prayed for his welfare. Yet the guru simply sat ever more still and silent, turned mentally inwards and unmoving in his seat, a niche padded with cloth and cushions in the hermitage's small shrine room. Finally, one evening he did not even get up to go and sleep in his hut next door. He looked far away and absorbed, yet calm and oblivious to the world. His eyes were closed and his breathing was barely discernible. None of the nuns dared to speak to him. One after another they threw themselves to the ground in front of him before they went to their huts for the night's rest. Still the guru did not move. It was unusual for them not to receive a gesture of farewell from him.

The nuns were even more worried the next morning when the

rinpoche did not return their morning trumpet greeting but remained still in his seat. Had he been there since the night before? It was not proper to stare at such a wise and high-ranking lama, so the nuns entered the semi-darkness of the shrine room with their eyes lowered. The room was lit only by a few flickering butter lamps and the shimmer of daylight falling through a low doorway. When Ape Rinpoche still made no movement, not even a twitch of his hand as a sign of greeting, Kunsang found the courage to address him. He remained silent and did not move. She repeated her greeting several times, but Ape Rinpoche gave no reply. Then she stepped closer to him and asked him a direct question, which he did not answer. Only then did she dare to raise her eyes and look into the face of a dead man.

'The guru's face looked the same as ever, relaxed and peaceful, yet there was something different about him,' she told me. 'His eyes were neither closed nor open, but at some point between the two, something I had not seen for a long time. His body looked stiff, there was no breathing, no rise and fall of his ribcage, only a sense of perfect and complete peace.'

Kunsang remembered her sleeping mother and how she had lain motionless on her bed, not breathing, not moving, not making a sound. She remembered the shadows that had come creeping out of the depths of the hut, eventually filling the room, and the heaviness and peace she had felt in her mother. She sensed the same peace now.

Her great teacher, her root guru Ape Rinpoche, had left this most recent of his many lives.

Other gurus came to perform *powa* for him and carry out the death ceremony – just as the hermit lama had done for Kunsang's mother many years ago, and as she and the older nun had done for her own father, and as it must be for every Tibetan whose soul is not to be lost and abandoned after death on the way to the next reincarnation. This time the ritual was much more elaborate. Hundreds of guests attended, some of them travelling great distances, and the entire village came up from the valley to pay the guru their last respects. For two weeks after Ape Rinpoche's death his body remained on its seat. Many of the countless visitors could scarcely believe he was really dead when they saw him sitting there as he had always done in the past. They fell to the ground before him and crawled on their stomachs until they were a few yards away from him, crying, praying, not daring to look at him.

Once Ape Rinpoche's spirit had embarked on the journey to his next incarnation, his mortal remains were burned and the crowd of guests descended to the valley.

Although Kunsang still rose before dawn every morning, still blew her bone trumpet and meditated on emptiness and the light nature of everything on earth, she no longer felt the freedom and emptiness she had felt during Ape Rinpoche's lifetime. The calm she hoped for did not come, nor the great peace that had ruled the lives of the nuns and their guru. She began feeling more and more negative energies and disruptions, glimpsing shadows and strangers and traces of the new age that she had never wanted to see. The news of Ape Rinpoche's death had spread far and wide and it was common knowledge that only a dozen nuns now lived in his hermitage, alone in the huts around his abandoned hut. Soon thieves appeared, thinking they could rob the defenceless women of what little they possessed. For Kunsang, these assaults were not as painful as the loss of her guru. His departure had left behind a deep wound in her heart.

In the next few years some of the nuns left the hermitage. But Tsering Dhondup, the monk who had fallen in love with Kunsang, returned. One day there he was, sitting in her hut. The two of them drank tea and talked about all that had happened since they had last seen each other. It was not long before Tsering moved in with Kunsang and they became a couple.

My grandmother has always loved telling me about her time with Ape Rinpoche, about the years she spent alone in her tiny hut, but she is reluctant to talk about the time when she lived with Tsering. Even today, she is ashamed of having given up her life of celibacy in that sacred place high in the mountains. Being with Tsering seems like an accident to her, a blow of fate. Her heart was with the gods, with her religion. She accepted Tsering the same way she accepted the snowstorms in winter and the rainstorms of autumn. She had never asked him to come to her, but neither could she do anything to send him away; he was simply there. She never felt the giddy sensations of romantic love, the skipped heartbeats, the butterflies in her stomach, but with Tsering's return, her life took a new direction.

Like Kunsang, Tsering came from a small family, but his had never been a real family. He was what the Tibetans call a bird-child. His mother had had an affair with a man from a wealthy and influential family, but she did not have the slightest chance of marrying him. Quite apart from the fact that Tsering's father had been married for many years to a woman of his own class, with whom he had children, a marriage across class borders would have been inconceivable in Tibet's feudal system of the time. Many rich men had affairs with other women. As there were no medical means of contraception, and abortion went against the Buddhist principle of protecting every life, there were many illegitimate children in old Tibet.

So Tsering's mother brought her son up alone. She had to keep his parentage a secret, just as his father did, with one difference: as an unmarried mother, she was exposed to the ill-will and malice of her neighbours, while her lover went on living with his family as if nothing had happened. She stood up against the rumours that her son was a bird-child, trying to take the sting out of the accusation by having Tsering examined for signs of his noble lineage. Back then, the Tibetans believed that a child's gestures and behaviour betrayed aristocratic origins, regardless of where and with whom it had grown up.

The examination was carried out by a civil servant roughly equivalent to a local mayor in the West. Other officials led the five- or six-year-old Tsering into a room where the civil servant sat, surrounded by his helpers. 'Go over there!' the man ordered the frightened boy. 'Now over there! Stand against the wall! Sit down on the chair!' Tsering stumbled around the room, eyed by distrusting faces. Before he knew what was happening, he was sent out again. Nobody remembers what the outcome of the test was, and Tsering never found out whether the officials recognized his parentage in his youthful comportment.

Old Tibet was not a utopian Shangri-La, the blissful paradise on earth that people in the West like to conjure up; it was a country where aristocrats and high-ranking clerics had many more rights than the simple people. Worldly and spiritual dignitaries in the Tibetan state had the knowledge and the power to construe ancient scriptures as they saw fit and could interpret the legal system to their own advantage. Kunsang, however, never had critical thoughts about the society in which she lived. She accepted everything that happened around her as divine will.

9

Obstacles

It wasn't long before my grandmother encountered what she calls an 'obstacle' in her life, which she feared might block her path to a fortunate rebirth.

In the decades that have followed, she has attempted to make up for this obstacle through intensive prayer, offerings and meditation, and by leading as sacred a life as possible. At the same time, she knows that obstacles can crop up in anyone's life, no matter how religious they are; they are ordained by fate, part of human karma, unavoidable and impossible to circumnavigate. Tibetan has a word for this: *barche*, and the prayer to overcome it is called *barche lam sum*. Strict Buddhists ask monks to recite this mantra on their behalf to clear such obstacles from their paths in life.

The first signs of my grandmother's obstacle were an ache in her belly and persistent nausea. At the time, Tulku Sönam Nyendak was staying at the hermitage. He was from the far eastern province of Kham and was travelling the very long distance to Pemakö in the south-east of Kongpo. He agreed to examine Kunsang's urine and feel her pulse; he knew immediately that she was pregnant.

This was terrible news for Kunsang. What was to become of her vocation as a nun? What about her life in the hut at the hermitage? A life like hers was not suitable for a newborn baby, and it was not fitting for a nun to live in such a holy place with a child.

Tsering was travelling and knew nothing about the pregnancy. Kunsang's first instinct was to leave the hermitage and get as far away as possible before he returned. She suggested to the tulku that she could accompany him to Pemakö. Pemakö was a holy Buddhist site in a huge canyon of the Yarlung Tsangpo river that separated the south-east of Tibet and the north-east of India. Surrounded by high snow-topped peaks, it was a pristine landscape of woods, meadows and glittering waterfalls. Kunsang thought she could live there, bear her child and start a new life in a new place.

The tulku had not yet responded to her request when her brother, Pema Lodroe, came to the hermitage to find out how Kunsang was faring. Relieved, she told him all about her pregnancy and her plan to leave. Both he and the tulku advised her against travelling. The journey was too long, they said, too dangerous; she knew no one there and she was too young. In fact Kunsang was nearly thirty years old, if not more. She thinks it must have been 1950, the iron-tiger year, when all this happened; or perhaps it was 1951, the iron-hare year. Since her brother was both older than her and a man, she received his advice as a strict order. A man's word bore more weight than her own opinion, just as it did for every Tibetan woman. Her brother had been her authority ever since their father's death. She remained at the hermitage.

Despite her despair, Kunsang still felt deeply connected to Tsering. On his return he wanted to live with her again, and they decided to stay together and withstand as a couple all that life presented to them. Marrying in a temple was uncommon in Tibet. Ideally, couples held a feast with many guests, but only rich people could afford this kind of wedding ceremony. Kunsang and Tsering had no money. More importantly, they did not feel they had anything to celebrate; they knew all too well that nuns and monks were not supposed to marry. If they did, they kept it a secret. Since they were living together, they already felt they were married. Kunsang was both happy and sad: happy to have Tsering, and sad that marriage would be yet another obstacle on her spiritual path through life.

With great concern, Kunsang and Tsering spoke with the *tulku* about their situation. He allayed their fears. They could remain nun and monk; they could continue to wear the red *chupa*, the traditional Tibetan religious clothing. The wise man recommended that they perform special rituals to weaken the negative consequences of their marriage, and held a ceremony for them before he left for Pemakö, saying the *barche lam sum* for the two of them.

When Kunsang sensed that she would soon be giving birth to her child, she left the hermitage and went to her brother's house in the valley, where her sister-in-law could help deliver the baby. Birth and menstruation are seen as 'dirty' in Tibet and must take place far away from sacred sites. A woman would never go into a shrine room or temple when she was menstruating in case she contaminated the sacred place and angered the local deities.

There were no gynaecologists in Tibet, nor even any trained midwives. Modern hygiene was unheard of. It was not always easy to find someone to help with a birth. Because of the blood involved, Tibetans considered this work impure and did not value it. A man could never have acted as a midwife, as men were regarded as purer than women and would never have contaminated themselves with a woman's blood. Tibetan men still avoid coming close to women just before and after birth, because they are afraid of *dip*, as they call such contamination. Tradition holds that if a man sees a woman's blood, one of his energetic channels, known as *tsa*, through which wind energy flows, will dry out. That can be very dangerous for a man. Small wonder then that most Tibetan women, including my grandmother, wish to be born again as men; men lead better, easier, less complicated and less painful lives than women. There are even special prayers for being reborn as a man, which my grandmother regularly recites. Not only are men spiritually higher than women in the Tibetan faith, they are also spared the difficulties of pregnancy and birth.

In Tibet, pregnancy, birth and lying-in were not seen as positive and joyful experiences, but as sources of fear and sometimes of sickness, suffering and death. When a woman gives birth, they said in those days, she is like a pea on the threshold: no one knows whether she will roll into the house or out of it, whether she will survive giving birth or not. The mortality rate was not only high for newborns but also for their mothers.

Everything went well for Kunsang. My grandmother and her sister-in-law immediately saw that the baby was special. Its birth was considered a kind of miracle because it came out as a little white ball, as if wrapped in gauze. They had to tear open this 'wrapper' before they could see the baby. It was a splendid-looking child with not one blemish or red mark, not a drop of blood or mucus on its tiny body. It had pale skin and black eyes – and it was a boy. Kunsang cried tears of happiness.

Later she learned that the villagers had seen several rainbows above the house where she gave birth. They lasted throughout the day, as bright as if they had been painted on the sky. Also the water from the stream next to the house had gushed milky white from the ground for several hours. These were clear signs that the baby was a reincarnation of a high lama or rinpoche. It was predicted that the child would one day become a great guru.

The villagers did not get a chance to see the baby until he was a few months old. In Tibet, newborns were not taken out of the house before that. When the time came for her to show the child to the villagers, Kunsang painted a wide black vertical line from the root to the tip of her son's nose, using a mixture of soot and butter. This old custom was to protect the child from the evil eye. Alas, it did not do so. He soon stopped drinking, grew weaker and weaker, and his skin changed colour. He died before he was five months old. Kunsang was later told that she should have torn open the white gauze with her thumb and middle finger; it had been wrong to open it with both hands. She feared her mistake might have caused her child's death, and was filled with great sorrow. Tsering too could hardly bear their misfortune, but there was nothing they could do but accept their fate.

Kunsang wound her dead baby into her chupa, where she had held him so many times, and walked up into the mountains until the snow and ice and wind prevented her from going farther. She found a cave, laid the child's body inside it and weighed it down with rocks.

Soon my grandparents returned to their old life in the huts, which were no longer a hermitage but a settlement of nuns and a few monks, rather like a religious community. Before long Kunsang was pregnant once more. Again it was a shock for her, and she was filled with doubts and self-recrimination. When she was about to give birth, she went back down to her sister-in-law in the village. The child was another boy, and this too was an unusual birth: a breech delivery, with the baby's legs coming out first. Once again the villagers believed a special child had been born.

After only a few months, this baby too developed health problems, which neither Kunsang nor anyone else in the surrounding area could heal. He died before he reached six months. Again Kunsang carried her dead baby up the mountain to lay him under a rock, hoping he would become one with the stone and the cold and the snow and the wind.

After the deaths of her two children my grandmother was very sad, but the mourning of a lost one is short in Tibet. For Tibetans, death is not final, but merely a transformation from one state into another. Despite their sorrow at bidding farewell to a loved one, it is more important to pray for a favourable rebirth and hold the correct ceremonies than to beat one's breasts and show pain. Doing so can be very detrimental to the dead, who can feel the tears of their relatives raining down on them like hailstones. It is taboo to mention their names, as that would only disturb their peace. To this day, my grandmother includes her dead children in her morning and evening prayers, along with her parents, her family and her friends – indeed the whole universe. No one is a stranger to her, every living creature, whether human or animal, her neighbour or a tiny insect on the kitchen table, may have been her father or her mother or one of her dead children in a former life. 'Being re-incarnated as a human is as rare as gold,' she always says. 'If you are born a human, you must not waste your existence.'

Kunsang was soon pregnant for a third time. She gave birth in the valley as before, this time to a girl. In Tibet, it is usually not the parents who choose babies' names, but high clerics. On the instructions of a very high lama, Kunsang's daughter was named Sonam Dolma. Most Tibetans are given two forenames; generally the combination of the two names tells people whether the child is a boy or a girl. 'Sonam' can be either, but the addition of 'Dolma' makes it clear that the baby is a girl, as Dolma is the name of a well-known goddess.

A few months later, when Kunsang dressed her daughter and folded her carefully into her *chupa* to return to the hut on the moun-tainside, she was overcome by dark thoughts. What if this child too were to die? Would she have to carry another baby to a cold and stony grave?

But Sonam grew as strong and healthy as any child could be. Long after she learned to stand, walk and talk, she was still drinking from her mother's breast, though she also loved the sweet *tsampa* Kunsang made for her. She grew up in harmony with the un-changing rhythm of prayer and ceremony that made up the everyday life of her parents.

When Kunsang became pregnant for the fourth time, she had a dream: the door opened and a young monk looked into the house, asking her if she would take him in as a guest. Kunsang agreed and invited him in. When she looked down at the palms of her hands, she found in them a beautiful coloured stone. But before she could thank the monk, he had disappeared into thin air. This dream convinced her that her fourth child would be a girl, and the prophecy proved true: Sonam Dolma soon had a healthy sister.

10

Life at Pang-ri

My grandparents led the life of a secluded religious family in the grounds of the former hermitage with their two young daughters. They still felt bound to their vows as nun and monk, but they were also obligated to one another, both because of their children and because their hearts were in harmony.

In the wood-sheep year, 1955, or the fire-monkey year, 1956 (my grandmother cannot say for certain), they were summoned from their seclusion by Trishul Rinpoche. This well-known lama had sent a monk to bring them to Pang-ri, a small monastery high above the Pang valley, about two days' walk from Ngabö. Trishul Rinpoche was a tulku, who was about to leave his hermit's life at Pang-ri because the king of Sikkim had called him to Gangtok, the capital of his mountain realm in the north of India. The king had asked the respected rinpoche to advise him, and Trishul Rinpoche wanted my grandparents to look after his sanctum during his absence. He needed people who could take care of the building itself, as well as the spiritual part of the hermitage. He didn't know how long he would be away: perhaps a few months, perhaps several years.

Neither my grandmother nor most of the other people in Tibet's remote mountainous areas knew anything about the military and political entanglements in which Tibet was involved with the Chinese. All they knew was that the Chinese had come into the country and that their soldiers had committed atrocities. Everything in their small world was the same as ever: the years came and went, the gods were merciful, and they had all they needed to survive. Only very educated people with far-reaching connections like Trishul Rinpoche had the faintest inkling that things would not remain as they were. Only they understood the strength and power of the huge Chinese empire and the weakness of the Tibetan army. They knew that monks and nuns were in particular danger, since communist China rejected anything to do with faith, believing only in the god it had created: the round-headed peasant's son Mao Zedong, who had stopped at nothing to achieve great power. This may well have been one reason why Trishul Rinpoche had obeyed the summons from Sikkim. 'Take good care of my monastery,' the tulku told my grandparents as he left, 'but if you feel it's getting dangerous, if the Chinese come here and want to kill and destroy, you must leave. If that happens, lock up the temple well and save your lives.'

Trishul Rinpoche had heard reports that the Chinese were attacking monasteries, destroying statues and ransacking temples. Kunsang remembered her trip home from visiting her sister so many years before, when she had seen a monastery destroyed by the Chinese. Now, herdsmen told my grandparents about marauding soldiers in the area, all wearing the same uniforms, with a red star on their caps. They had seen workers bringing stones from the mountains and piling them up in the valleys to build ribbons over the land, along which wagons rode on wheels. These wagons were not pulled by animals but by roaring machines built by the Chinese.

In the main hall of the Pang-ri monastery stood a precious and fabled statue of the Guru Rinpoche, also known as Padmasambhava, the Lotus Born, the founder of Tibetan Buddhism. Born in the north-west of India in the eighth century, he spread the religion throughout the Himalayas and Tibet. This statue had once stood in a large old monastery that had fallen into disrepair. The monks finally decided to tear it down and use the stones to build a smaller monastery right beside it. Legend had it that Padmasambhava refused to move to the new temple. No matter how many monks tried to lift the statue, no matter how young and strong they were, they couldn't budge it. In the end, the head of the monastery stood before Padmasambhava and shouted: 'Indian, get moving!' Finally the monks were able to lift the statue and carry it into the new temple.

In the consecration ceremony for the new monastery, the monks had ritualistically thrown grains of barley at the statue. The grains had not bounced off the smooth surface and fallen to the ground; they had stuck to Padmasambhava's face, sprouted and started to grow, looking rather like a beard. This miracle showed the monks the power of Guru Rinpoche, and also marked out Pang-ri as a holy site. On the day my grandparents took responsibility for the monastery, the rebellious Guru Rinpoche still stood in the main hall there.

Pang-ri was an ideal place for my grandparents, not just because their house next to the monastery was more comfortable than the old hermitage, but also because they could live together here without anyone objecting. Their only neighbours were a family – mother, father, grandmother and daughter – living in a hut on the other side of a fence to the west of Pang-ri. These neighbours were not welcome in the monastery. The rinpoche had long suspected them of an unsolved theft and had put up the fence to keep them out.

Occasionally herdsmen or villagers from Pang, the village down by the river, came to pray in the temple, bringing offerings to my grandparents. The house was very modest, consisting of a kitchen, a bedroom and a pantry. It also had a stone fireplace, solid walls and a roof that kept out the rain, wind and snow. After all those years living in huts made of branches, it seemed to Kunsang like the house of an aristocrat.

Kunsang's days began to take on a regular pattern. Her main task was maintaining the fire in the hearth, a symbol of the life in a house that was never to go out. At that time most people in Tibet had to go begging to their neighbours if their fire was extinguished, or light it anew using a complicated procedure. They had special fire-lighting equipment that had been used since ancient times, consisting of a square of metal and a small bag that contained tinder and a flint, which they had to strike against the metal. The sparks set fire to the tinder – easily flammable plant material – but it often took many unsuccessful attempts to make the fire.

'Good housewives don't have to beg for fire,' Kunsang always told her daughter Sonam. 'They keep their hearth glowing.'

Every evening Kunsang piled up the ashes neatly on the brick hearth and raked them over the still glowing embers, just as she had done at the hermitage. Covered like this, the fire could glimmer away overnight. Sonam slept next to the hearth in a fur sleeping bag that Kunsang had sewn for her. It held the wonderful scent of animals and was the best protection against the terrible cold that crept into the kitchen through the open chimney above the fireplace. If she stretched out slightly, she could see the stars shining overhead.

By the time Sonam woke, Kunsang was back from her early-morning chores in the temple and working away at the hearth. She'd push the ashes aside with a poker, throw a handful of twigs on to the embers, and soon a new fire was blazing. Then she would rub a few flakes of butter into tsampa, sprinkle it with finely grated cheese and pour tea over it. The resulting salty broth was their breakfast, midday snack, drink and main meal all in one.

After their meal, my grandparents went into the gompa, as Buddhist monasteries are called in Tibet. The Pang-ri gompa was a small building with a large room on the ground floor and a smaller attic room. Impressive columns decorated with colourful carvings rose to the high ceiling of the ground-floor room, which contained an altar and several wooden statues of deities, as well as printing plates and printed books stored in wooden bookcases. Masks hung high on the walls, their mouths agape, showing their pointed teeth and red tongues. On the tables before these frightening figures were offerings: balls of tsampa, painted red and decorated with flecks of butter: and butter lamps, which flickered over the deities. When Sonam ventured into the room, it seemed that supernatural beings with angry faces and many arms and legs moved in the light of the lamps, glaring at her. It was as if the gods were watching her wherever she went, and when she took a few hasty steps and turned back suddenly, their eyes were still fixed upon her.

The upstairs room was even more mysterious. It could only be accessed via a steep staircase and was always closed by a folding door. Only my grandfather was allowed to open it and enter the attic. He prayed twice a day in this temple to the protective deities, at sunrise and sunset. Before his prayers, he or Kunsang lit smoke offerings in the two sangbum, large receptacles that rested on stone plinths in front of the monastery building. Shaped like amphorae, each had an opening at the front, through which Tsering inserted juniper. When set alight, its fragrant smoke pleased the gods. These rituals drove away all ill-meaning forces and spirits and softened the hearts of the protective gods. Such ceremonies protected the well-being not only of the monastery but of the entire area.

Sonam was strictly forbidden from entering the attic, but sometimes her curiosity outweighed her fear. More sliding than walking, she climbed the steps and sat in the dark outside the door hiding its great secret. There she listened to the dull thuds of the drum rhythmically accompanying her father's prayers. One day, while her father was in the attic, she plucked up her courage, crept up the stairs and found the folding door open. She peered into the dark room. What a disappointment! All she could make out was another closed door, behind which her father was praying. She was seized with fear and beat a hasty retreat.

Every now and then her curiosity would drive her up the stairs again to catch a glimpse of the attic and the secret room, but she was never to see it. Only many years later did she learn exactly what happened in that room behind the second door: her father prayed to protective divinities and made offerings to them. These rituals were reserved for men, which was why even Kunsang was never allowed into the attic.

Kunsang herself recited her prayers and made her offerings in the lower room. With a series of prostrations she approached the large altar, upon which stood the statue of Guru Rinpoche, the Padmasambhava. By the dawn's light she placed seven large silver bowls in a row in front of him, with space between them for exactly one grain of barley. Then she filled the bowls with water from left to right, taking great care to make the distance between the surface of the water and the rim of the bowl precisely one grain of barley high. In the evenings she gathered up her bowls as she prayed, this time from right to left, threw the water outside, cleaned the bowls, dried them and placed them upturned in a pile on the altar.

In between performing these ritual tasks, Kunsang constantly moved her prayer beads between the fingers of her left hand. One bead after another slipped through her fingers whenever she was not filling the butter lamps, tending her little kitchen garden, gathering firewood, keeping the fire burning, stirring the daily tsampa broth, picking vegetables or taking care of her younger daughter. All day long she murmured om mani peme hung.

During this time, little Sonam often sat outside the monastery and gazed down at the sketchy outlines of the houses and fields that formed the village of Pang far below, where the black ribbon of the Pang Chu river ran through the dark valley. She grew up accompanied by the rustling of trees, the crowing of ravens and the babbling of a nearby stream. Only occasionally did she hear snatches of voices in the distance: herdsmen calling to their animals. The pure, cold air flowed around her as she waited on the threshold of the monastery, longing for her parents to finish their prayers. This patch of earth was populated only by Sonam, her little sister, her parents, the neighbours and the monastery dog, along with a few birds, distant yaks and the timid animals of the forest, which she rarely caught sight of.

Sonam was left much to her own devices in Pang-ri. Her parents were busy in the monastery, her sister was still a baby and slept half the day, and there were no other children around. Even the monastery dog, Gaba Lha Gye, whose name meant 'may the happy gods win out', was not much of a playmate; he was big and wild and slept most of the time. Sonam collected young acorns, still soft and green, which she made into tiny spinning tops. She created a whole world in her imagination out of stones, leaves and wood. Long stones were people, round stones were yaks, small stones were birds, and leaves became clothing and blankets, beds and cushions.

She often sat under a tree with her only friend, the old woman from next door, listening to the croaking calls of the pheasants and hoping to hear a cuckoo. Mostly she heard only the wind rustling in the grass and the buzzing of insects. Neither Sonam nor the old woman spoke as they sat together and Sonam played. The old woman had no teeth left in her mouth, only a few black stumps protruding from her gums. On her belt she wore a hollowed-out walnut shell that could be opened up and was filled with some mysterious substance Sonam was sure she had never come across before. The old woman stroked it across her lips and also put it into her mouth. Sonam watched her very carefully, but she couldn't fathom the mystery of the nutshell, and she didn't dare to ask her neighbour what it was. In old Tibet, children never asked adults questions, and adults explained very little to them. Children weren't supposed to know everything or meddle in adult affairs. They learned by watching and imitating what they saw.

Sonam abided by this rule, though nobody had ever explained it to her; she simply knew it. She never touched the neighbour's mysterious nutshell, as there are few greater taboos for Tibetans than mingling saliva with that of a strange person. Two unrelated Tibetans would never drink from the same bowl, never eat with the same spoon – that is impure. So Sonam went to her mother and begged for her own walnut shell: 'Please, Amala, just for me. I'd so like a nutshell like the old woman'.

Kunsang had very little time to see to her daughter's wishes; she had to pray and gather juniper, fill the lamps, fasten the wicks, take care of the household and Sonam's little sister. But Sonam eventually talked her around. Kunsang hollowed out a walnut and bored two holes in each half, threading a string through them to make a tiny container that opened at one side. Then she gave her daughter the nut. To her delight, Sonam discovered that it was filled with butter. Now when she sat with the old woman under a tree, listening to the birds singing and Tsering drumming, she too opened her walnut and smoothed a little butter on her lips to moisten them, and then licked it from her fingers.

The villagers' rare visits to bring food to the monastery were a welcome change to the monotony of Sonam's days. The peasants gladly gave the family their tsampa, butter and dried yak meat, as it meant that Tsering and Kunsang would make offerings and pray for them, which they were not able to do themselves.

In return for their gifts, my grandparents gave the villagers hairs they had collected from Trishul Rinpoche. Anything that had once been part of a lama or had been touched by one was considered holy. People either wore these precious spiritual items in amulets around their necks or burned them, inhaling the spiritually cleansing smoke. Monks even used the urine of their lamas to moisten tiny balls of clay, which they swallowed like magic pills in times of need, or to prevent sickness and harm. After Trishul Rinpoche had been gone for many months, Tsering's supply of hairs was running out, so he mixed hairs from yaks and horses in with those of the rinpoche to stretch his resources. When Kunsang noticed what he had done, she was angry, considering it deception. But Tsering told her it was perfectly legitimate – it was all for the good cause of helping the villagers in their faith. This represents one of the deeply human aspects of this religion as practised by simple everyday people. It makes no difference whether 'sacred hairs' come from a guru or a horse. The results make the people happy, and that is a good thing.

In the autumn, my grandparents stocked up for winter. They collected dry branches that had fallen from the bushes and sparse trees, piling them up for firewood. They stored labu (long radishes), yungma (turnips) and potatoes in a deep hole that Tsering had dug behind the house. Other supplies for the long winter were dried peas wrapped in cloth bags, the dried and chopped leaves of the yungma, and onions, which hung from the rafters in the kitchen. Kunsang pressed butter into clean pigs' and sheep's stomachs, which she then sewed shut and stored in a cool nook of the house. As long as it was still warm, the butter soon became soft and rancid, but in winter it froze into lumps as hard as stone and kept very well indeed. It is a myth that Tibetans like to eat rancid butter and make it into butter tea. They only do this if they have no way to keep their butter supplies cool over the summer.

In the winter, while the white storms raged outside, Sonam squatted by the fire and played one of the few games Kunsang had taught her, doing conjuring tricks with tiny balls of tsampa. She spent hours practising these tricks, and never grew bored of them. Since she had no toys, she made herself things to play with. She upturned a short-legged little table, wound a string around it and pulled it along behind her. This was her yak, which she would drag around the kitchen with loud bangs and crashes until her mother made her stop.

Sonam's games were not popular with her parents when they threatened to disturb the peace of the monastery. She found this out the hard way when she decided to build her own musical instrument, inspired by her father's drumming. She fastened shards of clay, wood, stones and metal to the wall of their house and began beating away at them with a stick, while she shouted and roared. Kunsang came running out of the kitchen and banned her from ever performing another concert, leaving the budding musician in floods of tears. This cacophony would not please the local gods and spirits, Kunsang told her. She did not mean to be cruel – for her, religion was the most important thing; everything else was unnecessary distraction and disruption. Her world had little room for fun and games.

Sonam's life improved with the arrival of spring. She and the old woman from next door sat outside, enjoying the first rays of sunshine and listening to the slight crackle of the crusted snow as it thawed. As it grew warmer, Sonam and her mother climbed the slopes by the monastery to collect wild mustard, onions, nettles and the leaves of a mallow-like plant called tshampa. After six months of winter, with no fresh food, eating plants again was pure bliss. Whenever they had their first nettle soup of the year, Kungsang would offer a prayer of gratitude to nature for giving her family fresh plants.

They also collected the leaves of ribwort plantain, which could be eaten only when young and fresh, before the first cuckoo called. The first time they heard a cuckoo, they had to put something edible into their mouths straight away. 'If someone has an empty stomach when they hear the first cuckoo of the spring, they will go hungry all year long,' Kunsang said. So at this time of the year, whenever Sonam left the house, her mother put something to eat in her pocket. A real luxury.

Kunsang planted lots of marigolds in her little kitchen garden. Sonam was not allowed to pick the bright, tempting flowers, which were used only for offerings. Instead she gathered wild flowers at the edge of the woods or in the meadows. Even those she should not pick unless she had a reason, her mother told her, so she collected them for the altar.

Summer was the most magnificent season. In summer Sonam went for walks with the old neighbour. Like her, she leaned on a stick as she walked; she wanted to do everything the way her friend did. She had to hold her neighbour by the arm, telling her where they were going and what she could see; the old woman was almost blind, so she was content to follow her little guide at every turn.

When the time came to look for wild caraway, Sonam knew that the wonderful warm days would soon be coming to an end. The clouds began to lower and the cold winds blew, announcing the arrival of autumn. Then Kunsang and Sonam climbed even higher into the mountains to gather the juniper they needed for the smoke offerings in the temple, and to exchange barley with the herdsmen for cheese, butter and yoghurt. They ate the yoghurt as they sat with the herdsmen, and brought home several kinds of cheese and fresh butter in holders Sonam had made on the way up, breaking off large leaves and folding them into containers sealed together with tiny sticks. Kunsang used cloth bags to carry grated cheese. Fresh cheese was a special treat that lasted only a few days. Mostly they ate dry grated cheese – *chuship* – with *tsampa*. Kunsang chopped *chura* (dried cheese) into cubes, threading them on to a string that she hung from the ceiling until the cheese hardened. Sonam sucked on these for hours, keeping them in her mouth for as long as possible so that they let out their flavour bit by bit. This hard cheese was the Tibetans' favourite snack.

My mother lived her childhood days in Tibet just like Heidi in the Swiss children's books. During her later years in Switzerland she loved to play the Tibetan Heidi. Even today she still feels most at home surrounded by nature; she can spend hours sitting in a flowering meadow, looking at the distant Alps and daydreaming to the sound of cowbells and birdsong.

One morning, Sonam did not feel like getting up and gambolling across the meadows. She wanted only to lie by the fire in the kitchen, wrapped tightly in her fur. She alternately shivered and sweated, growing weaker by the hour until she could no longer eat or even drink tea.

Kunsang tied her four-year-old daughter securely into her *chupa* and set off with a heavy heart. She was very frightened. She had lost two of her children to disease, and she feared for Sonam's life.

She had heard from the villagers that a rinpoche was staying in the valley, and she hoped that he would know how to deal with Sonam's sickness, that he knew how to make sacred pills out of herbs and speak healing prayers she could repeat at home. The rinpoche received her immediately. He reached for his prayer beads to perform *mo*, the magical divination that most rinpoches command. It wasn't long before he told her, 'Carry your child four times around the holy lake Basum Tso, and she will recover.'

The lake was a day's trek from Pang, and it was almost twelve miles long and three-quarters of a mile wide. With the weight of her daughter on her back, it would take Kunsang at least two days to walk around it, which meant that she would be walking for at least eight days if she wanted to go round it four times. It would be torture, a great feat of stamina, but she had no other choice.

She thanked the rinpoche and went to collect food for her journey. Then she set out, walking through valleys, wading through rivers and climbing over mountain pastures until she finally reached the banks of the sacred lake and threw herself to the ground. It looked like a huge shimmering emerald set between dark woods and snow-capped peaks. There was an island in the middle housing a small monastery with bright prayer flags strung out alongside it. The sounds of drumming wafted over to her. At both the foot and the head of the lake were villages where pilgrims could spend the night.

The beautiful surroundings were lost on Kunsang. She summoned up all her strength and willpower and kept walking, her back burdened with her quietly wheezing child, as well as a full sack of *tsampa*, a bowl of butter and a bag of tea, a pan and a ladle. Fortunately, the path was well trodden. Basum Tso had been an important Tibetan Buddhist pilgrimage site for centuries; it was considered particularly auspicious to begin a pilgrimage on the fifteenth day of the fourth month of the Tibetan calendar. Because it was later in the year, Kunsang came across few fellow pilgrims. It normally took a whole day to reach the upper village from the lower one, but Kunsang walked so fast that she circled the entire lake in a single day. At the halfway point she stopped to rest. She pushed three stones together into a triangle and lit a fire for her tea, a difficult and time-consuming process. After that she hurried on as fast as she could to reach the village at the other end of the lake. There she asked a villager to put her up for the night; it was very common for locals to take in pilgrims and give them a meal and a bed. The next morning she continued around the lake, walking so fast that the few other pilgrims could not keep up with her. Her whole body ached, her back was burning beneath her heavy burden, and she had no time to enjoy the beauty of the lake, the mountains and the sky. She was focused only on Sonam's recovery, praying silently for her to return to health.

Kunsang managed to walk four times around Basum Tso in only four days, half the usual time. Her pilgrimage worked: not long after she returned to the Pang-ri monastery, Sonam recovered. Soon she picked up her everyday life, dividing her time between the temple, little walks with the old neighbour and sitting by the fire. For days, every bone in Kunsang's body ached, but she didn't utter a word of complaint. Instead, she thanked the gods that she had not lost another child.

11

Disaster Looms

The peaceful life of Pang-ri was soon disrupted again. Herdsmen brought the first bad news to the monastery. There had been fighting and blood spilled in Kham, a two- to three-month trek from Pang-ri. The Kampas, my grandmother's ancestors from this region, who were famed for their bravery, had staged an uprising against the Chinese occupiers. But the Chinese had sent more troops to Kham and were overwhelming the freedom fighters. At the same time, they were combing the country for scattered rebels; no village was safe from their patrols. My grandparents listened to this news with great concern, although they did not feel threatened. The Chinese had occupied Tibet for eight years now, and not a single soldier had ever appeared at the monastery.

One autumn morning, they were awakened by the dog's relentless barking. Gaba Lha Gye rarely barked, he was generally happy just to lie in his corner at the side of the house in peace. But on this morning he barked and howled as if he had gone mad, in a way they had never heard before. When Kunsang went outside to see what was upsetting him, she discovered that strange things were going on. The bushes opposite the little house moved, the ground trembled slightly, a whistling rent the air. She saw something blue moving behind the temple. Once, twice, three times the blue leapt, and there was a blue shimmer behind the bushes too. Then the earth shook slightly again, and Kunsang caught sight of a Chinese soldier in green camouflage uniform, his face blackened. He was grasping a long rifle. A blue enamel cup dangled from his belt.

Kunsang rushed into the house to tell Tsering that the Chinese had come. The dog would not stop barking, so Kunsang had to go back out to tether him and calm him. Tsering stayed inside; they had heard that the Chinese were looking for Tibetan men, taking them away for forced labour. Outside, Kunsang spotted more Chinese soldiers with blue enamel cups. She pretended not to see them and hurried around the house. A Chinese soldier only a few feet away from her pointed his rifle and shouted in an incomprehensible language. Before she could look around, she was surrounded by Chinese.

A Tibetan man she had never seen before came up to her and told her that he was with the soldiers and would translate for them. They wanted to know if there were rebels hiding in the monastery. Kunsang shook her head and said they could look for themselves. The soldiers stormed into the house with their rifles, but found only my frightened grandfather, my mother and her sister. They went tramping through the monastery, disturbing the peace of the sacred rooms, knocking at the walls, calling out unintelligible remarks and banging their rifles against the statues. They left empty-handed, threatening my grandparents that they would come back and impose strict punishments on anyone hiding rebels.

Soon afterwards a storm blew up. There was a crash of thunder, and lightning struck the door of the monastery, leaving a black mark. Snow whirled through the air and, down in the valley, the storm tore the roofs off the houses. A large tent set up by the Chinese in the middle of the village was ripped to pieces. Everyone knew this was a sign from the gods, who were angered by how the Chinese had treated them.

Just as my grandparents had begun to recover from the shock of the Chinese soldiers, the next portent of disaster arrived. Once again there was noise in the early morning: growling and howling and crashing and banging that echoed across the mountains. Kunsang was more cautious this time; she opened the door a crack and peered out. She saw nothing unusual, so she opened the door wide and caught sight of what was making all the noise: a snow leopard was creeping around the house. She closed the door right away, and had to calm down a moment before she could tell the others what she had seen.

There was more banging and snarling. Carefully Tsering crept over to the tiny window and tried to get a look at the leopard. The huge grey and white cat was beating its tail against the ground, a sound so loud it reverberated off the mountains. No one dared set foot outside until it had left. When they did go out, they found the tracks of its huge paws in the snow that had not yet melted on the shady ground behind the temple. The rarely seen snow leopard was a harbinger of terrible things to come.

When they heard the thundering crashing again two nights later, my grandparents leapt out of bed and ran to the window, but there was nothing to be seen but a clear, starry night and the outlines of the mountains. They knew the snow leopard must have been walking around the house, but they didn't want to go outside to find him. The next morning, Kunsang waited and listened care-fully before she dared to fetch water from the spring. As she walked there, she called the dog, but he did not come. Later, when she took him his food, she found poor Gaba Lha Gye lying in his corner, drenched in blood, his stomach torn open, his entire body disfigured by bite wounds. The family dug a hole and buried the dead animal. They lit a butter lamp for him and included him in their prayers.

After all these bad omens, my grandparents were hardly surprised when they heard a flurry of clucking and flapping one morning outside the house. They opened the door to an astounding sight: a group of hens was rushing around the grounds. Kunsang soon spotted a villager, who told her that the Chinese soldiers had begun to catch live hens and throw them into boiling water. Since Tibetans keep hens only for their eggs, not for their meat, the villagers were appalled, and decided to drive their birds up into the mountains. He had brought his hens to what he hoped was the safety of the monastery grounds.

It was not long before the Chinese returned to the monastery and demanded that my grandmother give them the hens. She almost abandoned her usual composure and raised her voice, but she controlled herself and merely said that she could not give them the birds because they did not belong to her. The Chinese didn't care. They bagged up dozens of hens while Kunsang surreptitiously shooed away as many as she could. Some flew into trees, some on to the roof of the temple. Unfortunately, the birds not caught by the Chinese soon fell prey to eagles and other wild animals.

A few days later, Chinese soldiers returned to make a thorough search of the monastery. This time they were not looking for rebels or hens – they sought weapons, gold and other valuables, and were ransacking one monastery after another, trying to fill their war coffers. They removed ritual objects made of precious metals from the temple, valuable statues and thangkas, along with spears and knives, which they considered weapons even though they were only used for ritual ceremonies. They even took away the knives from Kunsang's kitchen, leaving her no implement to chop her turnips and onions.

After they had made a pile of everything that looked valuable, the soldiers went through the monastery building again, this time even more closely. They noticed a small window on the outside but couldn't find a room to match it, so they assumed there was a hiding place in the temple and ordered my grandparents to open it. The two of them were baffled. 'There is no secret room,' they told the soldiers. This only made the Chinese even angrier. They beat their rifle butts on the walls and ceilings of the upper floor of the monastery until they discovered a door hidden behind a heavy board. Using the axes and spears they had stolen from the temple, they broke the door down and discovered a secret room filled with dusty old masks, weapons and trunks. Even my grandparents had not known this room existed. The soldiers also found a Chinese enamel bowl containing a felt bag of silver coins. Their commander accused Kunsang and Tsering of having stolen these coins.

'But we knew nothing about the room, or the objects in it,' they insisted. 'Take what you want, these things mean nothing to us.' Though they truly had no interest in gold and treasure, they deeply regretted losing all the rinpoche's beautiful objects, which they were supposed to be protecting. The greedy soldiers took everything that might have the slightest value outside, then destroyed what was left of the room with their feet and axes. Watching how disgracefully the Chinese treated these holy objects was a terrible experience for my grandparents. Later they heard that two of the soldiers who had been involved in the looting had died miserable deaths.

It was after this incident that my grandmother began to think of escape. Should they leave Tibet, leave the country that could no longer be their own now that the Chinese controlled everything? Should they flee to India, the promised land of Buddhism? Or to Sikkim, where the venerated Trishul Rinpoche, the owner of their monastery, had gone? This new idea was so radical to her that she didn't even mention it to her husband. Only when she was alone before the altar did she begin to plan: on the pretext of helping with the harvest, she and her family could visit her younger brother and set out on their escape from there.

After these rude interruptions, peace descended over the monastery again, but it was a deceptive peace. Kunsang and Tsering repaired the broken doors as best they could and gathered up the scattered pages of the holy books, which are traditionally composed of loose sheets of paper tied together between cloth or wooden covers.

One day Sonam upturned a little wooden table from the kitchen, put her sister inside, tied a string to it and pulled her through the fields around the monastery, eliciting cries of joy. Kunsang was amazed to hear her say to her sister: 'Come on, let's go to India!' She couldn't understand why Sonam had said such a thing; she hadn't mentioned her plan even to Tsering. Was this a sign? She thought about all the terrible things that had happened and what might come next. Would the Chinese return to the monastery and destroy everything? Would they take Tsering away? Would they soon ban everything that was sacred to them? She had been told that the Chinese wanted to abolish everything religious; they even wanted to do away with the differences between aristocrats and peasants. She couldn't believe that was possible, but she was soon to see how it could be done.

12

Re-education

The Chinese had already begun to 're-educate' hundreds of millions of people in their own country, and they now began to apply their methods in Tibet. Soldiers had put up a tent in the village of Pang, where they held regular meetings. Not only were the villagers required to take part, but also the monks and nuns living in the remote monasteries, nunneries and hermitages in the surrounding mountains. Kunsang walked down to the village and squeezed into the crowd. The Chinese criticized the terrible condition of Tibetan society, lecturing about exploited peasants and evil landowners, good-for-nothing monks and grasping rinpoches. They claimed that Tibet was in a state equivalent to the Dark Ages, with the authorities forcing the common people to believe terrible things and carry out inhumane practices. Kunsang was horrified. No one forced the Tibetans to believe, they practised their religion freely and voluntarily and it made them happy to do so. The Chinese didn't care; all they wanted was for the Tibetans to submit to their authority.

Once the Chinese had finished their critique, the villagers were forced to speak. One after another the soldiers led them up on to the podium and ordered them to exercise 'self-criticism'. They were supposed to tell their life stories, describing the traditional Tibetan ways as feudal and backwards, and praising everything Chinese as correct, progressive and promising a bright future. Most of the villagers were terrified and said what the Chinese wanted to hear: that life before the invasion had been terrible, full of poverty and desperation, and that the aristocrats had oppressed them and the monks had exploited them. The Tibetans didn't believe a word of what they were saying so they didn't give convincing performances, merely reciting their sentences by rote.

At the end of the meeting they all had to chant the slogan 'Long live Mao Zedong'. But while Kunsang was wishing the comrade chairman a long life, in her heart she was praying that the Chinese would go home.

My grandfather had to take part in the next meeting. It was just as bad for him, except that because he was the monk responsible for the mountain monastery, he was interrogated by Chinese officers and bureaucrats seated at a table. 'Out with it, where did you get your food from all these years? Where did you steal it?' an officer shouted at him.

My grandfather knew perfectly well what the man wanted from him, but he pretended to be simple. 'We eat *tsampa* and drink tea,' was all he said.

'Nonsense!' roared the man. 'I want to know who gave you your food! And what work you did for it!'

The officer repeated his questions over and over, but Tsering simply answered that he prayed and raised his children, grew vegetables and collected wood for the winter. He went into such detail about his daily chores that the Chinese soon got annoyed and let him step down. That was precisely what my grandfather had wanted to achieve, and he was relieved that it had been so easy.

93

But as he walked through the village, glad that he would soon be back at the monastery, he saw soldiers patrolling everywhere. He was scared of the Chinese; he had heard rumours that they took Tibetan men prisoner at random, so he hid out with acquaintances in the village for a few days.

When Tsering didn't come home after the propaganda meeting, Kunsang grew more and more worried and frightened. Finally, on the fifth day, he returned. He had waited until things had calmed down in the village before he dared make his way back to the monastery.

Only Kunsang took part in the next meeting, during which the Chinese sprang their next surprise: they would be taking all the land from the monasteries and landowners. They wanted to divide the land, most of which had been administered for centuries by long-established aristocratic families, between the previously landless peasants, herdsmen, tradesmen and serfs, so that they could culti-vate it themselves. Like most Tibetans, Kunsang was appalled at this plan to upset the fundamental structure of their lives. According to Tibetan beliefs, all land was merely on loan from the Dalai Lama and the divine Tibetan state. For generations the peasants had served the aristocrats, admired them, feared them and relied on them to make decisions. The aristocrats told them how to work the land; they held authority on legal matters and provided admin-istration, order, even the pageantry in life. Everyone knew their place in society; everyone knew what to do to stay on the path to a better reincarnation, to which anyone could aspire.

Suddenly all this was to be abolished. The Chinese put the aristocrats behind bars or into what they called labour re-education camps. They allocated the expropriated land to the previously landless peasants, randomly parcelling up fields and meadows and then generously distributing what did not belong to them.

To her great surprise, a Chinese bureaucrat informed Kunsang that she and her family would be allowed to stay at the monastery and even to undertake the pilgrimages required of monks and nuns. She suspected this might be a trick to see if they tried to escape.

One piece of bad news followed another. Reports came of monks who had been sent back to their monasteries later being chased down, arrested and locked away. Temples and monasteries had been wrecked and burned, statues and holy scriptures desecrated. Lhasa was under siege. There had been a major uprising there because the Tibetans feared that the Chinese occupiers wanted to abduct the Dalai Lama. Chinese officers had insisted that he attend a theatre performance outside his residence – without his guards or his cere-monial public convoy. This violated centuries of tradition. Tens of thousands of Tibetans had gathered outside the residence to protect the Dalai Lama from the Chinese. This was an important day for Tibet. Although there had been smaller uprisings before, mainly in the eastern provinces of Kham and Amdo, 10 March 1959 marked the official beginning of the unrest. To this day, Tibetans around the world celebrate it as Tibetan Uprising Day, even though, with typical cynicism, the Chinese administration has attempted to make it a public holiday as the Day of Liberation.

After the uprising, the Chinese went on the offensive, shelling the Dalai Lama's palace. He fled to India with a few loyal compan-ions. Meanwhile, thousands died in battles against the Chinese, and countless Tibetans were arrested, tortured and murdered. Many weeks later, when Kunsang found out about these terrible events, she saw that the only hope for herself and her family was to escape to India, and made up her mind to follow the Dalai Lama into exile.

My grandfather, however, would hear nothing of it. 'Trishul Rinpoche has given us the task of looking after the monastery, and that is what we must do,' he told her. He ignored her objection that the rinpoche had advised them to leave if they were unable to live under the Chinese. 'They've already taken everything from us that interests them,' he assured her.

Kunsang told him everything she had heard about torture and prison camps, but Tsering thought it was all exaggerated. Months passed as my grandparents discussed whether or not to escape. Then Tsering had to attend another Chinese re-education meeting. When he arrived in the village, his heart stopped. Aristocrats from the surrounding area had been herded together in the middle of the square. Chinese soldiers were beating them, knocking them to the ground, kicking them and pulling them through the dirt by their hair. The villagers were horrified, but none dared to stand up to the soldiers. Some cried silently. A Chinese officer dragged several random villagers into the circle and ordered them to hit and kick the former landowners and their wives.

Now Tsering knew that the Chinese would destroy everything – and that he and his family had to get far away from this insanity.

Later my grandparents learned that the Chinese had arrested the aristocrats and crammed them into stables. They were forced to empty the peasants' latrines, spread manure on the fields with their bare hands and carry stones, firewood and water for their former serfs and servants. Many of them committed suicide. The Chinese forced monks and lamas to kill birds, insects, rats and other small animals, knowing that killing living creatures is the worst thing a Buddhist can do. Particularly high lamas had to beg for forgiveness in public for their wealth, which they had long since lost, had they even had any in the first place, since many lamas lived simple, modest lives. The villagers were forced to mock and jeer at them, beating them and torturing them at daily public meetings that the Chinese called by the Tibetan name of thamzing, which means something like 'combat meetings'. None of the villagers enjoyed these activities, but anyone who refused was subjected to brutal persecution himself.

The Chinese claimed to have liberated the Tibetans from the grip of an aristocratic and priestly caste, but that is far from the truth. Old Tibet was certainly not an egalitarian society, and there were many examples of injustice: the simple people had little to live on, and many servants were poorly recompensed, some even kept in a state similar to serfdom, which forbade them from leaving their masters' land and didn't allow them to make personal decisions for themselves. Despite all this, the population was held together by deep shared beliefs.

People accepted their fate as karma, the result of their actions in past lives. The poor hoped to change their karma in the next life through virtuous deeds, contact with the gods and spirits and having the right rituals performed at their death. The great ideological structure that shaped the lives of the common population of Tibet was less the scholarly Buddhism of the monks, nuns and rinpoches than a form of folk religion, a mixture of Buddhism and animistic and shamanistic practices. Just as the Tibetans revered their rinpoches, gurus, buddhas and bodhisattvas, so they also paid homage to thousands of ever-present local deities and spirits that lived in every rock, on every mountain, in every river or woodland. They worshipped their house gods, tent gods and hearth gods. If the milk boiled over on the fire, the angry house god had to be appeased. Anyone who crossed a pass piled a few stones at the highest point in homage to the local mountain god. The Tibetans feared the wandering souls of the dead, worried that their 'shadow soul' might be stolen by a *dongdre*, the lost soul of a dead person. Their world was inhabited by countless beings that were to be avoided or revered, appeased or warded off. This densely populated spirit world explained everything that happened around them.

All this the Chinese occupiers sought to destroy. They never understood that the Tibetans did not feel like a backward, subjugated people in the grasp of the clerics and aristocrats. Nor were they willing to believe that the Tibetans would have developed their society, of their own accord and in their own way, to meet the demands of a new era.

At first the Tibetans not only roundly rejected the new ideological structure imposed by communism, initially they simply ignored it. But as time passed, it became more and more difficult to maintain the old faith in the face of all the fundamental changes the Chinese made to the Tibetan way of life.

Both my grandparents were highly educated. They could read and write and had studied many Buddhist scriptures. Even so, they too trusted in folk beliefs and customs in many practical areas of everyday life. They would choose a particular day to set out on a journey. They relied on the power of objects touched by the holy breath of a lama. They saw no distinction between 'genuine' Buddhism and superstition. For them, everything was chö, true Buddhist faith. But they had to accept that neither house spirits nor gods could help them against the Chinese. They felt they had only one option – and that was exile to India. Though they did not know anyone on the Indian subcontinent and hadn't the slightest idea of what awaited them, they knew that the Dalai Lama had found refuge there, and their faith in him made them believe that India would be their refuge.

13

Escape

My grandparents kept to themselves their decision to escape, not even telling my mother or her younger sister their plan. Kunsang told the children that they would be visiting their uncle, then going on a pilgrimage. The risk of being betrayed to the Chinese was great. A few Tibetans sympathized with the new rulers and collaborated with their campaigns.

My grandparents couldn't leave the temple without providing sufficient offerings for the altar. They kneaded *tsampa* with water and butter to make dough. There was too little time to shape it into figures or artworks, so they made it into simple blocks, which they piled carefully before the altar. They filled all the butter lamps the Chinese had overlooked. During their prayers they took barley from their remaining stores and threw it over the deities. They had to do all this at night so that the neighbours did not notice.

One night, their prayers before the altar were interrupted by a child crying. Kunsang rushed out and found Sonam weeping outside the door to the temple, half carrying, half dragging her four-year-old sister with her. The two of them had woken up, found their parents missing and been scared. Kunsang tried to calm her daughters, worried that the neighbours might get suspicious. She had told them that they were planning a long pilgrimage as their younger daughter was sick, and had asked them to look after the temple during their absence. Kunsang was amazed that the neighbours didn't suspect anything and were obviously not thinking of escaping themselves. On the contrary, they were pleased about their new responsibilities, which broke the rinpoche's long-standing ban on them entering the temple.

Making arrangements with the neighbours opened an old wound. My grandfather had once had an affair with their daughter and she had borne his child. When Kunsang discovered the affair, she was angry and sad, and told Tsering he could move in with this woman and that she would go back to the hermitage with her two daughters. Tsering stopped her, refusing to let her go. He promised that he had finished the affair with the woman and wanted to stay with Kunsang. In time she forgave him and forgot all about it, until the time came to leave.

As they were making their final preparations, Kunsang felt sorry for this woman, who now had a child by a man married to another woman. She selected a couple of valuable objects from the little she possessed, placed them in a pile with some food, and told Tsering to take the gifts over to the neighbours and say goodbye. He also handed them the keys to the temple.

Just before they were due to depart, Tsering left the monastery armed with a stick, only to return late in the evening exhausted, covered in earth and mud, his clothes torn and his hands bleeding. He had been searching in vain for a bag of silver coins he had buried. Like many other Tibetans, he had been given the coins by the Chinese after they first occupied Tibet – a clumsy attempt to win over the population with petty gifts. But now he couldn't find

100

the coins, the only thing of any value they possessed. With this money, they could at least buy food. Tsering was plunged into doubt and wanted to call off their escape, but Kunsang stood her ground: she would leave without him and take the children with her.

At daybreak the next morning, Tsering again climbed into the mountains to the area where he had buried the money. That evening he returned home with his face lit up, the little bag of coins carefully hidden in the folds of his clothing.

Now they were ready to leave. Kunsang packed tsampa, butter, strips of dried meat, dried grated cheese, little cubes of hard cheese and pressed blocks of tea. She also took a pan with folding handles, a folding ladle, a small but valuable rug and a little round container with a mirror on its lid, which contained a red stone that was used as a disinfectant. If anyone was injured, she could wet the stone and rub it on the wound. She also packed the bronze mould used for making tsa tsa. Each of them carried their own wooden dish in the breast pocket of their chupa. Kunsang had a beautiful round wooden bowl with a lid that a well-known rinpoche had given her. They also rolled up a few blankets for protection against the freezing nights.

Neither of my grandparents had a precise idea of the way to India; they knew only that they had to head south. Their route would take them through one of the mountain ranges that surrounded the Pang valley. They knew that the mountains on the way to India were particularly high, but they didn't know that they are the highest mountains in the world: the Himalayas. Kunsang tied her younger daughter to her back with a large cloth, so tightly that neither wind nor cold could come between them, before they all paid one last visit to the temple. Tsering and Kunsang threw themselves to the ground, reciting a final prayer to the gods.

'His holiness the Dalai Lama has left the country,' Kunsang

murmured, 'and now we must go too. Please protect us and watch over us.'

They lit one last smoke offering outside the temple. Sonam stood beside them, crying, not understanding what was happening. She knew her parents were saying farewell to her home, but she had only a vague inkling of why they had to leave and where their journey would take them. My grandparents were absorbed in silent prayer. Tears rolled down Kunsang's cheeks too, tears of sadness and fear and uncertainty. Would she ever again see this place that was so sacred to her?

As the family walked through the village of Pang, they were keenly aware of the searching looks that seemed to be boring into their backs. At the outskirts of the village Chinese soldiers blocked their way, gruffly demanding to know where the heavily laden travellers were going. Kunsang told them they were on their way to her brother a few days' journey west, to help his family in the fields. The soldiers knew from the red clothing that they were a nun and a monk, and they thought that working the land would do them good, so they let them pass without further questioning.

My grandparents and Pema Lodroe often visited one another, as their villages were only two days' walk apart. This time they were visiting him to say goodbye. He was the only person who knew about their plans for escape, and he wanted to give them a horse to carry their heavy loads. Tsering's sack of *tsampa* and butter was nearly half as heavy as he was, and Kunsang's back was burdened by her little daughter, as well as dishes, blankets and the few small possessions they had brought with them. Only Sonam had nothing to carry. She struggled just to keep up with her parents.

For two days the family walked alongside the Pang-chu, the river that passes by Pang. When they reached Kunsang's brother's, they were given a warm welcome, though the promised horse turned out to be a broken-down old nag. The Chinese had conscripted all her brother's other horses for their soldiers.

They spent a few days with Pema Lodroe and his family, feeding the old horse *tsampa* and butter out of their supplies, hoping it would gain enough strength to be capable of carrying at least some of their luggage. The sad, uncertain farewell was nevertheless celebrated in style, with vegetables and *momos*, Tibetan dumplings, filled with meat. In the evening, Kunsang's sister-in-law served them *then thug*, literally 'pulled soup', a vegetable and meat soup with chilli, coriander and dough pulled into long noodles. The adults drank *chang*, home-brewed Tibetan beer. Kunsang presented her brother's family with her *daru*, the beautiful-sounding hand drum that she had used her whole life, and a bell that Trishul Rinpoche had given her. Both these objects were very valuable to her but too heavy to take on the long journey. Sobbing, Kunsang's sister-in-law accepted these spiritually important objects, promising to look after them, and in return gave Kunsang a silver bracelet. 'It will come in very handy if you have nothing to eat,' her sister-in-law explained. 'It's not heavy and you can always sell it.'

Before sunrise the next day, Tsering divided their *tsampa* supplies into two bags. He tied one to the horse's back along with the blankets and the kitchen utensils, the other he shouldered himself. Kunsang tied her little daughter to her back and off they went.

For the next few days they covered long distances, always walking alongside the Pang-chu river. They avoided the routes of the caravans and the large herds, which were usually used by Chinese soldiers as well. The terrain was easy to navigate, over dry grass and through bare bushes. They spent the nights in the protection of small groves of trees, hidden inlets by the river or abandoned huts. One morning they awoke to find that their horse had vanished, even though Tsering had tethered its legs together the previous evening. They searched for hours, but the animal was long gone. They presumed it had loosened its tethers and set off for home.

As they reached the foothills of the Himalayas, their path became more challenging, up one hill and down another. The swathes of mist parted to reveal Bön-ri, or Mount Bön – the sacred mountain of the ancient Tibetan Bön religion. The Bönpos believe that all Tibetans originate from the foot of this mountain. Eventually the moment arrived when the family had to cross the river they had been walking alongside for the past few days. As if ordained by fate, they spotted a man in a traditional leather-spanned wooden boat drifting downstream. They waved and he paddled over to the bank. But to their great disappointment, the man refused to ferry them across the river. He must have guessed where they were going and didn't want to risk getting into trouble. 'My father works for the Chinese,' he said, telling them that the army had posted soldiers all around the area to watch for refugees. Kunsang and Tsering decided to rest under the bushes at the edge of the river and wait until nightfall to continue their journey. To their great surprise, the boatman returned that evening and offered to take them across the water. Once they were on the other side, they carried on, hoping to reach a nearby monastery before dawn. Suddenly the quiet night was shattered by gruff shouts, clattering and the tramping of army boots. Kunsang and Tsering couldn't make out where the Chinese soldiers were; the sounds seemed to come from all directions. Afraid that the soldiers would shoot if they heard them, they spent the night hunkered down at the edge of a field.

When they set out again in the early morning light they heard nothing but the rushing of the Pang-chu River and the whispering of the grass in the cool wind. A few hundred yards on, they came across a group of Chinese soldiers. One of them threw some kind of ball into the river, where it exploded with a loud bang, while the other soldiers ran to and fro along the bank. Tsering and Kunsang couldn't understand what was going on. Today we know that the soldiers were brutally killing fish with hand grenades.

The soldiers immediately suspected the family of being refugees. One of them spoke a little Tibetan, and my grandmother explained to him that they were pilgrims on their way to the nearby monastery, from where they planned to walk around the sacred mountain of Bön-ri. The soldiers couldn't agree whether or not to believe her. She remained unintimidated, simply repeating the name Bön-ri over and over again, miming praying. It was always Kunsang who carried out such negotiations with the Chinese; being a man, Tsering was more likely to appear rebellious and dangerous.

One of the soldiers was already shouldering his rifle, but another of his comrades seemed to contradict him and signalled to the family to proceed. Perhaps the soldiers thought they would never make it to India, or perhaps they simply wanted to carry on fishing in peace.

The sun was high in the sky by the time the family finally reached the monastery. The imposing building was set on a hilltop with a small village at its foot. They were greatly relieved to be able to sleep under a safe roof again; monks and nuns were welcome guests there, as they were in any Buddhist monastery. After a deep and well-earned sleep, Kunsang awoke to find the preparations for the daily prayers already well under way. She quickly shook Tsering awake so that he could take part as well. Sonam woke with a start when she heard the long, low tones of the *dungchen* and the *dungkar*, metal trumpets rather like Alpine horns that called the monks to their prayers. It seemed to her as if the air and the floor around her were vibrating to the sound of the monks' drumming.

Not until the prayers were over did Kunsang begin to make cautious enquiries about the situation along their planned route.

This was no easy task: she couldn't reveal their plan to escape, as there could be Chinese informers anywhere, even in the monasteries. So she told everyone that they were performing kora, walking around the holy mountain Bön-ri three times.

To show that they were devout pilgrims, Kunsang and Tsering gave the monks some of their butter and tsampa and asked them to include them and their children in their prayers. Once they had gained the monks' trust, Kunsang dared to ask a few pointed questions. They were alarmed by what they were told. There were many Chinese soldiers stationed around the monastery, because the area was on one of the most popular escape routes to India. It was difficult to pass through the region unnoticed. However, the sexton told her, most of the Chinese soldiers would soon be withdrawing to fight Tibetan rebels elsewhere.

Kunsang was suspicious of what the sexton told her. They had stayed at the monastery for three nights now, and she had noticed that he never slept, instead walking to and fro while everyone else was in bed. It seemed to her as if the man were keeping a keen eye on them. She feared he might be working for the Chinese and had seen through their disguise as pilgrims.

She shared her fears with Tsering. They were both horrified to think that Chinese power and influence had penetrated even such a sacred place as a monastery. Was there no place left in Tibet where people could live in peace and without fear? Now they faced a dilemma. They knew that the route to India led over the mountains to the south of the monastery, and across Tibet's largest river, the mighty Tsangpo, but they didn't know which valley or pass to take. Because the sexton was behaving so strangely, Kunsang didn't dare ask anyone else in the monastery.

Days passed in idle waiting, until, as predicted, the Chinese withdrew one unit after another and only a few old soldiers were left in the area. Kunsang climbed up to a meadow above the monastery to think and pray undisturbed. Suddenly, high in the surrounding mountains, she spotted a thin white column of smoke standing out against the otherwise spotless sky. A sign, she thought immediately. This can be nothing but a sign from the gods for us, an offering to signal that we can now escape. Hastily, she gathered up her *chupa* and rushed back to the monastery to tell Tsering.

The next day, a Tibetan, a man she had never seen before, approached and asked her where she wanted to go. 'I'm here with my family to go on a pilgrimage,' she answered as calmly as she could. 'One of our children is sick.'

The man nodded and said, 'We'll be making an escape in a few days. Do you want to come with us?' Kunsang said no, repeating that they were on a pilgrimage. The man nodded again and told her to come to him if she changed her mind. Kunsang thought long and hard about this brief encounter. She had liked the man's quiet and friendly manner, but she knew she could trust no one. Nor did Tsering know what they should do.

When the man appeared again the next day, Kunsang summoned up all her courage. 'We want to escape too,' she whispered to him. 'Can we join you?'

The stranger was even friendlier now. 'Yes,' he said simply. 'We're leaving tomorrow evening. You can come with us if you like. I'm travelling with a group. Don't ask about us, it'll only arouse suspicion. And don't ask anyone from the group, they're all very careful.'

Overwhelmed by this stranger's kindness, Kunsang simply gave a silent nod, then hurried to tell her husband what had happened. On her way, she saw a group of people camped outside the monastery. She guessed these were the refugees, and when she saw among them a monk she recognized from another monastery, she felt her family would be safe to proceed to India with them.

107

The next morning, Kunsang met the man who had told her about the escape. 'We're meeting by the river tonight,' he said. 'We've got a boat.' Kunsang simply nodded. Tibetans never agreed to meet at an appointed time; nobody had a watch or a clock. Night began when mountains could no longer be distinguished from valleys, or woods from stones; it ended when the first, second and third cock crowed.

As soon as darkness fell, the family made their way out of the monastery. Other refugees were waiting below: men, women and children, a group of a dozen people. Some had horses loaded with supplies. Tsering and Kunsang had to carry their own belongings, as no one offered to load them on to one of the horses.

The refugees walked in silence until they reached the banks of the mighty Tsangpo river, which flowed as wide as a lake. A few miles on, they rested by the river while two men went to fetch a boat. No one had to remind them not to make any noise. They knew that there would be Chinese soldiers here.

It was not long before the men rowed back in a heavy barge, a traditional Tibetan wooden boat with high sides, at its prow a carved horse's head, staring proudly into the waves. With much clattering and scraping and snorting, the horses were led across a couple of boards into the alarmingly swaying boat, but they were soon calmed, and stood still alongside their wooden likeness. Then the refugees climbed in, silent and apprehensive. Sonam had never seen a river so wide, never imagined that a boat could be so large. As she looked at the alarmingly black water, roiling and gurgling in the light of the half-moon, she was glad that they all had to stand pressed close together. Feeling her mother on one side of her, her father on the other made her feel safer as the boat rocked in the current.

Soon the men pushed the boat away from the bank with their

oars, and all she could hear was the splash and roar of the water. As the current pulled them faster and faster downriver, Sonam gripped the side of the boat with one hand, her mother's arm with the other. Even the horses stood stock still. Perhaps they sensed how frightened the people were. The refugees knew this river was too deep to stand up in, and none of them could swim. As they reached the middle of the river, one of the horses suddenly began scraping its hoof against the bottom of the boat. One of the men managed to calm the frightened animal; everyone else remained frozen with fear until the boat reached the other bank.

Hurrying off the boat, the group quickly resumed their trek, hoping to reach a nearby wood before the sun came up. They were led by a Tibetan trader who had taken this same route on foot with his porters a number of times before. This was to be the last time he made the journey. He too was escaping to India to find a new future. He knew the paths well, and the best places to stop, safely hidden from the Chinese.

The first day's camping ground was damp, with a cold wind blowing across it. Kunsang distributed the daily ration of tsampa to her family, and despite the uncomfortable conditions, they all managed to sleep, especially Sonam, who was exhausted from the hard night's journey. Two men took turns standing guard, so that the group could set off at a moment's notice.

This day all was well, which was fortunate, as the next few nights' treks were to be more strenuous than the first. The refugees always moved by night. They had to steer clear even of their fellow Tibetans, for the local mountain tribes of the Loba worked as guards for the Chinese in return for a few sacks of rice or a crate of liquor. When the group saw the lights of their fires in the distance, and heard their piercing shouts of hoy hoy hoy, they quickened their pace.

During the nights that followed, the group crossed countless minor rivers. They were not broad like the Tsangpo, but in each crossing the adults got wet up to their knees. Tsering was burdened with too many bundles to be able to help Sonam. Sometimes one of the other refugees would carry her across a river; on one occasion, when she had to cross by herself, she got wet up to her shoulders. But it was her feet that suffered the most. Each day, when they reached their camp ground, she would take off her inadequate shoes and inspect the blisters, scrapes and bruises. After a few nights, when the others caught sight of her poor feet, they decided to put her on one of the horses. Though she was scared of the huge beast, she was very glad not have to walk any more. Tied to the baggage fastened to the horse's back with ropes, she crouched low between two sacks of tsampa, happy to rest as the group moved higher and higher into the mountains.

Lulled by the horse's regular movements, and unable to see over the cargo that was her nest, she fell into a grateful sleep, only to be rudely awakened when the horse lost its footing and plunged over the edge of the path. It almost turned a somersault, rearing up and just managing to come to a stop on its side before it slipped farther down the mountainside. Since Sonam was tied on, she couldn't struggle free. Nor could she see anything in the darkness except the sacks that now threatened to smother her and the horse lying on its side. She was about to scream when she remembered that they were escaping and no one was to say a word, let alone shout out. All she could do was groan quietly.

Luckily the adults had witnessed the fall and rushed down the mountainside. Tsering and Kunsang and two other men pulled and dragged wildly at the sacks until they found a silently weeping Sonam. She was unharmed, but badly shaken. Even so, there was no time to rest. The three men pulled the horse back to its feet on a rope and brought it up to the path. They fastened the load again, but Sonam refused to get back on the horse. Her feet might be raw and aching but she trusted them more than she trusted the horse. Once again she followed in her mother's footsteps, but soon she was again facing terror, when they were forced to cross a rope bridge over a raging torrent. After this there would be no possibility of riding a horse anyway, since there was no way the animals could cross the bridge. The men unloaded the sacks of supplies and abandoned the horses, trusting that their instincts would make them follow their own tracks back down to the valley.

The higher the refugees climbed, the more their fear of the Chinese was superseded by fear of the terrain they had yet to cross. Winter had arrived with full force. They no longer travelled by night, yet even by daylight it was hard to make their way between rocky outcrops, over steep drops and through fields of hip-deep snow. Ice-cold winds blew the clouds perched on the mountaintops down into the valleys, where they sat like heavy, damp sacks.

As they walked, Kunsang repeated her *peme hung* and focused on bringing her family to safety. Sonam thought of the cosy kitchen back home in Pang-ri, her warm fur next to the fireplace and the hot butter tea she had sipped there every morning. She had not known then that she was living in an earthly paradise. As she trudged on through the snow, exhausted, aching all over, she tried to think only of her happy past, of meadows full of flowers and treetops swaying in a warm spring breeze—

Then suddenly she lost her footing and was catapulted back to reality.

No matter how often my mother has told me this story, I still feel my heart pounding when she describes that fall through the snow, down into the crevasse. I imagine her lying there on the ice, looking up at the scrap of distant white sky, not daring to call out – knowing that she has to save herself because no one else will help her.

My mother described to me how, driven by wild desperation, she jumped at the wall of her icy prison, clawing her cold-numbed fingers into the snow, pulling herself up with all the strength in her arms, kicking her feet once, twice, once again, until she managed to heave herself over the edge of the hole. Sweating and panting, she lay flat on the snow.

Where were the others? She could make out only a group of grey shadows disappearing along the white path ahead. She jumped to her feet and hopped along the path from one footprint to the next as fast as her legs would carry her, stumbling and tripping like a mountain goat, landing over and over in the snow. Finally the grey shadows grew larger and she recognized her mother and father and all the others. She hurried until she was next to her mother and pressed her face against her *chupa*. Kunsang stroked her head absent-mindedly, not stopping, concentrating only on her steps. She can't have noticed anything, thought Sonam, and she vowed not to tell her mother about her accident and her great fortune until that evening.

The next morning the mountains towered before them not as dark, distant outlines, but like a wall of rock and snow. Sonam had never seen anything like it. She'd lived in mountains her whole life, but these were different. They had no wooded flanks, supported no green pastures. No yaks grazed on them. The refugees had to circle their way up, round countless hairpin turns and up ever-steeper gradients.

Above them rose the mountains, blindingly white in the sun. To look at them, as they stretched impossibly high into the brilliant blue sky, brought tears to Sonam's eyes. As her vision reddened, she pressed her eyelids together against the sting of this blinding light. Below her gaped an abyss. A misstep off the path would mean certain death.

It seemed almost a miracle when, after two harrowing days, the slope softened and a valley opened up before them dotted with a cluster of crooked huts. At first they were afraid that there were Chinese soldiers hiding inside them, but when they saw no footprints in the snow, they ventured closer. The doors were unlocked, the rooms empty. At last they could camp out on more or less dry ground, protected from the wind and snow. They even found a fireplace and broke a few small pieces of wood off one of the buildings to light a fire for their first hot tea in weeks. They were almost happy. Surely they must be near the border.

Suddenly the man keeping watch outside ran into the room with shock on his face: 'People! From the other side!'

With courage born of desperation, the men rushed outside, only to see three Tibetans coming up from the pass behind them. They seemed untroubled by the snow and the cold and the effort of the climb; they moved as fast as snow leopards. They were herdsmen who had taken animals across the border and were on their way back to Tibet to fetch a new herd.

The man who was obviously their leader warned the group, 'You can't possibly stay here. It's too dangerous. The Chinese were here a few days ago; they captured a group of our people and took them back to Tibet.'

'These houses are a trap,' said a second man. 'They know people are exhausted when they get here and want to rest. You have to carry on.'

Quickly everyone packed their things, shouldered their packs, thanked the three herdsmen and set off again. Having to go back out into the cold without so much as a sip of tea felt particularly bitter for the refugees, but there was no choice. Everything around them was swathed in mist and snow. A Chinese company could have been standing only a few hundred yards away and they wouldn't have been visible. Their only comfort was knowing that the Chinese wouldn't be able to see them either.

The mountainside grew less steep, and after a few more hours, shadows sprang out of the mist, changing first into green shapes, then into soldiers. Sonam was shocked. Were these the Chinese who wanted to take them prisoner and send them back to Tibet? Had all their agonies been in vain? The others were frightened too and huddled together to discuss what to do. If this was the border pass, they might be Indian soldiers. The refugees agreed that there was no turning back and that the soldiers would easily catch up with them anyway, so they decided to march on. The soldiers' faces looked different from the Chinese, they appeared friendly. Their language sounded different too. Even their uniforms were a different colour.

The trader who acted as the group's leader exchanged a few words with the strange men in a smattering of broken language. Then he said to the others: 'They're Indians!' He added something else about 'made it' and 'border', but his voice was drowned out by the refugees, weeping and laughing and praying and congratulating each other, and a chorus of lha gyalo, meaning 'Victory to the gods!'

14

The Promised Land

After almost a month of travel, the refugees had succeeded in escaping from Tibet, but they were far from the end of their journey. The Indian soldiers did not offer them tea, or anything to eat, and there were no huts to shelter them. Instead they had to continue on, over more ice and snow and rock. Nevertheless, my mother felt as if a heavy weight had been lifted from her. Even the wind that whistled across the pass no longer seemed so cold and harsh. The route was also almost all downhill now, and between the scraps of clouds they caught glimpses of distant green valleys, meadows and rivers. Sonam was overjoyed to see colour again, the familiar landscape she had missed for so many weeks. Everyone in the group was filled with optimism, hungry but happy. They had all made it to India; no one had frozen or starved or fallen to their death. As they clambered down the mountain, they were all in great cheer, convinced they would soon be in the care of the Dalai Lama.

Just below tree level, they reached an army camp, where they were finally given something to eat and drink and offered supplies for the next few days. The soldiers recorded the refugees' names and inspected their baggage. They even asked them to undress, but they all refused. Tibetans never appear naked in front of other people, especially not strangers.

Their sacks now stuffed full of rice, flour, tea and lentils, the Tibetans continued their trek downhill. As they descended, the air grew more and more humid. They were unaccustomed to such conditions, and the joy and lightness they felt in freedom soon gave way to sweaty exhaustion. Their route led over swaying rope bridges planked with bamboo poles and back up more steep slopes. After a few miles of strenuous walking, they came across a group of Indian herdsmen who offered to carry their supplies. Some of the refugees were only too eager to accept the offer, but they weren't glad of the unexpected help for long. The bearers walked faster and faster, and suddenly turned off on a side path into dense forest. Though several of the men attempted to chase them down, their efforts were in vain. Luckily my grandparents had kept their own supplies on their backs. The others were distraught at losing so much food, but finally they realized they would not find the thieves, and proceeded on to the valley. They expected that they would come across large villages of Tibetan refugees further downhill, and they looked forward to finding friends and relatives who had fled before them. Most of all, they were eager to come into the presence of the Dalai Lama, who would surely help them.

Before they arrived at any Tibetan settlements, however, they came to a military camp where soldiers intercepted Tibetan refugees. The soldiers led them into barracks where they could sleep. The group was grateful for shelter, but their thirst overcame their exhaustion. They had tea leaves but no water. How were they to explain that to their Indian guards? None of them spoke the language.

116

Kunsang had a sudden brainwave. 'Pani, pani,' she said to the Indians. The soldiers understood immediately and brought water. Kunsang had picked up the word in Tibet when Trishul Rinpoche had told her stories about India, and she had never forgotten it. The other Tibetans were amazed and very grateful, until they realized that although there was a fireplace in the barracks, they had no firewood.

'Lakhri,' Kunsang said next. Once again the soldiers understood and brought a pile of sticks. Pani and lakhri were the only Indian words Kunsang knew, but they were to be more than helpful, not only in this camp but in those that followed.

It was a short night. Early the next morning, the soldiers woke the refugees with yells. The Tibetans were still exhausted and could not understand what the soldiers wanted them to do. They felt like yaks herded from one pen to the next, until finally they were ushered into a strange-looking metallic box with what looked like immense dragonfly wings on top. Before they understood what was going on, the soldiers had fastened them to the floor of the box with thick ropes and closed the doors. They were left sitting in near darkness. Suddenly a mighty, ear-splitting roar, like nothing they'd ever heard before, assaulted their ears. Panicked, they shouted out questions to one another. Only Sonam, who sat next to a small window, saw what was happening.

'We're in an iron bird!' she yelled. 'We're flying!' She pointed out of the window, through which she could see the earth and the trees and the tents below becoming smaller and smaller. She was amazed, incredulous that they were really flying high in the air like birds.

'No!' Tsering shouted back at her. He was unable to see anything from where he was sitting. 'We're not flying!' After an hour or so there came a lurching jolt. Suddenly the roaring stopped and Tsering said, 'Now we're flying, I can feel it.'

117

In fact the transport helicopter had just landed. Soon the doors were opened and different soldiers were herding them out.

'Haven't we just got in?' Tsering asked. The soldiers didn't understand my grandfather and shoved him out too.

This new place was much hotter and more humid than the camp they had left, making the refugees fear that the hollow iron bird had flown them to some unknown country. Then they saw that these soldiers were wearing the same uniforms as the first ones; and they pushed, shoved and barked orders just as imperiously and impatiently as their comrades at the border. There was much confusion. The Tibetans didn't understand the soldiers' commands, and their shouting and prodding frightened them. They were led to a large truck, and herded into the back of it. The vehicle travelled for several hours along bumpy roads until it reached a town, the name of which my grandmother remembers vaguely as being Missamari. She does know that it was in the Indian state of Assam, in the far north-east of India, between Bhutan and Bangladesh. The soldiers took the group to a small settlement on the edge of town. Barracks woven out of bamboo were spilling over with Tibetan refugees.

In this region, the villages were as large as Tibetan towns, the towns bigger than anything they had ever seen or even imagined. The landscape was much greener and lusher than at home, the air much warmer and more humid. It was noisy, and everything moved so quickly. Here life was loud and fast, utterly alien to my family, who had lived their lives in remote mountain monasteries. The stiflingly hot, humid climate was the most difficult thing for them to adapt to. The heat was so unbearable it utterly obliterated all memories of the cold, snow and ice they had suffered just days ago. Although it was spring, it was warmer than the height of a Tibetan summer, and it seemed to become hotter by the day. The

Tibetans had no clothing but their now stifling woollen *chupas*, jackets and trousers, and customary modesty forbade them from disrobing.

At the camp, which housed several hundred Tibetan refugees, my grandparents and their travelling companions met acquaintances from Tibet. They approached these reunions full of happy anticipation – they had reached safety, they were free, and they would soon be with the Dalai Lama. But the friends they found at the camp were subdued. Like my grandparents, they too wanted to join the Dalai Lama. He had already set up a Tibetan government in exile in Dharamsala, but Dharamsala was far away, and no one had the resources to set out in search of their spiritual ruler. Life in the camp was a day-to-day struggle to survive, rather than the peaceful Tibetan haven they had imagined.

Obtaining drinking water was a pressing daily problem. In Tibet, it had been an abundant resource; everyone had almost limitless access to fresh, clear, cold spring water. Here the water was warm, cloudy, sometimes nothing but a brown trickle running from the pump in the middle of the Tibetan settlement. The unfamiliar heat and humidity made everyone extremely thirsty, but there was nothing to drink but this foul liquid. The Indians had given them tea, but it was a strong, bitter, reddish Assam blend that tasted terrible to the Tibetans. If only they had a little *tsampa* to mask the awful taste, but there was no *tsampa* to be had.

Only days after their arrival, the first of my grandparents' travelling companions was stricken by stomach cramps, diarrhoea and vomiting. First Kunsang, then Sonam's little sister fell ill. A week later there was no one in the group not complaining of nausea and diarrhoea. My grandparents soon learned that almost every day one of the several hundred inhabitants of the camp died. There was a pharmacy with a few medicines, but they seemed to be of little therapeutic value. Kunsang bought a bottle of sweet red liquid for her younger daughter, who for days had lain feverish and apathetic on her mat, but it didn't help her. Soon she was no longer passing stools, only blood. Kunsang tied the child to her back and took her to a hospital not far from the camp. There, doctors examined her but didn't treat her. When Kunsang returned to the camp the next day, she was not carrying her daughter on her back but in her arms. Sonam's sister had safely crossed the world's highest mountains but faltered on level ground, poisoned by dirty water or bad food.

'She's not a human being any more,' Kunsang told Sonam.

Kunsang wept bitterly, hunched over her daughter's tiny corpse. Sonam had rarely seen her mother cry. Tsering went in search of the monks in the camp to perform *powa*. Then he and Kunsang took the body to a place not far from the camp where a fire always smouldered. This was where the many dead refugees were cremated. They placed Sonam's sister on a small stone platform in the open air and gave her over to the flames. There were no curious onlookers; cremations were an everyday occurrence.

My grandparents used the metal moulds they had brought from home to shape their daughter's ashes into *tsa tsa*, which they placed on the banks of the river that flowed alongside the camp. For forty-nine days, as their religion prescribed, they prayed for their dead child.

Both my mother and my grandmother have forgotten the girl's name. It is not important to Tibetans to remember the names of the dead. My grandmother had even forgotten the names of her own parents. It was only after my persistent pressure and with the aid of my mother that she began to recall them. But she would never say them out loud. She believes that speaking a dead person's name or showing his or her photograph stimulates and summons

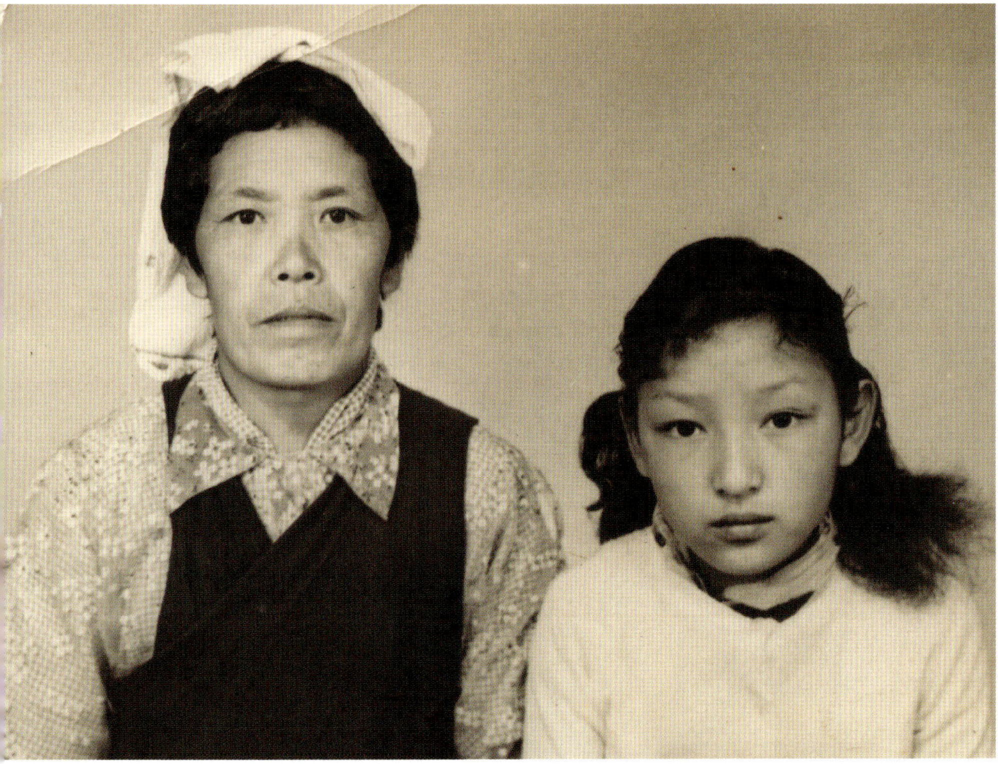

Kunsang and Sonam (aged 10) in Shimla. The first photograph ever taken of them.

Sonam (aged 12) with nameplate on her first day at Stirling Castle.

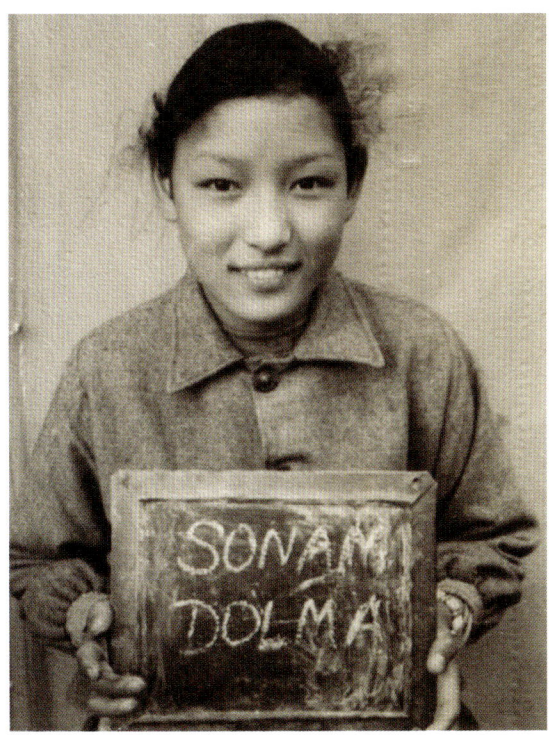

13-year-old Sonam (back left) with 7-year-old classmates.

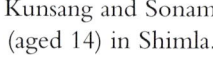

Sonam setting out from Stirling Castle for a trip to Delhi.

Kunsang and Sonam (aged 14) in Shimla.

Sonam and Martin by the Ganges in 1970, the year they met.

Sonam, Tashi
and Yangzom in
Nepal (1984).

Sonam at Pang-ri
on her first trip back
to Tibet in 1986.

Yangzom on a trip
to a monastery
in Thangbi, Bhutan.

Yangzom with two
Bhutanese friends
in the courtyard
of the monastery.

Yangzom helps farmers
with the harvest in
Thangbi, Bhutan.

Sonam beside the
ruins of her family's
old kitchen at Pang-ri

Kunsang reunited
with Puko Ani-la.

The Dalai Lama at the opening of Martin Brauen's exhibition *The 14 Dalai Lamas* in Zurich, 2005.

Sonam in her New York studio.

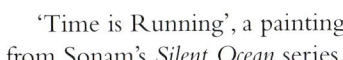

'Time is Running', a painting from Sonam's *Silent Ocean* series.

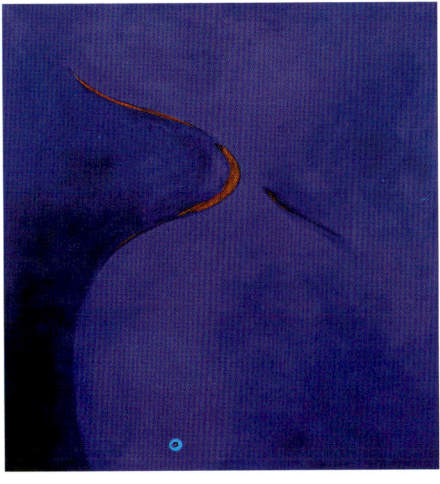

Sonam, Kunsang and Yangzom in 2010.

up that person's consciousness, and that is not to be desired. She believes her dead daughter's consciousness is far, far away and must be left in peace.

Not long after her little sister's death, Sonam fell ill. My grandmother couldn't bear the idea of losing her only remaining child. Had it been a terrible mistake to flee from Tibet? In an attempt to make something that resembled tsampa to comfort Sonam, she tried to roast the wheat flour they had been given. The result was dismal, but even so, it was closer to tsampa than anything else they had. As well as wheat flour, the helpers from the Indian government also distributed rice, lentils, sugar and oil, but Kunsang could make very little use of these ingredients. She threw the lentils away in secret because she had no idea how to cook them. She did know how to cook rice, but for Tibetans, it was a rarely served side dish, not a staple food. She searched everywhere for milk to make her own butter or yoghurt, but there was none to be found. Finally she found dried meat at a nearby market. Any Tibetan who still had a little money immediately bought up the meat, even though it hardly looked appetizing, with all the flies that constantly buzzed around it. Luckily Sonam didn't eat any of it – most of those who did fell sick, with vomiting and diarrhoea. Sonam's condition neither improved nor worsened.

About two months after their arrival at the camp, Kunsang heard that some Tibetans were being allowed to go to Shimla, the capital of the Indian state of Himachal Pradesh in the far north of India. Over 1,200 miles above sea level on the rim of the Himalayas, Shimla was warmer than Tibet but much cooler than where they were now. Milk and yoghurt could be found there, and even more important, the town where the Dalai Lama was living was not far away. Shimla seemed to Kunsang the solution to all her family's pressing problems.

Before they could leave for this haven in the Himalayas, however, they needed identity papers and they had to pass a medical examination. The Indians would not allow any sick or infected Tibetans to travel to Shimla, where the epidemics laying waste to the camps in Assam had not yet broken out. It was an absurd regulation, for it was the sick who were most in need of fresh air, clean water and uncontaminated food. But the refugees had no influence over the rules; they could only submit to them. Kunsang managed to secure identity papers for herself and her family. On the appointed day, they washed thoroughly, dressed in their best clothes and walked as tall as they could to the hut where the medical examination was to take place. My grandparents clung to the straw of hope that they and Sonam would not be overcome by nausea or diarrhoea at the very moment they faced the doctor.

In the hut, a doctor divided the Tibetans into two groups: on one side the supposedly healthy, on the other side the sick. My mother and grandparents were extremely lucky: they were placed on the healthy side, thus securing a place on the truck to Shimla. Others were not so lucky. Just as the driver started the engine, a nun my grandmother knew tried to scramble on board, only to be held back by Indian security forces. She had been eliminated by the doctor – a terrible piece of bad luck, as she was no more ill than Kunsang, Tsering and Sonam. Screaming and shouting, she chased the truck as it moved off. My grandmother leaned down from the back and tried to grab her hands to hoist her up, but she could not get a grip on her. Weeping and begging, the nun ran behind the truck. My grandmother screamed too, but even if her shouts were heard, the truck did not stop. Sonam watched the nun, of whom she was very fond, growing smaller and smaller, and tears ran down her face.

Kunsang later learned that the nun had died a few months after their departure, succumbing to diseases that could have been cured in Shimla. To this day, the image of her running in desperation after the truck is lodged in my mother's memory – a picture of a woman who knew for certain that she had been sentenced to death.

15

Rocks and Stones

Shimla seemed like a paradise to my family. A small Himalayan town close to India's much-disputed border with its unloved neighbour Pakistan, it had been built by the British in the early nineteenth century. Its cool summer residences had offered colonial officers an escape from the humidity and heat of the Indian flatlands. Elegant white-painted houses of a sort my family had never seen ranged heavenward along the steep wooded slopes. They featured large-paned windows, coloured metal roofs, pointed gables and verandas. Of course, my grandparents only saw the white summer palaces from the outside, but that was progress in itself, as in colonial times the promenade and the beautiful clean streets between the villas had been off limits to anyone not European. Indians and other Asians could admire this radiant paradise only from afar, from their own tiny houses and huts, which had to be built at a respectful distance.

When my family arrived in Shimla in the early 1960s, Tibetans were not allowed to integrate fully into Indian society. The Indians confined the frightened refugees to old wooden barracks. Doctors appeared at the barracks to examine them. They all had to bare their torsos, which they did only after long discussions and complaints that none of the Indians understood. The doctors pressed their cold stethoscopes to the Tibetans' chests and stabbed needles into their arms, as the uncomprehending refugees cried out in pain and alarm. At least there was plenty of fresh water available. Kunsang was delighted to find barley and milk at the market, and set about making *tsampa* and yoghurt straight away. Before long, everyone's health had improved.

Only a few weeks after their arrival in Shimla, my grandparents learned that Dudjom Rinpoche, the high lama whom Kunsang had met when she was at Ape Rinpoche's hermitage, had also settled in the mountain resort. When the government in exile was formed, the Nyingma leaders had asked the rinpoche to take the role of leader of the Nyingma school so that they would have a representative in the government. Though all the Nyingmapa trace their lineage back to Padmasambhava, since then there had been many diverse lineages, and practices often varied in each region. Because of that, they had never before appointed a leader.

Kunsang was overjoyed that Dudjom Rinpoche was staying in Shimla. Now she felt almost at home. A small group of Tibetans set off for his house, wanting to tell the revered master everything they had experienced during their escape.

Dudjom Rinpoche lived in a large house along with his family and some servants. He received the refugees warmly. Bent over in reverence, my grandmother and the others followed His Holiness into his chambers and sat on the floor. Her weeping eyes fixed upon the floor, Kunsang told him of her escape and the death of her younger daughter. At the end of the audience, she gave the rinpoche an offering and asked him to recite a special prayer for her dead child. The revered guru agreed, alleviating Kunsang's grief a great deal. Finally she felt her daughter's fate was in good hands; it had only been a few weeks since her death, and now this high lama would include her in his prayers.

After this visit, the refugees felt much better equipped for their new life in India, which was soon to prove very difficult. They were divided into small groups and taken by truck to construction sites on remote mountain roads, where they were to work from now on. This was a common practice at the time; more than 30,000 Tibetans were employed on road-building programmes that the Indian authorities had created because there were no other jobs for them. Many Tibetans died doing this work, either from exhaustion or disease or poor nutrition.

My family, along with about twenty others, were taken to a construction site in the remote forests behind Shimla, too far away from the town to return there every evening. Their housing consisted of a tarpaulin suspended between trees or branches stuck into the ground. This was their only protection from the frequent rainstorms of the approaching summer. Only the prayers my grandparents continued to say every day helped them to bear this harsh life. Every morning both would pray for over an hour, then Kunsang would make breakfast and lunch, wake Sonam, and set off for the day's work. They prayed again in the evening. On special occasions, the families would travel to Shimla to attend rituals at the temple there.

Their lives were ruled by rocks and stones. Their job was to break up rocks as large as pumpkins to make gravel. They had no machines and no tools other than small hammers, chisels and spades. They carried the gravel they had made in troughs to deposit it on the roadbed. Every day, they broke rocks, in the heat of the sun or in the pouring rain. Even Sonam joined in, hitting her smaller rocks with a hammer until they were finally transformed to gravel.

Kunsang and Tsering didn't have to force her to work on the building site; it was perfectly natural for her to help her parents. The stones were not only an occupation for her; they were her toys, imaginary friends, marbles and treasures.

Soon after the family had arrived, two envoys of the Tibetan government in exile had come to their camp to recruit children for a new Tibetan school. Sonam would have liked to attend school but she couldn't imagine leaving her parents, nor was Kunsang willing to let her go. The school building was several miles away, in Chotta. Kunsang was wary of the traditional Tibetan teaching methods, usually restricted to drill, beatings and strict discipline. She always did everything she could to protect Sonam, and she wanted to keep her daughter with her, to know she was safe and cared for. The envoys were not pleased by Kunsang's decision, and threatened to come back again, but they left without Sonam.

Living under the tarpaulin shelter by the side of the road became even more arduous when summer arrived and brought the monsoon rains along with it. Water flowed in broad streams from the tarpaulin, often soaking the family's supplies. The endless rains transformed the paths into raging torrents, the forest floor into a damp sponge and the gravel roads into washed-out, impassable tracks. The monsoons also set off mudslides, covering the roads with mud and stones. Some of the stones were so enormous and heavy that the refugees had to work as a group to push them clear. Then they had to spend days shovelling earth and scree from the roads before they could make new gravel to cover them again. They didn't have to worry about traffic – many roads were shut during the rainy season because of the threat of landslides. When one stretch was finished, the Tibetans rolled up their tarpaulins, shouldered their blankets, pots and pans and meagre supplies, and walked to the next construction site.

The strenuous living conditions and heavy work took a toll on Tsering's health, which was already diminished by the unfamiliar humidity and the lack of hygiene. He grew weaker and weaker. The rocks were too heavy for him, and soon he was no longer able even to swing his hammer. His Indian boss had no sympathy for his health problems; he cared only about how many rocks he had reduced to gravel by the end of each day. Even the best and healthiest workers earned no more than a few dozen rupees a month – about five dollars. The money was just enough to buy a little barley and milk; by going without food, Kunsang was able to save a few coins. They could never be sure they would receive their miserly wages, for their boss cheated them whenever he could. He knew they were refugees, with no rights. Every negotiation with him was a battle, fought in improvised sign language. No Indians understood Tibetan, and no Tibetans spoke the local Indian dialect. When the boss didn't turn up to give them their wages, there was nothing the refugees could do but go begging in the nearest village. The people there had little enough, but even if each of them gave only a spoonful of flour or rice or a piece of fruit, Kunsang could fashion from it a modest meal.

My grandfather was soon so weak he could hardly stand, and Kunsang was stretched to the limits of her endurance. From dawn to dusk she broke rocks; then she fought for her pay, acquired something to eat, cooked it and looked after Tsering and Sonam. Every few weeks she had to gather up her family's belongings and move to a new building site. Her husband could barely set one foot in front of the other any more, let alone carry anything.

Finally, Kunsang decided she had to take Tsering to Snowden hospital in Shimla. She hoped the doctors would make him well again. Sonam was sad that her *pala* was gone and worried about his health, but the extra room under the family tarpaulin brought her a bit of relief: for the first time in months she had a space of about ten square feet to herself, where she could not only stretch out her body, but had room to arrange her pebbles and sticks and roots any way she liked. When Tsering returned to his family, his health had improved, but was far from robust.

One morning, Sonam awoke shaking and trembling in a cold sweat. Her work on the dusty building sites had left many scratches and wounds on her legs, and some had become infected and begun to fester. Kunsang wanted to take her daughter to the hospital, but Tsering advised her against it, knowing from his own experience that the hospital didn't care for patients who could not pay. Instead they decided to go to Baghi, a nearby village, where an Indian doctor ran a tiny medical clinic that was reputed to be good and compassionate. Somehow Tsering gathered enough strength to shoulder his daughter and walk several hours up the steep forested road. Kunsang carried their shelter and the supplies they would need if the treatment took a long time. The doctor looked at Sonam, cleansed her wounds, gave her medicine, and told her parents she would need to stay at the clinic for a week. They set up camp next to his house.

While the doctor was treating Sonam, Kunsang and Tsering would go to the nearby orchards, for which Baghi was famous, to collect fallen apples. They didn't let Sonam eat any of them, as they feared they might raise her fever and make the infection worse. On one occasion when her parents weren't looking, she helped herself to one of the forbidden fruits, and ate it with great relish. She felt guilty afterwards, but her condition did not worsen. With them constantly watching over her, however, she was unable to try another. Tibetans also believe that fever will rise if a sick person falls asleep during the day, so Kunsang would wake her daughter every time her eyes fell shut during daylight.

Nonetheless, Sonam managed to recover. My grandparents were very grateful for the doctor's help. When Sonam was well enough to walk, they used their meagre savings, which included the Chinese coins they had brought from Tibet, to pay the bill for the treatment. Then they set off down the mountain again. A few days later, back at their camp, an Indian man returned their money to them: the doctor didn't take money from his poorest patients, he said. My grandparents, who could urgently use every rupee, were greatly moved by such kindness. It was the first time they had seen that there were people in India who helped others at no benefit to themselves.

My family spent two years breaking stones in the forests around Shimla. Once again Tsering fell ill and had to return to hospital. His undiagnosed condition improved only very slowly. Kunsang and Sonam took him regular meals and tea, as the hospital did not provide food for poor patients. Eventually Kunsang was so exhausted by the hard physical labour and the travelling back and forth to the hospital that she decided she and Sonam had to move back to Shimla. Ever resourceful Kunsang soon came up with a business idea that would enable her to earn the handful of rupees they needed to survive. She invested the little money she had saved from breaking rocks in some raw wool, which she painstakingly dried, carded, spun and knitted into sweaters, something she had learned to do in Tibet. She sold them in shops for Western tourists, who came to the Indian mountains without realizing it was often no warmer there than in the Alps.

Even when Tsering came out of hospital, Kunsang worked day and night to make money. Although the profit from each sweater was small, she sold enough to add up to more than the family needed for its essentials. Sonam, now eight years old, longed for many things, but especially for a satchel like the Indian children had. Kunsang was dismissive. 'Why do you need a satchel? It would use up all our savings in one blow.' But Sonam kept begging for so many days, and with so much longing, that Kunsang finally gave in. On the day she presented Sonam with a new satchel, Sonam was thrilled, stuffing it with old paper she had collected on the street and marching proudly around town with the bag on her back. Unfortunately that was all there was to it: as much as Kunsang would have liked to send her daughter to school, she couldn't afford it. Her income would never have covered the school fees, not to mention a uniform and books.

All this caused Kunsang great pain. In Tibet they had been far from affluent, but faithful Buddhists had always given her what she needed because she was a nun. In India, no one took care of Tibetan nuns, not even the Tibetans living in Shimla. They were all refugees themselves and had to struggle for their own survival.

16

Pilgrims

My grandparents may have lived in abject poverty, their belongings only enough to fill two suitcases, but their spiritual devotion was as great as ever. They recited their prayers every morning and evening, just as they had done their whole lives. Each prayed separately, usually for over an hour at a time. Sonam said her prayers only at night. Dudjom Rinpoche had given her a special mantra to ward off leprosy, and every evening before going to sleep, she dutifully repeated it 108 times as she counted down the beads of her rosary. They all missed far-off Tibet, the land behind the mountain ranges on the northern horizon, the land where they had once lived in peace. By this time, however, the peaceful Tibet of their memories no longer existed. It was the early 1960s, and the Chinese had long since destroyed the country's social and cultural structures. They had expropriated land from the nobility, destroyed the monasteries, driven out the monks, tortured high spiritual dignitaries, and broken up the state administration once headed by the Dalai Lama, locking the landowners away in labour camps and encouraging tens of thousands, later hundreds of thousands, of Han

Chinese to settle in Tibet. Not a stone of old Tibet was to be left standing.

My grandparents missed the rituals and teachings of Dudjom Rinpoche, who had travelled much farther east, to the town of Kalimpong on the border of the then Buddhist kingdom of Sikkim. At that time, Kalimpong was home to many Tibetan refugees, especially monks. Dudjom Rinpoche planned to hold a ceremony there, and my grandparents, along with a group of Tibetan friends, decided to take part and obtain the master's blessings. They packed up their few belongings and climbed aboard an ancient train bound for the east, which travelled at a leisurely pace through the Indian flatlands, stopping at many towns and villages.

To their great relief, they discovered that there was a tap on the steam engine, from which hot water flowed. At each of the train's numerous stops, they ran to the front of the train and filled their pots and kettles with hot water. Every time, Sonam was very frightened that the train might start again before her father came back with the water, so much so that she couldn't enjoy the exciting journey. Unfortunately, the pilgrims were often interrupted while making their beloved butter tea with tsampa. They were travelling without tickets, which were too expensive for them even in the cheapest class, so they had to leave the train in a hurry when a conductor appeared. They'd be caught up in a tangle of people, bicycles, donkey carts and cows in some nameless and unfamiliar Indian town, waiting for a new train to take them on towards their destination.

Eventually they arrived in Kalimpong. It was so far north, they felt as if they could reach out and touch the snow-white peak of Kanchenjunga, the third highest mountain in the world, flashing in the sunlight. Though their escape across the Himalayas had been harsh, the sight of the mountains brought a little piece of home to them, a longing that rose like a dream behind the wooded hills of Kalimpong into the flawless blue sky.

Hundreds of Tibetans had come from all regions of northern India and the neighbouring countries of Bhutan and Nepal to take part in the initiations offered by Dudjom Rinpoche. The rinpoche was now dividing his time between three different homes, in Shimla, Kalimpong and Lhasa, and this was an opportunity to see him while he was relatively close by. Next to the rinpoche's large white villa, pilgrims had built an improvised village of bamboo huts, their roofs covered with the huge leaves of a plant my grandparents had never seen before. Almost all the pilgrims had come empty-handed, but the mood among them was buoyant. Every one of them felt privileged to be in the presence of this most holy rinpoche, meeting relatives and old friends.

Dudjom Rinpoche was holding a *mani-rilbu* ceremony. *Rilbu* is the name of the sacred pills that most Tibetans swallow once a day, *mani* comes from the mantra *om mani peme hung*. The week-long ceremony in Kalimpong continued day and night, and consisted mainly of the complicated production of these holy pills, which were made of finely powdered sacred herbs, roots and twigs along with the ground bones of deceased rinpoches and hair, nails and clothing from very high gurus. The pilgrims worked in shifts, both day and night, praying alongside Dudjom Rinpoche. When they grew exhausted, they simply lay down to sleep and were relieved by other pilgrims.

The rinpoche had several daughters, who chose Sonam as their playmate. At every opportunity they asked for her to come and play. As soon as Kunsang heard the girls calling for Sonam she led her to the rinpoche's villa. 'Now you must do their bidding,' she would admonish her, 'and do not insult them. You must obey them and be careful with them so that they don't get dirty or injured during your games.' Sonam had no need for all these instructions; she knew all too well that these were the children of a divine reincarnation, to whom she owed the greatest respect at all times. She was proud and honoured to be chosen by the rinpoche's daughters, but she couldn't relax with them. She had never before been inside such a grand house, and her sense of inferiority made her uncomfortable and unsure of herself.

After *mani-rilbu*, Kunsang, Tsering and Sonam remained in Kalimpong. It was only eighty kilometres from the border, so Tibetans had been settling there long before the Chinese had forced many more to escape, and there was an established and affluent Tibetan community. My family visited religious Tibetans who gave them *tsampa*, dried meat and sometimes even a few rupees; every Buddhist is obliged to give gifts to poor pilgrims. On their walks through Kalimpong, the three of them admired the magnificent summer residences of the British, who had come here to escape the hot Calcutta summers. It seemed to them a clean, magnificent place, where thousands of flowers bloomed at every turn. Once an important trading hub, Kalimpong had long since been reduced to an insignificant provincial town. The British had left the country, and the border to Tibet had been closed since the communist revolution in China and the Chinese occupation, blocking off the old trading route. But it was the most beautiful town my family had ever seen.

One day my grandmother heard that white Christian missionaries were distributing powdered milk outside their church, and set out to fetch some of this valuable commodity – apparently they could make milk out of powder; what a remarkable thing! The missionaries filled Kunsang's container and explained to her how to add water to the white powder to make milk. Soon Kunsang went routinely to the church to collect powdered milk. When she was too busy, she would send Sonam. On many days, milk was the family's main food. Kunsang was grateful for the help but surprised by the papers the missionaries handed out along with the powder. 'They were written in Tibetan,' she told me, 'like my own holy scriptures, but they told odd stories about a father who lived in heaven and sent his son to earth so that he would die for mankind. These stories were very strange to me. I noticed that the Christians only gave their milk powder to those who took the papers, so I did too, but I didn't know what I should do with them. Tibetan letters are sacred, and must never be placed on the ground, stepped on or thrown away. I did not want to keep these stories about a father and son I would never know or see, from far away, so later I burned them.' That was the only appropriate way to dispose of papers with Tibetan letters on them.

In the autumn of the water-tiger year, 1962, the Sino-Indian War broke out and Chinese troops advanced into Indian territory. The Indian army failed to stop the aggressors, resulting in almost 2,000 deaths in a very short period of time. Dudjom Rinpoche was informed of these events and explained them to the pilgrims. Kalimpong was in the very north of India, in a small neck of land bordered by Nepal, Sikkim and Bhutan. The rinpoche feared that the Chinese might invade Kalimpong, threatening the Tibetans in their place of refuge.

Once again my family was forced to flee. Along with the eight other families in their group, they boarded the train, keeping a constant eye out for the conductor and mixing their tsampa with hot water from the steam engine. They decided to visit other holy Buddhist sites before they returned to Shimla. For two months they camped as a group, in makeshift tents, setting up their own tiny villages. Though they were often hot and dirty, they also felt peaceful and free. They went first to Tso Pema, the sacred lotus lake in

Rewalsar, near the town of Mandi, the place from which Padmasambhava, the guru rinpoche born of a lotus blossom, had set out to take Buddhism to Tibet. Then to Bodh Gaya, the site of the tree under which Siddhartha Gautama, the historic Buddha, had found enlightenment some 2,500 years earlier. They even went to Delhi, the capital of India, where they visited many temples, all of them larger and more magnificent than anything they had ever beheld. 'To be able to pray at these holy Buddhist sites was a most sacred gift for me,' my grandmother says. 'In my days in Tibet I had never imagined I would one day see these sacred places with my own eyes, yet here I was, praying where Buddha received enlightenment.'

In Delhi, however, Sonam began to weary of temples, statues and rituals. Instead she spent her time running around the unfamiliar streets of the vast city copying the children who begged for a few *paise*, the smaller denomination of the Indian rupee. She soon became as persistent as the Indian beggar children, who pursued their victims until they gave them something. But her mother didn't approve of begging, so Sonam usually did so in secret.

17

Survival

When my family returned to Shimla, a rumour was going round the Tibetan community that the group of refugees with whom they had come to India had been selected to travel on to a mysterious place called 'Swiserland', where it was said there were mountains almost as high as the Himalayas, covered with ice and snow and perhaps home to bears and wolves, if not yaks. It was apparently a great honour to go there. It sounded good, but what if there were no houses for them there either? What if nobody understood Tibetan? Though this was not the last she would hear of Swiserland, on this occasion Kunsang's karma gave the country the slip; the authorities chose a different group of Tibetans to go there. Instead, her family was to be resettled in the state of Orissa in the south-east of India.

The Indian government was giving the Tibetans a piece of land in the middle of a huge forested area that they were to clear and cultivate themselves. Nobody knew anything more precise about the plan, but my family prepared themselves for departure and headed to the station, even though they had not been told when the train for Orissa would leave. Tibetans were accustomed to accepting invitations of this type as soon as they were issued, and then waiting in the right place until the time came.

To the locals' amazement, the Tibetans set up their tents directly outside the station, lighting their fires, stirring their *tsampa* into hot tea and sprinkling a few flecks of butter over it. They had been told that the train to Orissa was expected any day now, but days, then weeks passed in this improvised camp. Tsering fell sick again. He was getting weaker by the day, with severe diarrhoea and blood in his stools. On the morning the train finally did pull into the station, Kunsang decided that he could not survive a strenuous journey. Although a monk called Tarchin-la had advised her to join the group travelling to Orissa, she could not risk it. As all the other Tibetans boarded the long-awaited train, this time not as stow-aways but as official guests of the Indian government, my family remained behind in Shimla. There were tearful and dramatic farewells, though my grandmother genuinely believed that she would come and join them as soon as Tsering's health improved.

It turned out that fate had treated my family well. The forest allotted to the Tibetans in Orissa was an impenetrable jungle filled with snakes and poisonous insects, the climate was tropical and the water was infected with diseases. Many Tibetans, incapable of adapting to the climatic conditions on the edge of the Indian Ocean, paid for their decision to go to Orissa with their lives.

Kunsang wanted to take Tsering to Snowden hospital, but he was far too weak to walk there. Desperate, she chased around town in search of help for her husband, but the Indian authorities felt no responsibility for the illness of a penniless Tibetan monk. It was only when she came across Save the Children that she began to make some progress. The white woman in the office of the British aid organization promised to send a car to take Tsering to hospital.

Kunsang found it hard to believe that she would keep her word, but the next morning a car did arrive to collect him.

Kunsang and Sonam now had to find a new place to live; they couldn't stay on the street outside the station. They had no money, and all their friends were on the train to Orissa. Telling Sonam to look after their belongings, Kunsang set out in search of accommodation. My mother vividly remembers that day. 'The morning passed, the afternoon came, and the evening set in. I was thirsty, my stomach was growling with hunger, and I was scared of the Indians bustling up and down the huge flight of steps below me. They stared shamelessly at me, and I'm sure they were wondering what this foreign-looking girl was waiting for. I was afraid of the Indian beggars, who gave me shifty looks. And they weren't the only ones. The salesmen sitting in their kiosks full of trinkets stared at me too.

'I crouched down between our luggage and clung tightly to our bags and I cried until my tears finally ran dry. By the time Amala came back, I was in a state of desperation.' Kunsang returned harried and exhausted, but she brought good news: she had found a place for them to stay.

The accommodation turned out to be a derelict house built against a steep slope. It had collapsed so far into the slope that it looked as if the next rain might wash it down the hill. The owners had long since abandoned it, and it had been blocked off because it was not safe. But no one was concerned about the safety of two Tibetan refugees in a small Indian mountain town.

The house was in such poor condition that only a couple of weeks later, Kunsang again set out in search of a new place to live. To her surprise and joy, she discovered that her old friend from the hermitage at Kongpo, Ani Pema-la, was now living in Kilti, a hamlet about an hour's walk from Shimla. And very close to Ani Pema-la's home was a hut with a small top floor that Kunsang could rent for the few rupees she made from her knitting.

Kunsang and Ani Pema-la had lived together in the hermitage for many years, and were very pleased to see each other again. They immediately resumed their old ways. Although as refugees they were both in the same predicament, Kunsang looked after her aristocratic friend. She bought supplies for her in Shimla, fetched water, cooked, washed and cleaned for her. Whenever Kunsang sold a sweater, she bought fruit not only for Sonam, but also for Pema.

What with working at her knitting, tending to her friend and visiting her husband in the hospital, Kunsang was so busy that she failed to notice how her daughter was neglecting her personal hygiene. Sonam got lice and was soon little but a bag of bones covered in pus, scratches, eczema and rashes. Appalled and afraid, Kunsang gave her a thorough wash, shaved off her hair and tended her wounds. Sonam hated being bald and spent the next few weeks in the hut with a scarf wrapped around her head, but she was glad to be getting her mother's attention and care. Pema had noticed Sonam's terrible state long before Kunsang did, but she couldn't have imagined doing anything about it herself. She was not a bad person – quite the opposite – and she loved Sonam very much, but it was not the done thing to take care of a child below oneself in the social hierarchy. The class differences of Tibetan society lived on – even in the wretched huts outside the gates of Shimla.

The four years she lived in Kilti were particularly hard for Sonam. During that time, her father was usually in the hospital, which was a two-hour walk away. He was only allowed out very occasionally. When he did visit, he brought boiled meat bones with scraps of flesh on them, still warm from the restaurants where he had bought them directly from the chefs.

141

Sonam helped her mother as best she could. Each day she gathered firewood. Then she would tie an empty coconut oil canister to her back and walk a good half an hour uphill to the closest spring. The large rectangular tin was half as tall as Sonam and she could only fill it partway, otherwise it was too heavy for her to carry back. The painstaking walk home took her twice as long as the trip up. Whenever she was in Shimla, she collected pieces of coal fallen from overloaded trucks. On one occasion, when the police saw what she was doing, she was so frightened she dropped the coal and fled as fast as she could, vanishing into the crowds.

My mother still remembers her happiest moments in Shimla. 'Amala rarely had time to take a walk with me along the lovely promenade, so for me that was the greatest luxury. There was a man there who sold balloons, and whenever I saw him I begged for one, but Amala always said they were too expensive. Finally, one day, she bought me one. I will never forget walking through town that day holding a balloon with one hand and Amala's hand with the other. The balloon didn't last long, but that feeling of happiness has remained with me all these years.'

When Kunsang needed more money, she came up with another business plan. She had noticed how much alcohol people drank in Shimla, and she remembered an old distillation technique for barley beer that she had learned in her childhood village. Buddhists frown upon alcohol and all other drugs. They are supposed to ascend to higher spheres through contemplation, meditation and prayer, rather than with the aid of substances. But this was an emergency. So Kunsang put aside her distaste and became a distiller of barley beer, working at it as diligently as she did at everything else. She could have watered down the beer, but that was against her principles. If people were going to buy alcohol from her, they should get the best quality for their money; anything else would have seemed even less honourable.

My grandmother believes it was the quality of her beer that made the project such a success, and she was soon having trouble meeting demand. One night a drunk customer turned up and started demanding more alcohol. She refused to sell him any more, upon which he became enraged and set alight the curtain at the hut's entrance. Kunsang rushed out, grabbed a bucket of water that was always on hand by the door and extinguished the fire. The next morning, the arsonist was still lying outside the house, sleeping off his inebriation. This put an end to her recently opened distillery. 'It was a sign,' she said. 'My un-Buddhist practice had brought bad karma.'

There was another incident that meant bad karma for my grandmother, this time involving Ada, a relative who visited her after he managed to escape from Tibet. Although Kunsang had hardly any food in the house, she welcomed him in and made him something to eat in the kitchen while he sat exhausted on her bed. When she brought him the meal he acted strangely, as if shocked or guilty, eating quickly and bidding her a hasty farewell. Instinctively Kunsang looked under the cushion where Ada had been sitting. This was where she kept her entire savings: a couple of Chinese coins and a few Indian banknotes. To her horror, she discovered it was all gone. It was a meagre reserve that nonetheless could have secured her family's survival for a couple of months.

She stood rooted to the spot, as if struck by lightning, incapable of thinking straight. Could her relative have stolen from her? Tsering was now living with them in Kilti, having been discharged from the hospital. When he came home that evening, she told him everything. Incensed, he wanted to find Ada right away and retrieve the stolen money, by violent means if necessary. It was all Kunsang could do to hold him back. She didn't want trouble, especially in her own family. Instead she went to Ada's wife and told her what her husband had done. At first the woman refused to believe her, but Kunsang stood her ground and wouldn't leave until she promised to confront her husband about the matter.

Nothing happened for a week. Several times Kunsang had to prevent Tsering from going to demand the money. Finally Ada's wife returned it, her face set in a deep frown and without uttering a word. Kunsang never mentioned the matter again. She has such a big heart that she even sent Ada and his wife money years later when she was in a more stable position – knowing that Ada was still just as poor as he had been back then.

Despite having left the hospital, Tsering was still in bad health. He walked with a stick like an old man. To help make money for the family, he painted Indian motifs on wooden boards: temples, mountains, women fetching water, or wild animals. Most days he would drag himself from the village to Shimla to sell his paintings to the middleman who in turn sold them to tourist shops. Sonam was always glad when he returned after a long day. 'My pala was very clever and very good at collecting things,' she said. 'He never came home empty-handed.' But the thing she most longed for was to go to a real school; she had her satchel, and she wanted proper books and schoolwork to fill it.

Not far away from their hamlet there was a village school where an old teacher presided over fifteen Indian children whose parents could afford the low fees. Most classes took place outside the one-storey corrugated-iron building; the children sat on the ground in the dust and scratched at tattered books with stumps of pencil. Sonam often wandered over to this school and sat beside the other children. She couldn't truly join in because she couldn't pay the fees, but she was glad enough that the teacher didn't chase her away.

When Kunsang found out that she had been going to the village school, she went to the teacher. 'I brought him tea and home-baked sweet bread, and I praised my daughter over and over until he said he would let Sonam take part in the lessons – as long as she always brought some of my sweet bread with her.' Sonam didn't learn a great deal. She had picked up enough Hindi in her five years in India to understand most of what the teacher was saying, but the other students were much more advanced than she was and the teacher didn't pay her a great deal of attention. Nevertheless, she was happy to join in a class of sorts at last. Her new life as a schoolgirl also brought her a change of name: the teacher couldn't pronounce Sonam Dolma, so he and the other children called her Shantakumari, which means something like 'peaceful girl'.

18

Stirling Castle

In the wooded Himalayan foothills that rose behind Shimla stood Stirling Castle. This legendary villa was run by Save the Children, the charity that had helped Kunsang to get my sick grandfather to the hospital. It was a large, rambling three-storey structure with tall windows and elegant enclosed verandas, which housed an orphanage, a clinic and a school for Tibetan children. Although Kunsang knew that there was help for the poor in India, she didn't know how to apply for aid for herself and her daughter. She had heard that Europeans who worked for Save the Children lived in Stirling Castle, and she knew that these people did many good deeds, but she viewed the grand house as a place beyond her reach.

My mother knew of Stirling Castle too, and she knew that Ani Pema-la's niece worked there. Finally, no longer able to contain her curiosity, she and a friend decided to make the hour's walk to the castle and beg for the coloured pills they had heard the nurses gave out to children there.

Pema's niece gave Sonam a very warm welcome and handed her a packet of pills, telling her to take one a day. She also gave her a long black dress, which she was to try on straight away. Sonam was far too shy to undress in front of someone she didn't know, so the woman just shook her head and let her take the dress home. By the time my mother got back to Kilti, it was almost dark. Her father was furious; he had been very worried about her and he forbade her to go back to Stirling Castle. Nevertheless, Sonam was delighted with the dress. It was much too large for her, but once she had folded back the sleeves and tucked the long skirt into a belt, she felt very grown up.

Despite her parents' orders, my mother went to Stirling Castle whenever she could. Sometimes she returned with the coloured pills, which she later found out were vitamins, and sometimes with more clothing. The nurses must have had a soft spot for her, for she never left the castle empty-handed. On one of her visits, she happened to pass the sick bay, and she was instantly entranced. 'I had never seen such a beautiful room. It was large, painted a gleaming white, with windows as high as a temple. There were two rows of white-sheeted beds with white pillows and white covers. I wanted to lie in one of those wonderful beds. I immediately decided I would find a way to come to the castle as an invalid and sleep in that room!'

A few days later, she told her parents that she wasn't feeling at all well and was going to spend a few days at the clinic at Stirling Castle. She was twelve now, practically grown up in her parents' eyes, so they were happy to let her go, knowing she would be well looked after there. The nurse took her into the sick bay right away – Sonam's was a familiar face by now – and soon she was lying in one of the beds she had so longed for. But it wasn't as luxurious as she had expected. The sick bay contained ten beds in all, and the other children there seemed very unhappy. One was wailing, another sobbing quietly; a third was staring at the ceiling apathetically. When darkness fell, the cries and moans of the sick children seemed to spread throughout the room like a cloud of misery.

'There was also something strange about my bed: the undersheet crackled and clung to my body, as if the sheet itself were crying and lonely. I couldn't explain it until I noticed that there was a rubber mat on top of the mattress, which was causing me to sweat so much I soaked the bedclothes. All night, in that magnificent bed, I lay awake, sweaty, uncomfortable, frightened by the sounds of the sick children all around me. In the morning I didn't dare to ask one of the nurses to remove the mat, lest I appear to be ungrateful.'

Finally, two days after she'd arrived, her mother came to visit and Sonam told her what was troubling her. As always, Kunsang solved the problem: she spoke to one of the nurses, who immediately whisked off the rubber mat.

But Sonam was suffering from another malady much more profound: homesickness. This was the first time in her life she had been away from her mother even for one night. The two were a unit and Sonam felt bereft without her *amala*. She missed her desperately. But not seeing her mother also meant that when Kunsang came to visit, Sonam saw her in a different way. 'For the first time, I saw how thin, poor and sad she looked. She wasn't plump and healthy-looking like the residents of Stirling Castle, but pale and tired. I was so miserable that I cried myself to sleep at night. I was used to being worried about my father, he'd been sick for years, but now I was worried about my mother too. What would happen to me if something happened to Amala?'

Everything about the adventure of staying in the sick bay at Stirling Castle ended up being much less pleasant than Sonam had anticipated. Every morning she was served porridge with brown sugar on top for breakfast; she had never eaten anything so sweet and sticky, being used to the salty things that Tibetans eat and drink. After breakfast, a nurse came round with a spoonful of cod liver oil, which tasted even worse than the porridge. Soon Sonam was plotting to leave. But that turned out not to be so simple. The nurses didn't want to let her go, and insisted she stay until she was in full health.

It was ten days after Sonam's arrival that Kunsang finally came to collect her and take her home. Though she'd been well cared for, she was relieved and happy to be going home with her mother. Their hut was a far cry from the large, clean, comfortable accommodation at Stirling Castle, but it was home.

Sonam's desire to sleep at Stirling Castle ended up having far-reaching consequences that would slowly begin to improve her family's life. When her mother had visited her there, she had met Ani Pema-la's niece and asked her if there might be any work for her at the castle. On the day she fetched Sonam, she was told there was indeed a job going, working for Save the Children. Kunsang could hardly believe her luck. This was her first official job and a turning point for her. She felt she was now on the road to making a good life for her family.

Kunsang was not to work at Stirling Castle itself, but at Summer Hill, a branch of the organization that cared exclusively for orphans. It was housed in an even more idyllic location, perched on a rocky cliff high in the forest. Like Stirling Castle, Summer Hill had been built as a summer retreat for the British. The salon with its high windows and balconies offered magnificent views of the Shimla valley below. The large, ornately carved room where once the British Raj drank and held court was now populated by Tibetan orphans, most of whom lay crying and whimpering in their beds. Kunsang would take care of these children in return for bed and board and a small wage.

On the first day of her new job, she took Sonam with her to Summer Hill; she didn't want to leave her behind in Kilti, and Sonam was more than happy to be close to her mother after her stay at the Stirling Castle infirmary. The English manager of the home gave Sonam a job on the spot; the staff needed all the help they could get, and Sonam was twelve – high time for a young woman to begin working.

But it was tough work. Mother and daughter had to look after the twelve babies who lived in the baby room, the former dining room off the salon. They spent the long day changing nappies and feeding and washing the infants. The babies, casualties of war, exile or poverty, were agitated and colicky and cried most of the time. Before their arrival, a Tibetan nurse had run the room. She was supposed to continue to help my mother and grandmother, but she managed to delegate all the real work to the two new employees. She had been at Summer Hill for some time, spoke a little English and had ingratiated herself with the Swiss matron, Lotti, who was head of the entire orphanage. Lotti was friendly and kind to her Tibetan helpers. When she learned that Sonam was only twelve, she gave her a pink plastic doll almost as big as a real baby. At first Sonam was frightened by its blue eyes, which opened and closed when she moved it. She had never seen a doll before, nor had she ever encountered blue eyes. It took her a while to reassure herself that the doll wasn't inhabited by some strange spirit. In the end, she had little time to play; she and her mother were working long hours, and when they weren't working they returned to the small room they shared and immediately fell into an exhausted sleep. 'Amala saw that the work was much too hard for me,' my mother told me. 'She did her best to do my share as well. She always took care of me.'

In the meantime, Tsering's health was getting worse and worse, and he returned to Snowden hospital, which was quite a distance from Summer Hill. Every day during her lunch break, Kunsang took him soup she had made the previous evening on a gas ring in the tiny room she and Sonam shared at Summer Hill. She only had an hour's break, so she ran immediately to a tea shop opposite the hospital, where they warmed up Tsering's soup for a few *paise*. She barely had time for a quick hello before she had to run back to Summer Hill. Once she got back, she snatched a moment for a cup of tea standing up and went straight back to work.

Things were hard for Tsering at the hospital. Few of the doctors took any interest in him, leaving him to lie, uncared for, on a mat in an empty room. There was one kind and good doctor who visited every few weeks. When that doctor was on duty, he examined Tsering, and gave him medication. In his presence the Indian staff were uncharacteristically friendly and caring to my grandfather. They allowed him to lie in a bed, gave him clean clothing and even something to eat. But as soon as the good doctor left the hospital, poor Tsering lost his bed and was left to rot in his desolate, empty room.

Kunsang and Sonam could only visit him together on Sundays, their day off, and each week these visits became more sad and alarming. Sonam was shocked to see her father lying on the bare floor with only a bloodstained blanket for comfort, his eyes wide with pain. His stomach was swollen like that of a starving child; his kidneys were failing, so he was bright yellow and unable to pass water. Kunsang was in a state of desolation that she couldn't afford better care for her husband. Sonam was terrified by the conditions in the hospital, and the screams of the other patients, who got just as little treatment as her *pala*. The stench of disinfectant, urine and vomit made her feel nauseous. On one particularly gruesome visit, Tsering was crying out in pain and a doctor finally came to lance

151

his abdomen. Water, urine and blood came flowing out, staining the already filthy floor. After that, Sonam asked her mother not to make her go to the hospital any more, even though it broke her heart not to see her father. These were hard days, weeks and months for my mother and grandmother, who could do little but watch as Tsering fell into a further state of decline.

After a few months, Matron Lotti found out that Kunsang was running down to the hospital and back up to Summer Hill every day at lunchtime, and generously offered to transfer her to Stirling Castle, where she could work in the kitchen and be closer to her husband.

19

Last Wishes

'You mustn't tell anybody we're man and wife!' Tsering whispered to Kunsang, who was crouching at his side and had to bend low over him to understand his words. 'When I'm dead, tell them I was just an acquaintance, not your husband. The hospital staff mustn't know we're a couple or you'll have to pay for my funeral. You can't afford that. You need everything you earn to buy food for yourself and Sonam.'

On his deathbed, my grandfather spoke only of his concern for his family. He couldn't focus on the prospects for his next life, as a monk was taught to do. He thought only of what would happen to Kunsang and Sonam after he had gone. His last wish was that Kunsang should deny her marriage to him. She understood why, but it still hurt her deeply. Soon after that, he lost the power of speech. The next time Kunsang came to visit, he could only make gestures.

'Don't worry about me and Sonam any more,' she told him. 'We have jobs, we are making money and things have begun to change. You know I will always take the best care of Sonam. It is time for you to prepare for your death and release yourself from all worldly things. You've been taught this all your life; now you must let go.'

Only minutes later, Tsering's breathing stopped and his consciousness began its way to a new life. Kunsang recited prayers but was afraid to stay too long in case someone found her with her dead husband. She hurried straight to Kathok Oentrul Rinpoche, an important spiritual man whom she knew from Tibet, to tell him of Tsering's death and ask him to carry out *powa*. She also asked him to take Tsering's monk's clothing – his red robe and cloak – to Dudjom Rinpoche, who was in residence in Kalimpong. This was the only offering she could make to the rinpoche so that he too would carry out the necessary rituals for a positive rebirth for Tsering.

The next morning a hospital nurse called at Stirling Castle and demanded that Kunsang come to the hospital to collect the body. 'That dead man is no relative of mine, only an acquaintance,' she told her, though she suffered greatly saying the words. 'I am a nun so I went to pray for him.'

It pained her to tell these lies, but she knew the hospital would now have to take care of Tsering's cremation, and that meant he would at least have a fairly decent funeral. Kunsang prayed for forty-nine days, lighting butter lamps, carrying out the required ceremonies and doing everything in her power to help my grandfather achieve a good passage to his new life.

Sonam was devastated by her father's death, but she could not show her grief. Though her mother was a comfort, there was no one else with whom she could share her pain. The two women had neither trustworthy relatives nor genuine friends in Shimla. Kunsang stayed in touch with other monks and nuns, and they would sometimes gather at the temple in Shimla for rituals on special festival days, but Sonam never felt a true sense of community. Her friends were peripheral, her mother her only constant. She often worried about what would become of her if anything ever happened to Amala.

Soon after this great sorrow, mother and daughter received some very good news. Stirling Castle had a new director, an Englishman who was very fond of Kunsang. He thought that Sonam should attend the school at the castle, along with the other Tibetan refugee children who lived there. She was thirteen years old now and she could neither read nor write; he was worried that she was falling too far behind.

Sonam was thrilled to be going to school properly at last. Every morning she lined up with the other children outside the castle to sing the Tibetan national anthem and recite Tibetan prayers, then they would march in pairs into the classroom. She was put into first grade, where she was two heads taller and twice the age of her class-mates. She learned the English alphabet and the multiplication tables. Tibetan teachers came to help the children learn English. Soon Sonam discovered books. She'd never had a book before. One day, she found a chest in the corner of the classroom full of beautifully illustrated volumes. 'Fairy tales, she told me. 'I loved the picture stories. I could sit for hours and dream myself into another world of princes, princesses and dragons.'

At Stirling Castle the senior staff members – the director, the head nurse and the teachers – ate in their own dining room. One day the waiter was sick, and Sonam was conscripted to help serve the dinner. 'I was amazed to see the food that was displayed on the beautifully set table: roast meat, baked potatoes, vegetables, followed by fruit and sweets. The next morning I took the break-fast into the dining room. There was butter, fresh milk and tea, along with a brown drink that smelled so heavenly that I couldn't help but try it,' she told me. 'I almost leapt with surprise, it was so delicious. I can still remember the taste on my tongue. It was only much later that I learned the drink was hot chocolate.'

The meals served to the Tibetan workers and the children they cared for were nothing like those in the dining room. Their daily diet consisted of tea with flatbread baked in oil and dripping with grease, or steamed dumplings with dhal and vegetables. They had the same soup every evening, with more fat than meat and more noodles than vegetables floating in their bowls. The dumplings and bread sat heavily on their stomachs all day. The drab food was filling but not healthy, and was supplemented only once a month by one egg per child. The adult Tibetan employees did not receive even that.

Sometimes Kunsang managed to improve their dull diet with fruit or other treats she bought at the market. They were no longer desperately poor. For the first time since their escape from Tibet, they had more than they needed for their day-to-day survival.

Kunsang even had a photo taken of herself and her daughter. She thought it was a great waste of money, but Kathok Rinpoche had suggested it, and she still did whatever a rinpoche told her. He thought he might be able to get Sonam into a Christian school, and he needed a photo to show the people who would pay for her tuition. It was the first photo ever taken of them. Kunsang was so excited at the photographer's studio that she forgot to remove her headscarf when she sat in front of the camera, a mistake that has annoyed her ever since. To this day, years later and on a different continent, whenever my grandmother picks up the tattered old photo and looks at it, she is disgruntled.

My mother treasures this photo. It is the only document of her childhood. But it never did get her into a new school. The rinpoche drowned while bathing shortly after receiving his copy.

20

Meeting the Dalai Lama

Ever since she had arrived in India, Kunsang had longed to travel to Dharamsala, where the Tibetan government in exile was based. There the Dalai Lama Tenzin Gyatso held audiences, gave blessings, carried out initiations and continued his spiritual life in exile as best he could. In Lhasa, he had had two huge palaces, the Norbulingka for the summer and the Potala, allegedly with 999 rooms, for the winter. Now he lived in a residence not much larger than a middle-class family home.

It had always been impossible for Kunsang to save enough money to make the long journey to Dharamsala, so she was overjoyed when she heard that Kundun, as the Tibetans refer to the Dalai Lama, was planning to come to Shimla and even to visit Stirling Castle to see the situation of Tibetan refugee children with his own eyes.

On the day of His Holiness' long-awaited arrival, Kunsang was churned up with anticipation and excitement. The Tibetans at Stirling Castle had worked hard to make sure everything was sparklingly clean, the children neat and tidy. Like the other employees, Kunsang wore her best white apron, which she had washed and hung in the sun for days until it was gleamingly white. As she stood in the row of employees and children outside the gates to welcome the Dalai Lama, she could hardly believe that she would at last see her spiritual and earthly leader in the flesh.

Suddenly His Holiness himself was standing right before her. She still remembers every moment of the encounter. 'He looked exactly like his portrait on the thousands of amulets and pendants printed with his face, but there was a presence about him that no picture in the world could capture. I felt a sense of warmth, love and intimacy emanating from him that I had never experienced with any other person. I felt embraced by the Dalai Lama's goodness. He stepped up to me and asked with a smile, laughing slightly, as he usually does when he speaks: "Are you a cook?"

'It was a small eternity before I could answer, for I had not been prepared for such a personal greeting. All eyes were on me, yet this bodhisattva, this enlightened existence in human form, expressed no impatience; he did not seem in any rush for me to answer. It was as if His Holiness had all the time in this world just to stand in front of me and look at me and smile and wait for me to answer his question.

'"Yes," I finally murmured. My body was bent low, my hands were folded at my chest, and I did not dare lift my head to look the Dalai Lama in the eyes. It would not have been respectful for a nun such as I to do that.

'"Show me your hands," the Dalai Lama said to me, and when I hesitated, His Holiness simply reached for them with an incredibly gentle gesture and pulled them towards him. Still smiling, he looked at my dry, chapped hands. They were rough from my work in the kitchen, from dishwater and scouring powder and floor cleaner, and the edges of my fingernails were black and brittle from handling coal. But the Dalai Lama held my hands for a long time, turning them over in his own soft, flawless ones. Then he patted them and said simply, 'They're so hard.' His words were almost lost in a chuckle of laughter. 'You've worked too much.'

'I was filled with happiness. Smiling, he released my hard hands, gave me a laugh and a nod and went on to talk to the woman standing next to me. Now I won't have to work so hard, I thought to myself, because he was here, because he touched me.'

For my grandmother, as for all Tibetans, just seeing the Dalai Lama in person once in her life was the highest possible honour. He had blessed her, and even if she never saw him again, his blessing would last her a lifetime.

The Dalai Lama's blessing did indeed take effect soon after this wonderful encounter. It was not long before Kunsang was told that she was no longer to work in the kitchen; instead she was to become the caretaker of a group of twelve children at the Stirling Castle orphanage, responsible for looking after them as if she were their mother.

At this time, Sonam's class went on an excursion to New Delhi. While the other girls were thrilled at this change from the school routine, Sonam was heartbroken to be separated from her mother for a whole week. She was terribly scared for her *amala*, whom she considered very old, even though Kunsang was only forty-five. So many of the mothers of her school friends were much younger than Kunsang, who was constantly telling Sonam how old and worn out she was, and how she didn't expect to live long enough to see Sonam with children of her own. Sonam's anxiety for her mother increased after her father's death. She always worried, somewhat irrationally, that if she were to go away from her *amala* for even a day, Kunsang might not be there when she returned.

In the photo taken of the group before they left, my mother looks like one of the teachers, towering above her classmates. She is wearing traditional Tibetan clothing, a colourful blouse underneath her *chupa*.

Sonam's friends adored the trip to Delhi. They wanted to see every palace, every temple; they wanted to visit every shopping street, go into every store. Sonam didn't enjoy the sights. Her socks soon wore through, and although her mother had given her a little spending money, she was much too shy to go into a shop and ask to buy new ones. She had no idea how much they would cost. So along with her worries about her mother, and her unhappiness about being away from her, she fretted about her feet. The discomfort brought about by the holes in her socks reminded her of the escape from Tibet, and that, in turn, made her think again of how much she missed her mother.

Things got happier when she returned from New Delhi. A new director of Stirling Castle, a former British army major called Mr Sweeny, was making many positive changes to life at the castle. The gulf between the senior staff and the lower workers was closing slightly, the children's food improved, and the atmosphere grew friendlier.

Sometimes Mr Sweeny showed films from England, a welcome distraction from Sonam's dull daily lessons. One of these films was about how children lived in Britain, what they had for breakfast, and how they went to school. 'For me, the most surprising thing was to see how they ate with knives and forks,' my mother told me. 'We only used our hands to eat, or sometimes a spoon if the food was too liquid. I had seen cutlery when I had served dinner in the staff dining room, but I'd never used it myself. This way of eating appealed to me, but I never imagined that I would have a future in which I too would eat with cutlery.'

Mr Sweeny became very fond of Kunsang and Sonam, calling my

mother 'Big Girl' because she was the oldest in the school. The children knew him as 'Uncle Sweeny', a kind-hearted man very unlike the typical Asian, for whom women were second-class citizens. On one occasion when he saw Kunsang carrying heavy luggage, he told her it was too heavy for her and carried it himself. Kunsang had never experienced such a thing. 'How could a high-ranking man carry something for such a lowly woman? In Asia, it was absolutely normal for women to carry heavy loads.'

Uncle Sweeny was also very generous. My grandmother discovered this when she asked him to buy a watch for Sonam on one of his trips home to England. She offered him her silver bracelet in return, the gift from her sister-in-law in Tibet. Uncle Sweeny refused, telling her to keep the beautiful bracelet. On his return he astounded her by handing her a box wrapped up in lovely paper. In it was a delicate ladies' watch that my mother wore for many years. Uncle Sweeny was a man of deep compassion who devoted his life to the Tibetans, initiating and implementing many humanitarian projects on their behalf.

One day, Uncle Sweeny came to Kunsang and told her he thought my mother should go to a different school, one for older girls, a quarter of an hour's walk from Stirling Castle. Sonam had often seen girls from Auckland House School. 'They wore smart school uniforms, brown blazers with a golden coat of arms embroidered on the breast pocket, brown skirts, yellow blouses and brown and yellow striped ties. Their matching yellow socks and brown shoes made them look even more elegant. Many of these girls came from rich Indian and even foreign families, and boarded at the school because their parents trusted its excellent reputation.'

'We can't afford it,' was Kunsang's first objection, but Uncle Sweeny promised to find a sponsor for my mother, an English family who would pay the school fees on her behalf, expecting nothing in return but a few letters from their charge. Soon my mother was attending school at Auckland House.

Because she was now fourteen, Sonam was put into fifth grade. The work was difficult for her; all the classes were taught in English, and she was still far from fluent in the language. Many of her classmates had spoken English from their earliest childhood. Not surprisingly, her examination results were not good; she was usually bottom of the class. Her mother couldn't help her, as she had no English and no knowledge whatsoever of mathematics, geography or chemistry. Her area of expertise, the world of the Tibetan rituals and deities, was not on the curriculum at Auckland House, but she used it nevertheless: before every examination, she performed a smoke offering, burning butter and tsampa to pacify ill-meaning spirits and reciting special prayers to help Sonam as she did so. All this was of little use – Sonam remained at the bottom of the class. 'But perhaps if it hadn't been for her prayers, I would have done even worse,' my mother says with a smile.

Mathematics was Sonam's particular weak spot. 'The sums and equations danced on the page when I looked at them. They seemed to jump up and down before my eyes, tangling together and filling my mind with utter chaos. The only subject I was good at was handicrafts. I could make lovely dolls out of scraps of cloth and had a natural talent for sewing and knitting. Perhaps my time at the monastery, fashioning my own toys, and my years in India in poverty had powered my imagination and made my fingers nimble.'

Uncle Sweeny saw that Sonam needed help with her English, so he asked one of the teachers at Auckland House to help her. Jessica Singh was married to an Indian man and was an excellent teacher. My mother was grateful to have such a kind, friendly person as her tutor, and the two of them stayed in touch for a long time. For some years Mrs Singh sent my mother twenty rupees every month to pay for fresh milk, and along with two other sponsors, Margret Davis and Margrit Steiner, she paid part of her school fees. My mother still thinks about these wonderful women with great fondness and gratitude. They made her life more bearable and showed her the true meaning of charity.

Sonam soaked up these acts of generosity and empathy. Her often harsh and cruel everyday life left her in desperate need of kindness from someone other than her *amala*, who did her best to comfort and shore up her daughter despite her own sufferings. She also learned some lessons about the sort of people who could be dangerous to a young girl's well-being. Diky-la was the Tibetan supervisor of the carers at Stirling Castle. This imperious woman submitted the children to all sorts of humiliations. For example, at the end of the day, once they had changed into their pyjamas, she would make them turn their underpants inside out and show them to her. Woe betide any child whose underwear was soiled! She would beat these poor children on the hands with a stiff rubber truncheon until their palms began to bleed. Diky-la carried out this ritual in secret, without the knowledge of the European staff. The Tibetan staff knew full well what was going on, but none of them dared report Diky-la's sadistic behaviour, lest she cause them to lose their jobs.

Nevertheless, Sonam was happy. For the first time since she had left Tibet, my mother was free to play whatever carefree games she liked. Every day when she came home from school she threw her satchel in the corner and raced outside into the spacious grounds of Stirling Castle. She and the other children chased around the garden, and climbed up on to the roof to watch the white students, usually volunteers from England, who sunbathed up there stark naked. With their skin as pale as freshly skinned chickens, they were a wonderful source of hilarity for Sonam and her friends. They speculated whether the students were boiling or burning inside or even dead already as they lay there motionless and sizzling in the sun. When darkness fell, and Sonam finally went inside to her mother, she was greeted by a thorough interrogation on where she had been for so long.

Sonam was never a rebellious teenager; her mother was everything to her, and she never tired of hearing her stories about her family and her life in old Tibet. 'Amala was such a wonderful storyteller. All the time when we were together she would tell me stories of her life in rich detail.' And Kunsang's prayers, every morning and evening, provided a constant anchor for her daughter. 'I admired the strength of my mother's beliefs, and hearing her pray for hours every day gave me a sense of safety and peace.'

The year Sonam began attending Auckland House, Kunsang bought her a pair of shiny new brown leather shoes for New Year. To buy them, she had sacrificed fifty rupees – a whole month's wages. 'For me these shoes were so beautiful and valuable that I decided only to wear them for the New Year's celebration. I put them on display in my room like jewels for the rest of the year. How disappointed I was when the shoes didn't fit me when the next New Year's festival came around!'

For Sonam, more important than lessons was getting to know the previously unfamiliar culture of the white people. Every morning she and her classmates went to chapel; Auckland House was a convent school. The prayers and hymns seemed to her less a religious invocation than an interesting anthropological experience. 'Not for one moment did I think that Jesus and Mary and all the saints I got to know in church had anything divine about them. I couldn't imagine that they might have anything to do with religion as I knew it. I enjoyed going to church – it was interesting and I liked the hymns – but for me it was just as much a performance as the first play I ever saw, a Shakespeare drama that the girls in the upper forms put on in the school hall.'

The tickets to that play would have been much too expensive for her, but Uncle Sweeny took her by the hand and said, 'Don't worry, Big Girl, we'll go', and soon she was sitting next to him in the best seats in the house, as pleased as Punch. 'I very much enjoyed watching the older girls acting out their strange complications on stage. My only regret was that my mother couldn't be there, sitting among the proud parents, most of them rich Indians in their best clothing, many of the fathers in uniforms studded with medals, the women in colourful saris. I was the only Tibetan child at Auckland House and the only girl from a poor background.'

That year, when Sonam was fifteen, she had to choose a second foreign language, either French or Urdu, one of India's twenty-two national languages, which was spoken by some 200 million people around the world. She decided on Urdu, which seemed much more practical to her than French. Why on earth would she ever need French? But her idyllic life at Stirling Castle was soon to come to an end. Save the Children was closing the Tibetan refugee aid project.

Kunsang and Sonam were distraught. Without Kunsang's job at the castle they would be out on the street, and they had been in that situation too often to want to go through it again. Kunsang immediately began making frantic enquiries, asking everyone she knew if they had a place or a job for her and her daughter. Neither neighbours nor teachers nor the staff at Stirling Castle, who were also losing their jobs, could help them, until Geshe Damchö-la, a Tibetan monk and one of the supervisors at the project under threat, had an idea. This very well-loved monk advised Kunsang to go to Mussoorie, a village some 125 miles south-east of Shimla, also in the foothills of the Himalayas. Like Shimla, it was a former British summer resort, over 6,000 feet above sea level. The monk gave Kunsang a letter of recommendation for Rinchen Dolma Taring, an aristocratic Tibetan exile who had founded a school and a children's home in Mussoorie with her own money and international donations.

Kunsang and Sonam again found themselves on board a train, this time with proper tickets. Once again they carried all their possessions, which had not increased much since their last train journey. Kunsang had a suitcase of clothes and a bundle of sheets and blankets, Sonam a bag containing her few clothes and the beautiful brown leather shoes. Once again they had to leave behind all that was familiar. Their only glimmer of hope amid the uncertainty was the letter that Geshe Damchö-la had given them, along with Kunsang's knowledge that the Dalai Lama had stayed in Mussoorie after his flight from Tibet, now eleven long years ago.

21

Separation

With their hearts heavy and their thoughts dark, Kunsang and Sonam disembarked from the train in Dehradun and took a bus to Mussoorie. Yet when they arrived at the children's home, their spirits rose. Mrs Taring welcomed them warmly. She had shiny black hair and wore a Tibetan *chupa* and the traditional apron of a married woman, made of three vertical panels of brightly coloured striped material, with the upper corners bordered in a floral tapestry pattern. She read Geshe's letter attentively and studied the excellent reference Kunsang had been given for her work at Stirling Castle. My grandmother told her about their escape from Tibet and how she and Sonam had fared in Shimla, although it was not easy for her to speak to such a highly revered woman, whom most people called *ama lhacham kushok*, meaning 'divine noblewoman'. During the entire conversation, she bent low in a bow, showing proper respect.

Despite her high standing, Mrs Taring seemed warm-hearted and generous. She told my grandmother about the 'children's village' she had established, with twenty-six residential houses.

In each house, twenty to twenty-five Tibetan orphans lived with a married couple, who cared for them like a mother and father. Mrs Taring offered Kunsang a job as a carer. She would live in House 13. The 'father' of the group had died not long ago, and his widow couldn't cope with the workload on her own. Kunsang would help her take care of the children. Sonam could move into the girls' hostel that Mrs Taring ran, and attend an Indian school. All classes at the school were held in English, but as Sonam had already been to an English school, Mrs Taring didn't anticipate any difficulties. Kunsang and Sonam were extremely relieved and grateful: this was more than they had expected.

The only down side was the fact that the girls' hostel where Sonam was to live was in Dehradun, some thirty-five miles away. The children's village was much too far away to travel from there to the school every day, and even if Sonam had wanted to make the journey, Kunsang would not earn enough to pay her daughter's bus fare. Mother and daughter had never been apart for longer than ten days in all their lives. They had always lived together, had overcome all their problems together, and were as close as only brothers and sisters or parents and their children can ever be. And now Sonam was to live in a different town. Kunsang understood that this was a great opportunity for her daughter, and she knew that she must take anything Rinchen Dolma Taring proposed as an order that she couldn't refuse. In old Tibetan society, the suggestions of a noblewoman such as Mrs Taring would always be followed to the letter, and she expected the same here.

Kunsang was glad that her daughter was to continue her education. The world of old Tibet, where a girl could aspire to being nothing more than a hardworking farmer's wife or an attentive herdswoman and a good mother, was gone for good. She wished that Sonam might become a nun herself, or marry a religious person, but this was clearly not possible, given their circumstances. All she could do was keep Tibet and its past alive by telling Sonam stories. Kunsang had found out from Tibetans who had escaped later than her that her ancestors' land was now being cultivated by strangers. She knew that both her brothers had tried to escape, but had been captured by the Chinese and put in prison. She realized that she and her daughter were completely on their own, and had only each other to help them make their way in the world. They were convinced they would never see their relatives in Tibet again. It was very clear that there could be no return to her old homeland and that she and her daughter had to stand on their own two feet. And that meant that nothing was more important for Sonam than a good education.

Once they had left Rinchen Dolma Taring, Kunsang took her daughter in her arms. 'Sonam, we're going to do it,' she said. She had accepted that the two of them would be separated, and that her daughter would live in another town in order to go to school. Sonam knew that a new chapter in her life was beginning.

While Kunsang settled into her new role as the 'mother' of twenty-five Tibetan orphans, my mother moved into the girls' hostel in Dehradun, filled with fear and suffering terribly from the separation from her mother. She cried silently into her pillow by night so that no one would hear her misery. She had no contact with her mother: telephone calls would have been much too expensive, and of course neither had access to a phone of their own. There was nothing she could do but accept her fate and look forward to the next vacation. There was one happy surprise: the language spoken in the corridors and rooms of the hostel was Tibetan. The home housed only Tibetan girls, 105 refugee children divided into two groups, each group looked after and supervised by a married couple.

Sonam went to school at Cambrian Hall, whose well-tended modern buildings looked almost like the schools she had seen in the film about children's lives in England. On her first day she was given a uniform: blue blazer, grey skirt, white blouse, blue and yellow striped tie, yellow socks and a pair of brown shoes, as well as a thin pale grey summer dress for hot days.

Once again, she was the worst pupil in the class – because she was less fluent in English than the others, because she had been at school for far fewer years than they and because the numbers again danced before her mind's eye as soon as she bent over mathematical sums, rows of figures or her slide rule. She ended up in such a panic every time that even her well-meaning neighbour couldn't help her, and nor did her mother's prayers for better math grades bring any notable improvement.

In her early days in India, at Stirling Castle and Summer Hill, Sonam had been amazed at the luxury of her surroundings, enjoying the blessings of running water, toilets, freshly washed laundry and regular meals. In Dehradun she was slightly more critical of the conditions. She saw how strictly the Tibetan carers ran the hostel. The food was meagre. The hostel had an eastern and a western block, and the eastern block, where Sonam lived, was locked during the day so that nothing got dirty. The girls had to spend all their free time in the yard; no great pleasure in the usually searingly hot temperatures of Dehradun, which was at a much lower elevation than Mussoorie and fully exposed to the tropical climate.

It was at this time that Sonam's nascent sense of the inequalities and injustices in society began to grow. Only the children of richer Tibetan families and the few married girls who strangely enough also lived in the hostel had the pleasant alternative of going into town in the afternoons and sitting in the local cafés. Sonam's weekly pocket money from the hostel, one rupee, would not have bought her a single drink there. She and the other poor girls couldn't even buy sanitary towels, although all of them were old enough to have regular periods. Feminine hygiene was unknown in Tibet, where women simply let their menstrual blood flow into the generous undergarments of their *chupas* or used old, often dirty rags. Such methods were unthinkable with their smart school uniforms and in the hot Indian temperatures, so there was nothing the girls could do but tear their T-shirts into strips, use them as sanitary pads and wash them as best they could in between. They would never have dared to ask for sanitary towels. The carers at the hostel were tight-lipped and unapproachable, usually leaving the girls alone with their worries; they were not people to whom obedient Tibetan girls could ever mention subjects such as menstruation or other bodily matters.

On one occasion, my mother could stand the heat in the yard no longer. Her heart thudding, she went to the carer and asked her for the key to her room. The woman refused at first, but when Sonam pleaded with her she finally gave in. 'There was one condition, though,' my mother said, 'and this I will never forget: I must not tell anyone, or she would never give me the key again. I was happy to escape the unbearable heat for a while, but I felt guilty creeping into my room when the other girls didn't have that privilege. Every time I fetched the key, my heart raced. Sometimes I'd let a few of the other girls into my room. We all felt like thieves.'

For my mother, the whole key business was unfair, and she would have liked to tell the delegate from the Swiss aid organization about it when he came on one of his regular visits to India to check up on the hostel. But she was afraid that if she dared speak up and rock the boat, she might be thrown out of school. All the girls were afraid of the Swiss visitor; he seemed to be a very special person who deserved great respect. The hostel staff prepared them for his arrival a few days in advance. They had to sweep, clean and polish particularly thoroughly, and when the important guest finally arrived, they all put on freshly washed dresses and lined up in two rows to greet him.

Amid cheers and waves, the man got out of his car and called out to the girls, 'Hallo, how are you?' They all had to answer, 'Fine, sir!' They didn't dare to mention the poor food, the lack of sanitary towels and the locked rooms.

All the injustices my mother witnessed left her with a deep feeling of powerlessness. She did not feel safe enough to ever express her anger over bad conditions or unfairness, so she learned to swallow it. She felt she always had to be careful to protect what little she had been given – and she was very grateful for the opportunity to go to school and live in the hostel. Unlike Kunsang, who always accepted things as they were, my mother's early years have shaped in her a deep and fervent longing for justice, a fervour that has stayed with her her entire life.

22

The Mouse King and the Prince

Sonam was counting the days until the summer vacation, but first she had to endure the end-of-year examinations, which caused her many a sleepless night. She did not do well, and to make matters worse, the headmaster read every pupil's grades out loud in front of the entire school.

After she had endured this humiliation, she was at last able to escape the heat, the hostel and the endless mass drills of the school and move for the summer up to Mussoorie, to her beloved mother, whom she had desperately missed for many months. As she sat in the bus and saw the first glittering peaks of the Himalayas in the distance, she felt great happiness, and her joy was even greater when she finally held her *amala* in her arms.

Sonam spent the summer vacation, which in India lasts for more than three months, with her mother and the other widowed carer in House 13 of the children's home. She noticed how her *amala* worked from morning to night while the other woman spent her time sitting lazily by the window, watching people come and go along the path outside. Whenever this woman spied Rinchen Dolma

Taring or another important person, she put on her apron quick as a flash, wetted her hands at the tap and rushed towards the visitor, drying her hands on her apron as if she had just interrupted some task. But in reality she left Kunsang to do all the work, and on one occasion even accused my grandmother of stealing food.

That summer, a young Tibetan man who worked at the children's village began paying Sonam visits. He was known as the Mouse King because he was thin and delicate, with huge ears and big, heavy-framed glasses. Tibetans are good at giving nicknames. They enjoy renaming people behind their backs, based on prominent physical features. The Mouse King spent hours in the kitchen of House 13, asking endless questions about the children, acting as if they were particularly dear to his heart. He chatted with Kunsang, drank the tea she offered him and watched Sonam's every move out of the corner of his eye. Sonam wondered what he really wanted, why he sat there for hours, constantly talking but not really saying anything. She discovered the reason when he sent her a letter telling her in cautious words how much joy it gave him every time he saw her.

Sonam didn't know how to react, so she told her mother about the letter. Kunsang had nothing against the Mouse King, but she thought Sonam was too young for him. Sonam was relieved; she felt exactly the same way, and threw the letter away without another thought. Girls no longer married as young as they had in old Tibet. If a man was interested in a woman, he first paid a visit to her parents to drop subtle hints about his interest, or he wrote the woman a letter. Sonam, who was only seventeen, didn't feel mature enough for love. When she received a second letter from the Mouse King, she threw this one away too, unanswered.

Men had begun showing interest in her several years before, when she was only twelve and still lived in Kilti next door to Ani

Pema-la. The first had been the nephew of the Indian landlord, who lived next door. It was a most unpleasant experience. This man was at least twice as old as she, and to make matters worse he was a butcher, a disgusting job to any Buddhist. Whenever Sonam walked past the landlord's house, the nephew and the men he hung around with would make suggestive comments. Although she couldn't understand them (she still didn't speak colloquial Hindi that well), she could sense that they were making romantic insinuations about her and this butcher, who evoked nothing in her but fear and repulsion. One day as she was passing by, the butcher grabbed her arm. Sonam panicked and instinctively screamed, then tore herself away with all her strength and ran into her house as the nephew and his friends looked on, laughing and jeering. From then on she tried to avoid the neighbours whenever possible, hiding away if the butcher or his uncle gave any sign of visiting her family.

In Mussoorie, a wealthy Tibetan had presented a marriage proposal to Kunsang in the traditional way, along with a large dish of magnificent fruits and a *katak*, the white scarf that Tibetans present to one another as a welcome gift or an altar offering. The man wanted Sonam as a wife for his two sons. Sharing a wife was a practice common in old Tibet: if one son died prematurely, which was not unlikely given the tough living conditions in the mountains, a shared wife prevented the family structure from collapsing. A dual marriage also meant that there was always a man in the house to protect the wife while her other husband spent months in the highlands with the herd. It had the further advantage that possessions didn't have to be divided up between two sons, as both lived in the same house.

Now that she was in exile in India, Kunsang saw no need to follow such outdated customs. Though she adhered to almost all the customs of her beloved old Tibet, when it involved protecting

Sonam from a less than perfect marriage, she let the old ways go and told the man in no uncertain terms that her daughter was not available for his sons. Nor was she interested in another traditional marriage offer that came from a second wealthy Tibetan, a restaurant owner and horse breeder who she thought was much too old for her daughter. Besides, Sonam still showed no interest in men or marriage, and Kunsang was more than happy to keep her daughter with her as long as she could.

Nevertheless, romance would come to Sonam from an unexpected quarter.

A few weeks after her vacation started, Mrs Taring informed her that she and another girl had been selected to serve in a Tibetan restaurant until the end of the summer. The two of them were to work without wages; their entire income would go to the children's home.

Sonam was amazed when she saw where she was to work. The restaurant was in the Savoy, a luxury hotel opened by the British at the beginning of the twentieth century, when it had certainly been the equal of its counterparts in London, Paris and Rome. By the early 1970s, when Sonam went to work there, its glamour had faded slightly, but it was still the best and largest hotel in Mussoorie. Its carved wooden verandas, red-roofed towers, wide curving staircases and vast carpeted hallways made a great impression on Sonam. In the restaurants, rich Indians in magnificent clothing ate from plates of fine white porcelain with knives and forks. Cutlery again!

Sonam had often passed by the restaurants in Mussoorie with her mother, both of them admiring the crisp white tablecloths and glassware and all the knives and forks on the tables. The rich European and Indian patrons of such restaurants inhabited a different world. She and her mother talked about how wonderful it must be to eat like that, and how unlikely it was that they would ever have such an experience. And now Sonam was to serve in just such a restaurant! She was thrilled, and not a little apprehensive.

The Savoy's Tibetan restaurant was tucked away in a corner of the hotel. It distinguished itself from the main restaurant, a temple of Indian cuisine, by its Tibetan wall hangings, and the fact that its two Tibetan waitresses wore traditional dress. Sonam was relieved to find that she was familiar with the dishes on the menu, all of them cooked to perfection and beautifully arranged on the plates. When not serving in the restaurant, she delivered room service, which she did not like doing. She felt very unsure of herself every time she walked along the long corridors with her tray and knocked at one of the many doors, not knowing who or what awaited her behind it. She was particularly afraid to bring food to the rooms of men travelling alone, who seemed to inspect not just the food but also the young waitress. But nothing untoward ever happened to her, and she sometimes made her way back to the restaurant with a small tip, which she saved for the next school year in Dehradun.

One day the Mouse King appeared at the Tibetan restaurant with a young European man whom Sonam had never seen before. The man was extremely tall but his manner was rather shy. Sonam brought them their menus, and in her heavily accented English asked them what they wanted to eat. She acknowledged each request with a whispered 'yessir'. She didn't like the fact that the Mouse King had come to her workplace, but she put on a polite face to hide her annoyance. And who was this young man he had brought along with him? He didn't look like the white tourists she had served before at the Savoy. He was much younger than them, and he was not wearing a good suit or bright tourist's clothes but a simple brown shirt and trousers. He looked rather poor, with his long hair, straggly moustache and worn-down shoes. He was thin, his cheeks almost sunken into his face, but his eyes sparkled and it seemed he could not prise them away from Sonam.

Sonam surreptitiously observed the man all evening. He seemed to be finding it hard to concentrate on what the Mouse King was saying; his gaze kept sweeping the restaurant in search of something. When the Mouse King got up to leave, the man stayed and took out a book. Sonam wondered why this guest was not departing after his meal like everyone else. He stayed seated and read and read until she had to tell him that the restaurant was closing. He was the last guest to leave.

Little did Sonam know that the mysterious young man had stayed so long in the restaurant because he had fallen in love with her at first sight.

Martin Brauen had been in Mussoorie for a week. He was a student from Switzerland who had been studying Buddhism at Delhi University, and had come to spend the summer in Mussoorie – Happy Valley, as it was known to the Europeans – to escape the oppressive heat of New Delhi and to do some work for Swiss Aid to Tibetans. He was immediately taken with the place. The dense woods, steep mountainsides and fresh green grass between the smart houses on the top of the hill reminded him of his home in Berne, though this landscape was more lush and colourful, and certainly a lot more hot and humid. He was particularly struck by the swathes of mist crouching around the hills like snow-white cotton wool. He loved the name Happy Valley, though when he arrived he could have had no idea how soon its meaning would come true for him, in the most literal sense of the word.

The Swiss charity had asked Martin to convey his impressions of the children's homes that Mrs Taring ran. He stayed initially in a guest room at the children's village, and it was here that he met the Mouse King. When his new friend suggested they go out to eat at the best hotel in town, the Savoy, Martin was happy to accompany him.

'They have a wonderful Tibetan restaurant,' the Mouse King had told him, adding with a wink, 'with two lovely Tibetan waitresses.'

The following night Martin returned to the restaurant. And the next. From then on he spent almost every evening at the Savoy. He came alone, armed with a book and a notebook. He couldn't afford much more than a bowl of noodles and two cups of tea, over which he spent hours reading and making notes. But whenever Sonam came in his direction he looked up from his work, gave her a big smile and tried to engage her in conversation. My mother was very shy and reserved. For her, white people were creatures from another world, of whom one did not ask questions but only answered 'yessir' or 'no sir'. She did everything she could to fulfil their wishes without another word. This white man was different, he wanted more from her, but Sonam couldn't imagine what that might be. Despite being aware of men's interest in her, it had never occurred to her that she might some day befriend a man who was not a Tibetan; that was beyond her wildest imagination. Traditional Tibetan women accept only Tibetan Buddhists for husbands. Sonam's mother was a very traditional Tibetan woman, and Sonam supposed that eventually she would meet a man of whom her mother approved. However, she was in no hurry.

It was not only Sonam who had firm convictions; Martin had his own. From his earliest childhood he had been used to getting what he wanted. He was as stubborn and determined as the people of Berne are generally reputed to be, perhaps even more so. Even though Sonam refused to be pulled into conversation with him, every evening Martin stayed at his table in the Savoy until the restaurant closed so that he could walk her home. He had rented an apartment from an old Indian couple in Happy Valley, not far from where Sonam lived with her mother at House 13. He had become completely smitten with Sonam's lack of artifice, not to mention her natural beauty and her smile, which lit up the room. 'Perhaps it was the challenge, too, that made me so interested,' he says. 'There was such an aura of sweetness about her, I just wanted to be around her.'

Martin's perseverance gradually overcame Sonam's shyness. He looked so thin and hungry that she began serving him extra portions out of sympathy. She would occasionally enter into a conversation with him, and when Martin invited her to the movies, although she first said no, and then maybe, finally she agreed to go, although she insisted that a chaperone, the other waitress, accompany them. The three of them watched a Bollywood melodrama in Hindi, Martin understanding almost nothing but not minding at all. He sat on the worn plush seat next to Sonam, who, knowing that he had little money, felt bad that he'd had to pay for three tickets. After the film they stood around in the mild Mussoorie summer night, no less embarrassed than before. The tearjerker had featured several actors and actresses falling into each other's arms in fits of joy. Then the three of them walked back to Happy Valley together, said good night and went their separate ways.

Any other man would have given up, but not Martin. He realized that the route to Sonam's heart was not via her friend the other waitress, but via her mother. So he invited Sonam and Kunsang to tea at his lodgings. He was almost surprised when the two of them turned up at the arranged hour, and this time the ice broke. Now the roles were reversed, with Martin rather than Sonam serving the tea. He tinkered clumsily with the tin cups, pouring tea the Indian way. The cups were so hot that no one could touch them, which prompted much merriment on all sides. The most amazing thing for my mother was the dog with six puppies that Martin had taken into his apartment and allowed to make her bed in the only armchair. Although she found the smell off-putting, she was fascinated by the way Martin played with the dog. She had never seen anything like it; for her, a dog was an animal to be used as a guard or for herding livestock, not something to look after and play with and certainly not to be allowed into one's living space. In Tibet, dogs were usually left to forage for themselves, but this one was spoiled and cared for like a baby. Kunsang too found it strange, but honourable – a good Buddhist should have sympathy for all living creatures, which this unusual young white man obviously did.

Martin didn't understand much of what Kunsang said, as they had no common language, but he noticed that she was touched by his care for the dog. He already knew that she placed her Buddhist principles above all else. That was an advantage for him: not only was he a student of Buddhism, he was deeply interested in everything about the Tibetan culture and religion.

To say that Martin came from an aristocratic and accomplished background is an understatement. His family tree contains seventeen emperors, more than 100 kings and several saints. It includes the English King Henry II and monarchs from the House of Plantagenet as well as Kings of Portugal and King Lothair and his father Emperor Lothair, the son of Emperor Louis the Pious, son of Charlemagne. Another branch goes back to the reformer and founder of Protestantism Martin Luther, as well as to the artists Lucas Cranach the Elder and Younger, the most significant German painters of the Renaissance.

Nevertheless, his forbears had also been forced to flee their homeland. During the first half of the sixteenth century, the French theology student Jean Cauvin converted to Martin Luther's newly established Protestant religion. In the absolutist Catholic France of the time, the young student narrowly evaded arrest and fled to Switzerland. Over the following decades, more than 200,000 other French Protestants, known as Huguenots, followed him. In exile, Jean Cauvin changed his name to Johannes Calvin. Martin's forefathers were among those strictly religious, hard-working Huguenots who made successful lives in Switzerland.

His great-grandfather was Elie Ducommun, a liberal journalist, businessman and state chancellor in Geneva, who became head of the Berne International Peace Bureau, for which he won the Nobel Peace Prize in 1902, only a year after the award was instigated. This man, whose main concern was world peace and the fate of other peoples, became something of a role model for Martin in his youth, and he still wears his gold ring engraved with the letters PAX.

There was in Martin's family a deep interest in Asia. His grandmother, Jeanne Schreck-Ducommun, was fascinated by Asian philosophies, Buddhism and the suffering in the world. She became another important role model for Martin, introducing him to Asian thought when he was quite young and fostering in him a passionate and abiding interest in Buddhism and the East. Before meeting his father, his mother Ula had been deeply in love with an Indian man called Raja. Their relationship ended when Raja was forced to return to India on the eve of the Second World War, but Ula never forgot him. Martin's father was also interested in Indian philosophy and ideas, particularly yoga, which he practised intensively. And so it was that Asia, and particularly the Indian subcontinent, was not alien to Martin but familiar and beloved ever since his youth.

It was no surprise, then, that he developed an interest in Tibetan refugees when he heard about their oppression by their Chinese occupiers. The Swiss generally became aware of the Tibetan catastrophe in the early 1960s, when the first large wave of refugees arrived in their country. In 1961, Switzerland had granted asylum to up to 1,000 Tibetan refugees, as a gesture on the part of one peace-loving mountain nation to another. One group was from the camp that Sonam, Kunsang and Tsering had lived in when they arrived in India. Another was made up of small children, most of them orphans. A cousin of Martin's grandmother organized a vacation camp for Tibetan children, where my paternal aunt worked for a summer.

Martin found this project fascinating and quickly developed an abiding interest in Tibet. He had previously known nothing of the country, but when he visited the camp, he found the Tibetan children wonderfully friendly and cheerful despite all the suffering they had endured. He felt he must some day travel to Tibet, and he began to study Tibetan Buddhism, seek out Tibetan art and artefacts, and collect money at his school for Tibetan refugees, sending it to India via the Red Cross.

Martin became more and more committed to helping other people, and decided to study medicine. Still Asia didn't lose its hold on him. He wanted to organize a major exhibition of Tibetan art in Zurich, where he was a student. It was to be the first of its kind in Switzerland and the largest in all of Europe. The fire of idealism burned bright in him: a nineteen-year-old student, he went to the mayor's secretary in his jeans and Ho Chi Minh-style moustache to apply for a venue for his exhibition. He wanted no less a location than Zurich's venerable Helmhaus Art Museum, an imposing late-eighteenth-century building directly on the River Limmat. The secretary sent him packing, having been advised by a museum director that Tibetan art was not real art but only handicrafts. Nevertheless, Zurich's cultural representative gave him hope; he would consider letting the exhibition be shown at the Helmhaus, provided Martin first managed to hold it elsewhere. He organized a much-admired and highly praised show in the neighbouring town of Winterthur, which was later shown in an expanded form by various Swiss museums including the Helmhaus.

Inspired by the great success of his Tibetan exhibition, Martin decided to give up his pursuit of a medical degree and devote himself to his interest in Asia, Asian culture and Buddhism. Armed with Latin and Greek, French and Italian but little English and even less money, he set off, now aged twenty-two, to study Buddhism at Delhi University. In this scorching-hot, overcrowded city, he lived in a squalid hut on the roof of a high building. Some of the neighbours suspected he was a spy, for the simple reason that his watch had three buttons rather than one, allegedly a clear sign that it could be used to transmit secret information abroad. It was during this stay that Martin met the Dalai Lama in person, interviewing him for a Swiss Tibet newsletter, a publication read only by friends and people interested in Tibet and practically ignored by the rest of the world. Back in 1970, the West was not yet even vaguely interested in the leader of all Tibetans, living in Indian exile.

Under his corrugated-iron roof, which glowed in the tropical sun, Martin engrossed himself in his books. He was plagued by diarrhoea, mosquitoes and poor food. But as fate would have it, his work on the Tibetan art exhibition had gained him the trust of the secretary of the Swiss aid organization that helped Tibetans, Schweizer Tibethilfe, and so he came to Mussoorie, met the Mouse King and fell in love with my mother.

23

Courtship

Martin became a frequent and welcome guest at House 13. After meeting Sonam and Kunsang, he began attending a nearby Buddhist temple every day, spending hours in contemplation. He deliberately passed by House 13 on his way so that Sonam's mother would see him. He could have saved himself this detour – Kunsang often went to the same temple herself and was given regular reports on Martin's visits by the sexton. He too had taken note of this deeply religious European. One evening Martin stayed in the temple so long that the sexton felt sorry for him and brought him a bed so that he could sleep in the *gompa*.

Kunsang began to think seriously about Martin. The poor boy, she thought, he's praying to get my daughter. But how could such a relationship develop? Sonam was too young to marry, that was clear. And the young man lived in Switzerland. Where was this all to end?

Martin would soon have to leave Mussoorie to continue his studies in Zurich. He spent every moment he could with Sonam, wanting to share all his feelings with her. That was not easy, as the two of them were never left alone together. Kunsang was always nearby, and if not Kunsang, one friend or another. Whatever he suggested, whether a trip to the Ganges or the cinema, Sonam always came accompanied by a friend. On the way back from one of these excursions, the door of the ancient taxi Martin had ordered for the journey would not shut, so he had to do the gentlemanly thing and put his arm around Sonam's shoulder to hold it closed, which he enjoyed a great deal. Sonam sat as stiff as a rake between Martin and the broken door for the entire journey, scarcely daring to breathe and desperately worrying what to do about the arm around her shoulder.

Martin's strategy of involving Kunsang in his courtship proved to be a wise one. She began to trust this strange foreigner more and more, and soon developed maternal feelings towards him. Whenever he came to visit, she made him noodle soup. She would also fetch half a cup of expensive milk from the Indian milkman, which she gave him with the soup. She knew he was having trouble digesting Indian food and she wanted to fatten him up. The growing friendship between Kunsang and Martin was expressed entirely by means of gestures, facial expressions and sounds – Martin spoke barely a word of Tibetan and Kunsang only a few dozen words of English and not a single syllable of German.

Martin even took my grandmother and my mother out to one of the expensive restaurants they had both so admired. A nervous Sonam sat at the beautifully laid table with all the knives and forks and spoons in front of her but no idea of when and how to use them. This was a terrible embarrassment for her. Kunsang felt the same way but gave no sign of her discomfort, watching Martin out of the corner of her eye and doing whatever he did. Unfortunately, she liked the food just as little as Sonam did and they sent almost everything back to the kitchen, leaving poor Martin to pay a large bill for food not eaten – a lot of money for a student.

But he didn't give up. He had found out that Sonam wanted to train as a nurse, and he began to work on a plan to take her with him to Switzerland when he returned home after his year in India. Nurses' training in Switzerland, he thought, would be much better than in India anyway. Of course Kunsang would have to come too. He knew both women well enough to realize that they came as a pair; neither would even begin to consider any suggestion that would separate them for more than a day or so, much less by a continent. He went so far as to ask his own mother to contact an acquaintance in the Swiss Red Cross. 'You'll have to make a bit of a drama out of it, tell them about our "love" . . . so that they invite both of them.' He knew from experience that it was not always easy to get Tibetan refugees into Switzerland, even though the quota of 1,000 had not yet been reached. 'She's terribly young,' he admitted in a letter to his mother. 'What do you think? Though she looks older than she is, her character, I've noticed, is still quite childish, in line with her real age. Not an ideal girlfriend for the time being.'

Finally Martin got up his courage. 'I'd like to take you and your mother to Switzerland,' he said to Sonam one night on their way back to House 13 after an evening out. 'You can train as a nurse there. The situation here in India is uncertain: there are so many domestic problems and there's a threat of war with China or Pakistan.'

Sonam realized now that Martin had serious intentions and she began to think carefully about his suggestion. For someone who had already lived in so many places, none of which had felt truly like home, it was possible to imagine relocating again, especially to somewhere as wonderful sounding as Switzerland. What was more, her mother was not against the idea.

Martin was full of hope. He was grateful that Kunsang was so open in her willingness to take such a leap. This traditional Tibetan woman was willing to travel halfway across the world if it would improve the life of her daughter. 'Isn't it wonderful?' he wrote to his mother. 'But now the greatest of all difficulties: persuading the Swiss Red Cross to let them both come. It's immensely important to me that Sonam Dolma and her mother enter the country. Not that I'm stupid enough to be thinking of marriage already. No, but Sonam Dolma is a person who would perhaps, to put it mildly, be suitable for marriage in three or four years. I don't know, and that's precisely why I want to have her in Switzerland: to get to know her. And a stay in Switzerland would have personal advantages for her as well: she wants to be a nurse and the training in Switzerland is much better than in India.'

But Martin's elation didn't last long. Kunsang may have been considering a highly untraditional path, but she still insisted on following the traditional custom of asking her guru for guidance on major decisions. Dudjom Rinpoche played this role in Kunsang's life. She had studied with him not only in Tibet, but also in Indian exile in Shimla and Kalimpong. So she wrote a letter asking her revered spiritual master for advice, and Martin had to accept that no decision could be made without his answer.

The rinpoche's response arrived a few weeks later. Sonam came to Martin's lodgings one evening extremely upset. 'My mother is very troubled,' she told him. 'The high lama has written to her that my health will suffer if we go to Switzerland. He has foreseen it. He says my mother's health is also at risk in the next one to two years; that the two of us ought to stay just where we are.' Sonam's tears flowed. 'If we went to Switzerland, we would not be following the rinpoche's advice.'

Martin was devastated and had to fight back tears of his own. He, Sonam and Kunsang spent several sleepless nights wondering what to do. Finally Martin decided that he himself should write a letter to Dudjom Rinpoche, after receiving Kunsang's permission to do so. In the letter, he pointed out a number of reasons why a journey to Switzerland might be beneficial to the two women. Sonam had a weak constitution, and the Swiss medical system was much better than that in India. The political situation between Pakistan and India was very unstable and he was worried that war was on the way; mother and daughter would always be safe in neutral Switzerland. He also followed the Tibetan custom of offering to finance a special prayer to remove and destroy any evil influences threatening the two of them. A lama he knew in Mussoorie had suggested to him that he do this.

Martin waited and waited for the rinpoche's reply, but it did not arrive. His job in Mussoorie was nearly over and his visa was soon to expire. He was to start studying Cultural Anthropology and Religious Studies at university in Zurich in a few weeks. His departure from Mussoorie was heartbreaking. From the window of his taxi he watched Sonam and Kunsang recede. As soon as they were out of sight, he burst into tears and wept all the way to Dehradun.

In Dehradun, Martin had one final task before leaving for Switzerland: he was to check up on the management of the hostels financed by Swiss Aid to Tibetans. He made some alarming discoveries. It seemed that the manager of the boys' hostel was cooking the books. He had two invoices made out for every food delivery, one higher than the other. He paid the lower bill, handed the higher in to be recompensed by the charity, and kept the difference for himself. When Martin told Rinchen Dolma Taring and the representative of the Swiss charity about the fraud, they refused to believe him, but when he presented them with proof they couldn't ignore, the charity's entire administration was soon up in arms.

He also found irregularities when it came to the school fees received from the generous Swiss donors who sponsored the Tibetan refugees. Like Sonam, all the children whose school fees were paid out of such donations had to write a letter every month to their sponsor. This was no easy task for the children, so to make matters simpler the teachers wrote a text on the school blackboard, which the children copied down as best they could: 'Dear benefactor, thanks to the grace of the Dalai Lama I am very well. I am glad you are enabling me to attend school. I am studying very hard and I always do my homework. I did well in an examination and I hope I will one day return to Tibet.' When the letters were finished, the teachers wrote the addresses on the envelopes. Some children, Martin discovered, wrote not just to one benefactor but to several. It was not clear what happened to the extra school fees that the organization collected for these children.

It was a sad conclusion to his time in the Happy Valley. He flew back to Switzerland and began his studies in Zurich, but his longing for Sonam only increased with each passing day.

24

The Decision

As autumn settled over Mussoorie, the days remained sunny but lost their heat. It was time for Sonam to leave the green mountain ranges and return to Dehradun, to the hot lower elevation. School was starting again.

With a heavy heart, she boarded the bus. Now she felt doubly lonely. Not only did she miss her mother during the long months of separation, but her heart ached for Martin too. Common sense told her the friendship was over, but something inside her refused to forget him and no other man interested her.

She had met a Thai man at a picnic the previous summer, and he began sending her regular declarations of his love. In one of his letters he wrote that he was standing in Mussoorie and looking down towards Dehradun, wondering which of the millions of lights down there must belong to Sonam. These romantic letters left her cold. It was hard for her to tell him 'I don't love you!' on her next visit to Mussoorie, but he left her in peace after that.

She had another admirer, a long-haired Tibetan who came from a good family. Though he looked both elegant and exciting, Sonam had to tell him too 'I don't love you!' Her third admirer, a soldier some twenty years her senior, was no more fortunate. This was one of the men who had been courting her when she lived at Stirling Castle. She had long since forgotten her old admirer when one day some of the other girls in Dehradun told her she had a visitor. She had no idea who it might be, so she crept over to a window to peer out cautiously. When she saw who was standing there, her heart began to beat out a wild rhythm: it was the soldier from Shimla! In a panic, she ran into the toilet and waited for what seemed like an eternity. She was terribly afraid that the hostel staff might find out a man had come to see her, which would surely have meant her being thrown out of the hostel and the school. To make matters worse, the toilets, simple earth closets, were blocked as usual and stank to high heaven. Sonam could barely suppress her nausea as she waited.

It was around this time that she received her first airmail letter from Switzerland. Hastily she tore open the blue envelope and pulled out several sheets of thin typewritten paper. Martin wrote at length about his life in beautiful Switzerland, his studies at Zurich University, and his longing for her.

Sonam was very impressed by his descriptions. She was debating with herself how to answer when another envelope arrived. Once again it contained pages-long descriptions of Martin's plans, hopes and feelings for her. Sonam was just about to answer the two letters when a third arrived, handed to her by the manager of the girls' hostel along with an extremely disapproving look. At that time it was very unusual and almost indecent for a woman to receive letters from a white man, so it was all the more embarrassing for Sonam to receive so many, and to be handed the letters by the hostel manager. In the end she went against her feelings and wrote to Martin, telling him not to send her any more letters. 'I was afraid they would end in trouble. I had been through so much that I expected tragedy more than happiness. I was always on guard against anything bad that lay ahead, lest I suffer terrible consequences.'

'Please only write to me if it's really important,' Martin read in his Zurich student apartment. 'Don't write me any unimportant things.'

But he wasn't deterred, continuing to send long letters to Sonam. She would take them into the toilet, the only place she could read undisturbed. She was scared that the other girls might gossip if they found out about her mail. She answered hardly any of Martin's subsequent letters, making him all the more worried and restless. He wrote to all kinds of people acquainted with Sonam whom he knew from his visit to India. Even the Mouse King got a letter from Zurich, instructing him to go to Sonam and ask her why she wasn't sending any replies.

Martin's letters had become a huge embarrassment for Sonam; the whole school believed she was having an affair with a Swiss man, naturally imagining much more than tame chaperoned trips to the movies. The matter became even more unpleasant when Rinchen Dolma Taring found out about it. After every semester examination my mother had to go to Mrs Taring's office and show her report card, a terrifying prospect because of her poor grades. But this time the director vented her rage at her, shouting in front of all the office staff: 'Why do you want to go to the West?' Sonam felt humiliated and ashamed. As the tears streamed down her cheeks, Rinchen Dolma Taring continued: 'What do you want from a white man? We have enough aristocratic Tibetan sons here; you can marry one of them. Aren't our men good enough for you?'

Sonam was horrified and speechless, feeling powerless and angry at the same time. She had never expected such a reaction from the founder of the children's home in Happy Valley. It had never even

193

occurred to her to consider whether Tibetan men were better or worse than white men. She had never been interested in men. Martin had stepped into her life like an unexpected prince in a fairy tale; she had done nothing to prompt his interest. She liked him, but he was from another world; she had never longed for him to come along and rescue her. In this way, her experience was similar to her mother's with Tsering: a man had suddenly come into her life and declared himself in love with her. She stammered an apology, sensing as she did so that something inside her was growing firm. She felt an inner core of herself standing by Martin, no matter what her benefactress and all the others might think of her. Nevertheless, the exchange of letters remained unbalanced: Martin wrote long missives; Sonam answered only briefly.

Though Sonam was feeling more and more attached to Martin, her mother was still the focus of her affections. 'I'm a lucky girl if I can come to Switzerland soon,' she wrote. 'If I was an unlucky girl I would be left behind in India . . . I will never forget your friendliness. But why do you always think of me? I don't understand what you mean by that. You shouldn't always think of me, you should think of your mother. You're so far away from me. In my opinion, a mother is more important than friends. You can always find new friends, but there is only one mother in the world. And when you write to me, please write my address in different handwriting so that the janitor doesn't notice you're writing to me.'

Then, in late autumn, like a thunderbolt from the blue, Martin received a short message from Sonam:

'Please don't be angry. I can't come to Switzerland. I'm going to see my mother on the 10th of December, then I'll talk to her again and perhaps she'll change her mind. But I can't tell you any more now, because I have to decide together with my mother.'

Then silence. It was only after a letter to Kunsang (which, along with her reply, was translated for her by an acquaintance) that Martin found out that my grandmother had obviously had a radical change of mind, although she gave him no explanation of why. Had the pressure from those around them got the better of Kunsang and Sonam?

Martin was absolutely distraught. In the few letters he received from Sonam she was once again as shy and reserved as when they had first met. Perhaps there was nothing he could do but go along with her wishes. But he couldn't help negative thoughts creeping up on him: hadn't his mother Ula once been in love with Raja? When he returned to India, hadn't she regretted this missed opportunity her whole life long? Wasn't her relationship with Martin's father little more than a panic marriage to help her forget her true love? Was Martin to face the same fate, carrying his impossible love for the vanished Sonam for the rest of his life?

He wrote more letters, to Sonam, to Kunsang. Finally he received another letter from Kunsang, again translated into stilted English by an Indian acquaintance. This one gave him hope.

'Everything depends on God,' she had written, 'and on my destiny. We would both be very glad to see you soon, for many things have now happened.'

This was just what Martin had wanted to hear. He had already been planning to travel to India and Sikkim, at that time still an independent monarchy, to make some short films there with a German filmmaker. Now he could combine the filming with a visit to my mother and grandmother. The filmmaker later accused him of going to India only to meet Sonam, but that didn't bother Martin; he did his work for the film properly, though only relatively success-fully, because they couldn't film the Tibetan oracle in Sikkim as he was constantly drunk, and because some of their footage of the Tibetan New Year that they filmed near Dehradun was confiscated by the police.

At Dehradun, Martin had a touching reunion with Sonam, though it was limited to a few embraces, tears and mutual declarations to stand by one another. He asked her and Kunsang to accompany him on a filming trip to the north-east of India. Sonam didn't want to miss school, but to his surprise Kunsang wanted to come along, which was to prove very fortuitous for Martin. During their travels the two of them became good friends. Though neither of them spoke the other's language, they continued to communicate using mimes and gestures. Both of them were convinced that they understood each other perfectly.

The trip took them first to Darjeeling, from where Kunsang went on alone to Kalimpong to meet Dudjom Rinpoche and present him once again with Martin's marriage proposal, this time in person. At a private audience, she told the rinpoche Martin's story and asked if he would agree to her and her daughter going to Switzerland with him. Dudjom Rinpoche listened patiently, nodded several times and then sent her away with instructions to return a week later.

My grandmother returned to the rinpoche's villa after a week and, bending low in a deep bow, handed him a gift of a scarf. He had good news for her. With the aid of his prayer beads he had reached a prophecy: 'Trust him, go to Switzerland, and all will be well!'

Kunsang was very happy, for she was now firmly convinced that Martin and Sonam made a good couple. She thanked the rinpoche again and again and left him a donation for his prayers in favour of the young couple.

She returned to Darjeeling to meet up with Martin, who in the meantime had gone to Kalimpong on a misunderstanding, thinking that my grandmother was waiting for him there. On hearing that she had left already, he went to Dudjom Rinpoche's home, hoping he could change the rinpoche's mind and convince him of his love and good intentions towards Sonam. The monks who lived with the rinpoche refused to let him in, but the rinpoche knew who it was outside requesting an audience, and asked his monks to give Martin one of his books of teachings and a scarf. When Martin caught up with Kunsang again and she saw these valuable and rare gifts from her rinpoche, she knew that he was the right man for her daughter, but she did not yet share this feeling with Martin. She wanted to let it settle in her own heart first.

The next day the two of them went to Delhi; Kunsang perfectly calm, Martin rather unsure of himself, still not knowing whether he could marry Sonam or not. As the two of them sat in an unprepossessing café, he took a napkin and drew on it a large person, next to that a slightly smaller one, and then another even smaller one. Then he drew a plane. This picture confused Kunsang, who had only ever seen planes as tiny dots in the sky and had no idea what they looked like close up. So Martin spread his arms and flapped them in the air like a bird, repeating in his more than broken Tibetan 'iron bird' and *nam druk*, 'sky dragon' – the Tibetan word for plane – until she finally understood him. Then he started pointing at the sky and asking, 'Switzerland? Switzerland?' Kunsang nodded more and more emphatically, shaking with laughter and snorting, 'Yes, Swiserland, yes.'

Finally Martin knew that he had succeeded in winning Kunsang's approval for his marriage to Sonam.

In the train on the way back to Dehradun, Martin was preoccupied with working out how to get Kunsang into Switzerland. He knew that Sonam would have no trouble entering the country as his wife, but he doubted the Swiss Red Cross would let her mother enter as part of its contingent of Tibetan refugees. He knew the

Red Cross was still angry with him because several years earlier he had prevented a group of relatively wealthy Tibetans from entering the country, discovering that they had been incorrectly classified as poor refugees. Although the Red Cross had acknowledged its mistake and ultimately had given the places to poor and needy Tibetan road workers, there were still some in the organization who had not forgiven him for his intervention. The fact that a young student could achieve so much had annoyed a number of long-serving bureaucrats within the Red Cross so much that they wanted revenge.

On the train to Dehradun, Martin had the desperate idea of suggesting to Kunsang that he marry her instead of her daughter. Then both of them could enter Switzerland: Kunsang as his wife and Sonam as their daughter. My grandmother even agreed to go along with this plan – as soon as she trusted a person, she was willing to do anything for them.

Fortunately, Martin wrote a letter to his godfather in Berne, telling him about the plan. Barely a week later, he received a telegram:

'Don't do it: firstly Sonam would be your stepdaughter if you married her mother, and you'd never be able to marry her. Secondly, the Swiss authorities would see through this marriage of convenience and send both women back to India.'

When Kunsang and Martin arrived in Dehradun, Sonam was awaiting them anxiously. As she watched the two of them getting off the train, she saw that they moved together with postures of complete trust and familiarity, and one look into her mother's eyes told her that everything would be fine. From now on she would never have to be ashamed of being with a white man; she had gained not only the rinpoche's blessings but also her mother's.

Now all signs of her shyness vanished, and she was able to visit

Martin's hotel room in Dehradun for the first time. Although she was careful that none of her fellow schoolgirls found out – she didn't want to overdo her new self-confidence, for they were not yet married – finally she and Martin were able to express the fullness of their feelings for one another. From then on, they both felt they were a couple, destined to be together.

25

The Wedding

Martin was a very conscientious person, and he was well aware that among Kunsang and Sonam acquaintances there were great reservations about a white man marrying a Tibetan woman. To be on the safe side, he wrote to the Dalai Lama, with whom he had been in contact since he had interviewed him. In his letter, he asked the head of all Tibetans whether there was any hindrance to his marriage to Sonam from a Buddhist point of view. He was greatly relieved when he received a reply, immediately showed it to my mother and grandmother. 'Our congratulations on your wedding,' the Dalai Lama had had his secretary write. 'His Holiness has given his approval.'

Now he couldn't resist writing to Rinchen Dolma Taring, the director of Sonam's hostel, telling her that even the Dalai Lama had given his blessing to the relationship of which she had so disapproved. She never acknowledged receipt of the letter.

Martin soon had to return to Switzerland, where he worked diligently and contacted everyone he knew for help getting an entry visa for his future mother-in-law. Again his efforts ran up against a brick wall. The Red Cross refused to help him, as he had feared they might. The Swiss immigration authorities were initially deaf to his attempts to bring not only his future wife but also his mother-in-law into the country, and not even a well-placed lawyer friend or any other acquaintances he asked could do anything to help him.

His head full of worries and worst-case scenarios, he began planning his next trip to India. He knew the wedding would go ahead while he was there; the two women had already made all the preparations. Sonam had officially announced the marriage to the Indian registry office. The procedure was to write on a piece of paper that she was getting married and pin it to a tree in the square outside the town hall.

Still Martin had absolutely no idea how he would get Kunsang to Europe. It seemed he would have to rely on the goodwill of the gods, since the authorities had so far been no use whatsoever. Then the gods did intervene. Through his work for Swiss Aid to Tibetans, he met Switzerland's top immigration officer. Appalled at the Red Cross's attitude, the woman contacted her brother and managed to get special permission for Kunsang to enter the country.

Martin flew to India. On the appointed day, he and Sonam and two witnesses took a scooter taxi to the registrar's home, as it was a Sunday and the man didn't want to go to the office to officiate just one marriage. He received them informally in white pyjamas and a dark blue robe, inviting them into his living room. He didn't want to see their papers or speak to the witnesses, he simply signed a sheet of paper, and less than five minutes after they had entered the house my father and mother were man and wife. After their wedding they went for lunch, and then Martin had to return Sonam to the girls' hostel. Even though she was now married, she was still not allowed to spend the night out.

There remained only a few more bureaucratic hurdles to jump. An official who was supposed to provide the Indian emigration papers refused to issue them until Kunsang could prove she had previously lived in Shimla. Time was running out, and Martin was angry and at his wits' end, arguing and arguing to no avail. He was just about to set off for Shimla, although it seemed highly unlikely that Indian bureaucrats could come up with the document in such a short time, when a Tibetan friend stopped him. 'Give me a hundred rupees,' he told Martin, 'and you'll have the paper in two days.'

Martin certainly knew that officials took bribes, but he couldn't imagine it would be so simple. Kunsang and Sonam kept urging him to try it. Finally he gave the friend the money, an amount close to what Kunsang was paid for two months' work. Much to his surprise, two days later the papers arrived at the hotel where he and Sonam were staying.

Now my grandmother, my mother and my father could prepare for their departure for Europe. Sonam spent almost Kunsang's entire savings, three thousand rupees, on a Tibetan apron of the kind only married women wore, and two Tibetan carpets. The little that remained Kunsang gave to Martin to put towards the cost of the tickets to Switzerland and the hotel in Delhi.

'Now you're responsible for us,' said Sonam as she looked trustingly into his eyes. Martin's free-living days as a student had come to an end, and he was happy for it.

The women packed their belongings: the new carpets and apron, a few pieces of clothing, the silver bracelet from Tibet, a rug they had brought with them from the old country, and a little round mirrored box. This was the same box that had travelled with them from Tibet, with the red stone that healed wounds. They also had their wooden food bowls, the bronze tsa tsa mould, and two pairs of shoes each. That was the entire sum of their possessions.

At the last moment, they had to face an unexpected bureaucratic challenge at the Swiss embassy in New Delhi. The consulate officer initially refused to issue a Swiss passport for Sonam, even though all the papers they showed him proved that Martin and Sonam were man and wife. Martin had every single document he could ever need on his person, all of which proved that the officer was in the wrong. Finally, after hours of debating and my father's refusal to leave the office until Sonam had a Swiss passport in her hands, the officer clapped his fleshy paws together and said: 'I wash my hands of you.'

The three travellers finally set off for the airport in the early hours of the morning. At the very moment they stepped out into the street, a man came towards them carrying a huge load of wood on his back. Kunsang was thrilled; this was an excellent sign for the future.

'If I had a Tibetan good luck scarf, I'd lay it over his wood,' she said.

Before Martin could ask what this good omen meant, my grandmother saw the next sign: a group of milkmen walking in their direction. That made her even more elated.

'The worst thing would have been a man with empty milk cans – that would have meant poverty,' she said, registering Martin's questioning look. The man carrying the wood was a sign of wealth and well-being, she added. It was always hard to find enough wood for a well-fuelled hearth in Tibet, and passing a man carrying such a load foretold great future prosperity.

26

A New World

The journey from Mussoorie to Zurich not only took the brand-new family from one continent to another, it also catapulted the two Tibetan women into a new age. During their twelve years in India, my grandmother and my mother had come across many of the blessings of modern technology, but even so their Indian life had little in common with what awaited them in modern Europe. In India they had travelled by train, bus and car, they had been to movie theatres and eaten with knives and forks. They had listened to the radio and read newspapers, they had visited huge cities and stayed in magnificent old villas. They had gone on pilgrimages to the most holy Buddhist sites and come into contact with Indian Hinduism. Yet the world to which they were travelling was beyond their wildest imaginings.

On the aeroplane, Sonam could hardly believe that such a vessel could contain so many people and things and still fly. When the noise of the engines grew to a loud roar and she no longer felt the rumbling and rolling of the wheels she was accustomed to from Indian train carriages, she grabbed hold of the armrests in terror.

Kunsang took it all in her stride. She sat placidly in her seat, passing the wooden balls of her prayer beads between her fingers, her gaze peaceful and unfocused. When she saw the stewardesses demonstrating the life jackets, she joked: 'I won't be able to put that on fast enough if we crash, and I can't swim. If we fall into the sea, I'll die.'

Kunsang remembered the ancient prophecy attributed to Guru Rinpoche, which said that the Tibetans would have to leave their home when the iron bird flew. For her, she felt, that time had now come. The prediction that the Guru Rinpoche had made so many centuries ago said that Buddhism would then travel to the West, and she believed this wholeheartedly. She felt she was fulfilling the ancient Buddhist prophecy.

Sonam had a less Buddhist approach, seeing things in a more practical light. She took little for granted and knew that to get along in the world she had to think logically. For her, the first mystery of the new world came in the form of two friendly stewardesses pushing a cart loaded with drinks. Drinking in mid-air? Sonam couldn't have imagined such a thing, but soon she was holding a transparent plastic glass of bright orange juice. But what was this? Her lips shrank back on contact with the liquid and she nearly lost her grip on the glass. This wasn't orange juice! It looked like orange juice but it tasted sickly sweet, sticky, and very different from the fruity drink she was used to.

Martin explained that it was not the same as the freshly squeezed orange juice on sale on almost every street corner in India, but concentrate with water added to make it last longer. He looked over at Kunsang, who had long since emptied her glass without so much as blinking. That was typical of her. She took everything as it came, questioning nothing.

The new family had hardly left Asia, and already the cultural discrepancies between the three of them had been made manifest by a glass of orange juice. Martin viewed the world as an enlightened Westerner; Kunsang, rooted in her Tibetan Buddhist traditions, was unshaken by even the strangest products of what we call modern civilization. She lived in the eternal world of the Tibetan divinities, unchanging with changing circumstances. Between these two poles was Sonam, uprooted from her Tibetan childhood at the age of six, having to adjust to life in India and one temporary home after another, and now at the age of nineteen catapulted into the modern West.

This dislocation was to have a profound effect on my mother. She has been uprooted and transplanted into so many different cultures that no one culture makes any more sense to her than another. There is nothing fixed she holds on to. Kunsang has been the only constant in her life. My mother questions and broods over whatever she is presented with. She does not simply accept anything; she is by far the most sceptical person in my family. I sometimes think that life for her is harder than for the rest of us; for a long time she had no solid ground on which to stand, no reliable traditions or conventions to steady her.

For me, everything has been easier from the outset: I am a child of the West. Tibet is only a small part of my life. I'm Swiss, I'm Tibetan. My upbringing and my spiritual approach to life are founded on Tibetan culture, but my life has been lived in the West. My *mola*, my *amala* and I are like three layers of an exotic sandwich: on top is Kunsang, a slice of Tibetan *tsampa* dough, at the bottom is me, sliced wholewheat bread; and in the middle is Sonam, the juicy filling that takes from and gives to both sides without belonging to either.

Amala and Mola will never forget their arrival in Zurich. As soon as they walked into the terminal, they were assaulted by a host of new sights and sounds and smells and technology. Immediately they had to get on to an escalator, something neither had ever seen before. Kunsang was both mystified and frightened by this moving staircase and had to make several attempts before she managed to get on. She had barely stepped off it again when Martin had to grab hold of her to stop her from walking into an automatic glass door that didn't open fast enough. In the restaurant where they waited for the bus to Berne, Sonam was baffled by the food she saw on people's plates. She gave Martin a cautious nudge, pointing furtively at a woman tucking into a large bowl of salad at the next table. 'What's that?' she whispered.

No Tibetan would eat raw vegetables, certainly not leaves, let alone in such huge quantities. Martin's explanation did little to settle Sonam's questions. 'Is she going to eat it all?' she persisted. She was amazed when she saw, only a few minutes later, that the woman had cleared her plate.

Her next surprise came on the bus to Berne. All the other passengers were Swiss, and they seemed to be hissing, rasping and croaking. Soon Sonam realized that these noises were the Swiss speaking their native language. She had never heard Swiss German before; she spoke only English with Martin. Was this the language she was going to have to learn? 'I can't imagine I will ever make sounds like that!' she whispered to him.

It seemed perfectly natural to both women that they were all going to live with Martin's mother, Ula, when they arrived in Berne. What did surprise them was that my grandfather, Harald, did not live there too, but in a much larger house. Martin's parents had been separated for many years, and though Martin got on equally well with both of them, Ula was the one who had graciously offered to take them in. Even though he knew the three of them would have to share a cramped attic room, Martin thought this was a good solution. As a student, he couldn't afford to rent a place large enough for three people.

Martin's sister Bice, who herself had recently separated from her husband, was also living in their mother's house with her two children, which was why there was room for my family only in the attic. Though the house wasn't large, it seemed to Sonam like a king's palace, with wood and upholstered furniture everywhere. Even sitting in an armchair seemed odd. So used was she to the ingrained hierarchies, where people always bow in order not to be taller than others, that she felt she was suddenly sitting on a throne. When her new mother-in-law served her coffee with cream and sugar, she was astonished: she'd never tasted such a thing before, nor been served in such an elegant manner.

Adjusting to their new life turned out to be harder than either Sonam or Kunsang had imagined. Martin had anticipated their difficulties and wasn't surprised by them. He did all he could to help his Tibetan wife and mother-in-law to acclimatize. Soon after their arrival, he and his father organized a small wedding celebration to which they invited all their Swiss friends and relatives. The party was a great success; everyone was very impressed by the two friendly and charming Tibetan women. Having never before encountered any Tibetans, they found Sonam and Kunsang very exotic. My parents believe they were the first Swiss-Tibetan couple in Switzerland. The guests all decided that Martin looked much better now he was married – younger and healthier, not as pale and drawn as he had been before.

My father spent weekdays at university in Zurich, only returning to Berne on Friday evenings, so Sonam and Kunsang were left to themselves. The house was crowded, the atmosphere tense, and misunderstandings were a daily occurrence. Sonam and Kunsang had never seen modern appliances such as washing machines and vacuum cleaners. The day after Kunsang saw Bice vacuuming, she thought she should use the vacuum to sweep the floors every morning, as was the custom in Tibet. So she vacuumed early each day until Bice told her it wasn't necessary. The kitchen was a source of further problems. Because Kunsang revered the hearth god, she wanted everything around the stove to be arranged according to special Tibetan rules and kept spotlessly clean. The other occupants of the house kept violating these rules and messing up her arrangements. When cooking, Martin's mother and sister would put a spoon directly into the pan to taste the dish, even though the food was for everyone. This was more than unappetizing for Tibetans, who would never think of letting their saliva mix with anything that was to be eaten by another person.

Mealtimes presented further challenges. Kunsang and Sonam didn't know European customs and were terribly unsure of themselves. After one meal, they were informed by Ula that the Swiss did not speak with their mouths full, make noises when they ate, or slurp their tea. Sonam had to learn to cook from scratch, not even knowing how to make tea or boil an egg. It was no wonder: Kunsang would never have let her near the fire as a small child, and in India they had spent the last years living in places where the food was cooked for them.

When the whole family gathered around Ula's oval table for a meal, Kunsang and Sonam found it disturbing that Bice's children Rita and Paul, who were only six and eight years old, talked constantly; in Tibet only adults talk during meals. And there was strange food to get used to: Swiss muesli, which seemed very odd to the Tibetans, who never ate raw food; hard cheese that smelled rancid; and strange cold lettuce leaves sour with vinegar that tasted like wet straw and were hard to swallow. They were not usually full when they left the table because they were not used to serving

209

themselves. In Tibet, the mother serves up the food, and now that they were expected to serve themselves they were very hesitant, afraid to appear rude. Tibetans wait to be offered second helpings several times before accepting, and they followed this tradition even if they were still hungry. By the meal's end there was nothing left over for them.

Sonam couldn't understand why Martin spent so much time on the telephone. Even worse, it seemed he was talking to women. Who were these women? What was he talking about? Who sent him all the letters he received every day? Martin explained patiently that it was all to do with his work, but Sonam was still suspicious. She was often overcome by sadness and jealousy and reduced to tears, for which the others in the house had little patience. It was only later that she realized Bice had problems of her own to deal with – and that the six extra people in the house were a major burden on Martin's mother.

Kunsang often came into conflict with Swiss values and customs. After her daily prayers she offered rice and crackers to the gods by throwing them out of the window, as she was accustomed to do in Tibet and India. After a few days the landlady knocked at the door and gave the entire family a severe dressing-down for feeding the birds. Birds did not need feeding in the spring, she told them.

Kunsang didn't like to stay indoors, and she often got lost while wandering around the town, unable to find her way home in the tangle of streets with their brick houses that all looked the same and street signs she couldn't read. In the supermarket, she was thoroughly astonished by the mountains of food; she couldn't imagine where it had all come from and who was supposed to eat it. She found it almost impossible to believe that she could help herself to whatever she wanted and only had to pay at the checkout counter at the end.

She was also alarmed by how often people showered and washed. In Tibet, this would have been a sign of excessive pride and arrogance. There, she had only washed herself and her children at night, to make sure the neighbours wouldn't see. She was familiar with showers from India, but she could never have imagined taking one on a daily basis, let alone several times a day as some Swiss people did.

The clashes and misunderstandings began to affect Sonam's relationship with Martin. When Martin innocently pointed out to her that he thought she was actually left-handed, the two of them had their first major fight, and Sonam refused to speak to him for three days. How could he say such a thing to her? For Tibetans, the left hand is impure; no one in Tibet accepts being left-handed. All children try their hardest to do everything with their right hand, no matter how difficult that may be.

Nevertheless, Sonam soon felt accepted by most Swiss people. Although she did meet people who seemed to reject or mistrust her, she often noticed that their faces brightened as soon as they found out where she came from. 'The Dalai Lama!' they said then, and 'Tibet is that wonderful mountain country.' It was only after some months that she realized that some Swiss people had a selective view of foreigners. There were some whom they welcomed and others they did not, such as women from Thailand or the Philippines, whom many Swiss automatically assumed were Asian prostitutes. And because Sonam barely spoke their language, she found it difficult to judge whether the people she was talking to were open-minded or not. All the Swiss looked the same to her.

She was baffled when all sorts of different people seemed to want to speak to her about politics or social issues; she was entirely unfamiliar with such topics for conversation, and was overwhelmed by the many different political parties, opinions and views. In

Tibetan society a small group of people determined things; the others obeyed without discussion. Now Sonam was frequently expected to give her opinion, even in writing – there was always something to be voted on in the Swiss direct democracy system: building schools or nuclear power stations, expelling foreigners, restructuring the unemployment benefits system or even founding a new canton. To begin with, she didn't understand any of these things, but gradually she began to approach the subjects and in time became more and more comfortable with them. Kunsang, on the other hand, lived far too much within her spiritual world to worry about such earthly matters.

Not long after they arrived, Sonam's sister-in-law Bice recommended that she should get her hair cut. At that time, in the early 1970s, almost all women in Switzerland had practical, short hairstyles. Sonam was only familiar with short hair on nuns; all other women in Tibet and India had long hair. She found the masculine-looking haircuts unattractive, but obedient as ever, she went to the hairdresser's. She still did everything her elders told her to do and she wanted very much to fit in to her new society. The haircut was a disaster. When she saw herself in the mirror with short hair, she felt like a stranger. She was so upset she refused to enter a hair salon again. Over the next forty years, she probably had her hair cut only three times. Even now, she prefers to cut her own hair.

She was also bewildered by all the cosmetics she was given for Christmas and her birthday: night creams and day creams and eye creams and hand creams, and more. To begin with she enjoyed the lovely pots and bottles, but soon her enjoyment was replaced by stress. There were so many different ways to apply the cosmetics, she couldn't read the instructions properly, and those she could make out were too complicated. In Tibet she had washed her face with soap and water and then rubbed it with butter, for which she had substituted Vaseline in India. It wasn't long before she left the new creams and potions aside and went back to her old regimen. Much later, when she had been further assimilated into the West, she began to realize how many unnecessary products the market thrusts on consumers.

As Sonam no longer got her hair cut, her black curls became more and more unruly, straying out of the tight ponytails and buns they had been constrained in back in Tibet and India. They too were vehemently demanding freedom. This disturbed Kunsang, who regarded Sonam's hair as an unfortunate explosion, one among many. Sonam didn't even want to pray any more! During their early days in Switzerland, she still used her *mala* beads to say her anti-leprosy mantra every evening, simply because she was used to doing so; her praying had always been done more out of obligation to her mother than conviction. After a time she decided the prayer was pointless: she didn't have leprosy and she was highly unlikely to contract it in Switzerland. True to her nature, Kunsang took over her daughter's prayers against leprosy, adding another fifteen minutes to her own protracted prayer times.

Sonam wanted to concentrate on her new life. She enrolled in a language course to learn all the hissing, rasping and croaking that was Swiss German. She and Kunsang agreed that Kunsang was too old to learn a new language; it wouldn't be worth her while. My grandmother was in her early fifties at the time, considered a woman of very advanced age in her home country.

Besides, Kunsang was happy to cling to her old ways. And very soon, the old ways came to her. Dudjom Rinpoche was travelling through Switzerland. It was at this time, in the early 1970s, that Tibetan lamas first began to travel to the West. They not only wanted to be there for the numerous Tibetan exiles, but also enjoyed giving lectures and teachings for Westerners interested in Buddhism.

Kunsang and Sonam could hardly believe their luck that their most important guru could be so close by. In India, they had had to travel long distances and wait days for an audience with him. Kunsang was delighted to see how easy it was to contact her spiritual adviser in Switzerland: she and Sonam and Martin took an hour's train ride to Zurich, and there was her beloved rinpoche.

27

A Home of Their Own

After three months of living at his mother's house, Martin was presented with a wonderful new opportunity. The canton of Zurich had purchased the Tibetan collection of one of the most famous Western travellers to Tibet, the Austrian writer, climber and geographer Heinrich Harrer. The collection was given to the University of Zurich, and my father was offered a job as an assistant at the Ethnographic Museum. Soon he, Sonam and Kunsang were able to move into their own apartment in Zurich. After living in close confines with Martin's mother and sister in Berne, they were all relieved to finally set up a household of their own.

Moving to Zurich was wonderful for Kunsang. She no longer sat bored and lonely at home; she went out and found a job as a cleaning lady at an old people's nursing home. Sonam was initially against her mother working, thinking her too old. 'That may be your personal point of view,' Kunsang told her, 'but I feel perfectly fit. I can earn eleven Swiss francs an hour, which is an immense sum. And I must contribute to the family's income, as I have always done my whole life long.'

Every day Kunsang mopped and scrubbed at the nursing home. She enjoyed her work: everything was so clean and well organized there. The old people lay in soft beds; they were even served their meals in bed.

Sonam took a job as a nursing assistant on the geriatric ward of a psychiatric clinic. After a while she found a job for Kunsang in the same department. The two women were impressed that a hospital would have special wards for old people, people with disabilities and even the blind. They had never come across similar institutions in Tibet or in India. It was only in Switzerland that they learned that the deaf are not stupid, as Tibetans generally assumed, and that the blind are incredibly skilled at finding their way around in the world, providing they are properly trained. However, there were things about the hospital that shocked them.

At that time there were so few Tibetans living in Switzerland that a radio station asked for an interview with Kunsang, and questioned her about her work at the psychiatric hospital. 'I have a nice job,' she told the interpreter, 'it's very good for the people here.' Not wanting to upset anyone, she had to be somewhat creative with the truth. In reality, she couldn't come to terms with the way some patients on her ward were treated. Many of them were incapable of eating unaided. They were tied to their chairs at mealtimes and the nurses spooned food into their mouths as fast as they could, looking forward to a cigarette break. Kunsang took pity on these patients. She didn't understand what they said to her and they didn't understand what she said to them, but they all sensed what she meant. They felt her big heart. One woman waited by the door every morning for her to arrive, giving her a handful of clay pebbles from the plant pots in the corridor and insisting they were coffee beans. Kunsang played along, thanking her warmly. A woman of 105 would let no one but my grandmother touch her bed; others would let only her wash them. When the nurses took a break, she sat down with the patients to feed them slowly and patiently with the food they had not eaten in the rush. She loosened the ties binding them to their chairs and handed out holy pills and herbs from Dudjom Rinpoche behind the doctors' backs, helping her patients to a better reincarnation. She held their hands and spent her time alongside them in deep sympathy and compassion, as every good Buddhist should.

For Kunsang, the worst thing was that the staff didn't leave the patients in peace when their time came to die. They pressed tubes into the helpless old people, pricked needles in their arms and connected them up to electric machines that beeped, rattled and flashed. Dying is very important for Buddhists and the dying should be allowed to go in peace and with dignity; we make no noise around them, neither holding them back nor speeding their departure. Death takes place in calm surroundings, preferably in the presence of the person's closest relatives and a monk. When Kunsang saw how much the old people were disturbed while they were dying and how alone they were, she feared they would have difficulties travelling on to a positive new life. So whenever someone died on her ward, she held surreptitious rituals and prayers for their reincarnation. She felt she owed it to the dead.

These conditions upset Kunsang so much that the work began to make her very unhappy. Nevertheless, she stayed at the hospital for three years before she switched to childminding, looking after the children of a couple who were friends with Martin and Sonam. She got on very well with the little ones. Even though she could hardly communicate with them, she spoilt them rotten. Since she knew only a few words of Swiss German, the children soon began to pick up Tibetan. They were always giddy with anticipation when Kunsang arrived – that meant they could stay up late, playing with her, and learning exotic songs they had never heard before.

28

Happy Events

After they had been living in Zurich for more than two years, Sonam started pressing Martin to move. 'I don't feel at ease in a rented apartment,' she said. 'We could be thrown out at any moment. We need a house of our own – how else are we to live in peace and security?' All Martin's arguments about tenant protection, tenancy laws, the housing market and notice periods were no use: these terms were meaningless to Sonam. She had had to leave too many homes throughout her life to retain any trust in landlords or neighbours. The only thing she trusted in was the power of ownership; during her years in Switzerland, she had learned that property is sacred to the Swiss.

So Martin began reading property ads. He found what he was looking for in Münchwilen, a village in the east of Switzerland, fifty minutes from Zurich by train. Anything closer to the city would have been too expensive, and apart from that, the location had its advantages: a number of Tibetans lived in the area, many of them Nyingmapas, followers of Dudjom Rinpoche.

Martin had been promoted to curator at the University of

Zurich's Ethnographic Museum, taking over the Tibet/Himalayas department. He now earned enough to keep all three of them in comfort, so Sonam left her job on the psychiatric ward. Her new work was renovating the house and designing the garden. Now her time revolved around chipboard, wallpaper, door frames and DIY-store special offers. She savoured the knowledge that every brick in the new house belonged to her, that within these four walls she could feel safer than she'd ever felt before.

When Kunsang's guru Dudjom Rinpoche and his family came on one of their visits to Switzerland, Sonam met his daughters again, now grown up just like her. She remembered well when she had been their playmate for a time in India and how they had ordered her around. Now she was living in a country where everyone had the same rights. According to Tibetan custom, she would have bowed low when she greeted the rinpoche's children, and they would have laid their hands on her head in blessing. But Sonam no longer accepted this hier-archy; she was no longer capable of subjugating herself to others simply because they were allegedly born into a higher position. When she arrived at their house she hesitated for a moment, unsure whether to greet them in the European way by shaking hands, but in the end, she simply nodded and pressed her hands together in front of her chest. Perhaps the rinpoche's daughters were just as glad to have avoided the embarrassment of a formal Tibetan greeting.

Kunsang, however, stuck to the old ways. One day while Martin and Sonam were away, she received a visit from a Tibetan aristo-crat she knew from India. The women were chatting animatedly when the aristocrat caught sight of the beautiful rug my grand-parents had carried all the way across the Himalayas on their escape from Tibet. Kunsang treasured this rug; she had not sold it even in their times of greatest need.

'What a wonderful rug! That would be perfect for my daughter,' said the noblewoman. 'She's a high reincarnation and will soon be enthroned. Would you sell me the rug so I can give it to her?'

Kunsang was unnerved. The only two objects to which she was really attached were this rug from her homeland and her prayer beads. What on earth was she to do? Sonam and Martin would have prevented the sale of the carpet, but they were not there. Kunsang was too trapped in her conventions to turn down her visitor's request, especially as the rug would be going to such a high-ranking reincarnation, which would be good for her own karma. So she accepted a few hundred francs for it, even though it was worth several thousand, quite apart from the fact that she would have never have sold it under any other circumstances.

Sonam was very upset to hear what had happened. Of course there was no way to get the rug back again. Once again my mother felt she was a victim of the old Tibetan class system. In India or Tibet, this noblewoman would not have visited Kunsang, she would never have set foot in the home of a lower-class person. Kunsang came across this woman again in New York in 2008; neither of them mentioned the rug. On this occasion my grandmother again experienced the archaic power of the aristocracy; when she said goodbye, the woman remained seated, ordering Kunsang to bow down to her and touch her forehead against her own. She did as she was told without a word of complaint.

Sonam's dreams came true when she found out she was pregnant. The child she had wished for, with the man of her dreams as the father, in her own house, her beloved mother by her side to help her – life couldn't get any better. She knew little about pregnancy and birth, and had no idea of the physical and mental changes she would be going through; these were more or less taboo subjects in Tibet. From her old homeland she had brought along the fear that giving birth was related above all to pain, complications and danger. Nothing gave her more pleasure than banishing those fears. She had worked in Swiss hospitals and knew how efficient they were. She read books about birth and pregnancy, talked to other young mothers and mothers-to-be and attended pre-natal classes with Martin, learning how to use all the miraculous inventions of modern baby care such as disposable nappies and bottle warmers.

When the big day came and my mother was taken to hospital with contractions, a midwife came into her examination room. The first thing she asked about was not Sonam's well-being or pain, but her health insurance and her husband's name and date of birth. My mother was understandably under some stress and couldn't answer all her questions, partly because birth dates are meaning-less for Tibetans. This immediately angered the rather brisk midwife.

'How can you not know your own husband's date of birth!' she shouted at the utterly perplexed Sonam, slamming her hand against the table. My mother burst into tears, while the midwife matter-of-factly linked her up to a machine, not wasting another word. Sonam had no idea what was going on and felt very humiliated until Martin was allowed into the room. My father wanted to be with her for the birth, which pleased Sonam, even though it seemed very odd to her because, in Tibet, women are regarded as impure during and after childbirth, and have no contact with men.

The birth went well and soon the midwife slapped the wet, blue creature covered in blood and slime on to my mother's belly. She was exhilarated, crying as so many women do at such a moment. Yet this slimy embrace was a more than curious experience for her; in Tibet, newborns are washed, dried and wrapped up warmly before they are handed over to their mothers.

Shortly afterwards I was bathed, scrubbed, weighed, measured, checked and swaddled. Everything was strictly regulated, as was the fashion at the time. When the nurse took me to my *amala* to be breastfed, she disinfected Sonam's breasts and hands with an unpleasant burning liquid, putting a mask over her mouth and nose and handing me to my mother as if I were a highly infectious dangerous creature. Breastfeeding was done according to schedule, regardless of whether I was sleeping, full or hungry at the prescribed time. If I didn't wake up until later and then screamed with hunger because I hadn't finished or even started feeding, that was my bad luck; the hospital schedule took precedence. My mother was in despair because I was not allowed to sleep alongside her, because she was finding breastfeeding difficult, because her breasts were hurting, because she was scared I would suffocate in my barred cot, because she was much too young and inexperienced to stand up to the hospital regime. She bit into her pillow at night so that the other six sharing the room didn't hear her crying.

We were kept in the hospital for ten days, even though my mother had no physical problems whatsoever. At that time birth was regarded as a medical condition that had to be treated in hospital. Tibetan women went back to their routine shortly after giving birth, but Sonam didn't dare to protest and was incredibly happy when she and I were finally discharged.

Once at home, her initial trouble with breastfeeding was forgotten and she became calm and happy. She only had to interrupt her idyll once a week, to take me to the district nurse, who weighed and measured me and reproached my mother. I was too fat, she said, I weighed so many ounces too much, because Sonam had fed me too much. My poor mother went home feeling guilty, and the next morning went on doing just what she felt was right.

Swiss district nurses at that time had very precise ideas about

223

taking care of babies, and they had been put into practice across the nation. The only rule Sonam agreed with was to do with how long the baby should be breastfed: six months was enough for her. Her mother told her that she had been suckled until she was almost three years old, even though not a drop of milk was to be had. Kunsang had often tried to stop Sonam breastfeeding by mixing ash and water on her breasts in the hope that it would put her off. She emphasized the effect by telling Sonam it was Chinese poo, but her daughter was unimpressed. She simply wiped the black mess off and went on sucking with relish.

My mother brought me up with both Western and Eastern methods of child-rearing. When she read in a clever book that little children have to be left to scream now and then, she let me do so for a few minutes until she could stand it no longer, and then picked me up. No mother in Tibet would leave a child screaming; most babies are carried around all day long. She read that babies need their own beds, but when she noticed that I didn't like my cot, she let me sleep in with her and my father every now and then, as was the custom in Tibet, where there were no cradles or cots. She took me to mother-and-baby gymnastics classes and joined in with enthusiasm, enjoying the exercise and the relaxed contact with other mothers. But she had a shock when all the mothers were instructed to line up and form a tunnel between their legs so that one baby after the next could crawl through it. Tibetans would never crawl between another person's legs. They regard the area beneath a person as dirty, especially below a woman, who might be menstruating. But Sonam just closed her eyes for a moment, clenched her teeth and repeated to herself like a mantra, over and over: 'You have to do it, it's good for your child, you have to fit in!'

According to Tibetan custom, it was Dudjom Rinpoche who chose my name. Kunsang had written to her guru, now back in India, asking him what to call her granddaughter, and he had recommended the name Tashi Yangzom. My parents found using both names too complicated. Thinking of the difficulties Swiss tongues would have, they decided to call me simply Yangzom, which means something like 'united luck'. They reserved the second name, Tashi, meaning 'auspiciousness' or 'bliss', for the child they planned to have next. Strangely enough, the registry office didn't raise any objections, even though in Switzerland every name has to clearly indicate whether the child is a boy or a girl – impossible for Tibetan names, which can apply to either sex.

It was two years before my mother became pregnant again and gave birth to my brother Tashi. Then our Swiss-Tibetan family was complete, and Kunsang was transformed into Mola, our grandmother.

29

A Pippi Longstocking Childhood

How different my childhood was from my *amala*'s and my *mola*'s!
The first years of my life flowed like a fresh, sun-dappled river.
There was no fairground we didn't visit, no circus we didn't go to.
We lolled on beaches. We were regular visitors to the theatres in
Berne and Zurich. Birthdays and holidays were celebrated with
gusto. Our parents gave us the very best they could offer. Perhaps
most important, we were a happy, intact family, and in our house
family life came first.

When we spent our first ever beach holiday on the Spanish
Mediterranean coast, my *amala* was astounded to realize that she
had become the mother of a bourgeois family with nothing to do
but have fun with her children in the sand, the sea and the ice cream
parlour. She had to learn to enjoy this life of leisure. Meanwhile,
our family nun had to get used to paddling in the shallows in a
bathing suit, kitted out with bright-red water wings. The art of
swimming was as alien to Mola as the mysteries of Tibetan
Buddhism were to the other bathers on the beach.

Mola always remained loyal to her Tibetan values. The fact that

I am left-handed troubled her for some time during my childhood. She tried again and again to train me to use my right hand, but was only partly successful. Amala too thought it a shame that I was left-handed; the idea that the left hand is bad and the right hand good was as deeply rooted in her mind as Mola's. Though she'd read in plenty of books that this old prejudice was nonsense, she still half believed it. This, as with so many other things, was always my mother's way – half following Tibetan tradition, half accommodating herself to modern Swiss life. In the end, she forbade Mola to continue her meddling, which meant that my grandmother continued to train me in secret, succeeding in teaching me to write at school with my right hand but use my left hand for everything else.

At a Tibetan school, it would have been perfectly normal for the teachers to treat left-handed children with scoldings, punishments and beatings until they used only their right hands. A Tibetan acquaintance of my parents in Switzerland was more clever about encouraging me to use my right hand. She gave me a little job to do, and then asked me, 'Yangzom, which hand did you use?' Of course I shot my right hand up in the air, calling, 'This one, this one!' and promptly received a two-franc coin. Even today, Mola is convinced of her left and right system; Sonam no longer understands what is so bad about being left-handed, though she still favours her right hand.

Mola learned very little German, believing she was too old to start a new language. At least that was her official reason. I think there was another: the language of her host country was not important to her. She could make herself understood in her everyday life, and her speaking only Tibetan was a great motivation for us grandchildren to learn the language, so that we could communicate with her. That was just what she wanted to achieve; it was hugely important to her that her traditions would live on through Tashi and me. Above all, she considered it essential for our karma and our souls that we learn Tibetan prayers and were able to read a little of the ancient holy scriptures.

Because Mola spoke so little German, it was sometimes difficult for her and Martin to understand one another, which also had its good side. Mola is of the opinion that everything her religion says is true, that the rinpoches' sacred pills work, their prophecies have to be obeyed and their memories must be honoured. She didn't understand Martin's view that gurus are intelligent but not infallible individuals and don't possess supernatural skills. Despite this, she loved Martin as her own son, and my *pala* too held Kunsang and her kindness in great esteem. This mutual respect has continued through their lives. But my father knows that when Mola expresses an opinion on matters of Buddhism, any discussion is pointless: Mola always knows the exact truth on the subject.

During my childhood, Mola remained a devout nun who withdrew for her prayers every morning and evening, not to be disturbed by anyone, even us children. She was also the funniest, most playful grandmother a child could wish for. For many years, she and my *pala* would chase each other and play tag, until once Mola fell over during a game and Amala had to intervene. Mola loved playing hide and seek with us, or rough-and-tumble games, which was a special joy for me, as I was much wilder and more impetuous than my little brother. But I also loved the quiet moments when Mola told us one of her many Tibetan stories. It was through Mola and her stories that we learned Tibetan without even noticing. During the first six years of our childhood, Amala often spoke Tibetan to us as well. But when I started school and had problems with German, she began speaking more and more Swiss German. Then everyone in the family, except for Mola, spoke the same language. My brother and I never learned perfect Tibetan, but enough to get by in everyday life.

Despite looking distinctly Asian, I never suffered any prejudice or teasing because of my appearance perhaps because a number of Tibetan families had settled in the area, so the locals were used to us. Nor did I ever feel torn between my Tibetan and my Swiss heritage; for me it seems completely natural to be part of both cultures. Even though we didn't believe in Jesus or the Christian saints, we celebrated Christmas, Easter and St Nicholas' Day. My parents arranged these festivals to make me and my brother happy and so that we grew up like all the other children in the village. I invited my friends to birthday parties, garden parties and sleepovers, occasions that don't even exist in Tibet. But we also celebrated *losar*, Tibetan New Year, the most important festival for Tibetans.

Two days before *losar*, we ate *guthug*, the soup of nine ingredients, which can vary from one family to the next: meat, spinach, peas, radish, *doma* – the roots of the potentilla – bulgur wheat, noodles and salt. To go along with it, Mola or Amala made various kinds of dough balls, rolling tiny slips of paper into them bearing the words 'chilli', 'coal', 'salt', 'wool', 'peas', 'moon', 'sun', 'glass' and 'onions'. We ate the soup in the evening, sometimes inviting friends to join us. My brother and I loved guessing which dough balls were floating in our soup; each of the words inside them had a particular meaning. A ball with the word 'chilli' in it meant that whoever had it possessed a quick temper. Salt indicated laziness, coal meanness, wool denoted gentleness, and best of all, the sun or moon meant that glory and fame were on their way.

On this *guthug* day we women had to wash ourselves. On the next day, the day before *losar*, it was Martin and Tashi's turn, while

229

Sonam and Mola prepared all the food for the occasion, as no one in a Tibetan family should work on New Year's Day. On the last day of the old year, my mother fried New Year pastries in hot oil. These biscuits are called 'donkey's ears' in Tibetan, and that's just what they look like. On top of a beautiful old chest of drawers Sonam placed them one across another to form a tall tower, its tip decorated with a half-moon and a sun baked out of the same pastry. She topped the tower with candies and chocolate, then threaded cubes of dried cheese on to a string and hung it over the tower. She does exactly the same every year, to this very day, even though the chest is now in an apartment in the Chelsea neighbourhood of New York City. All these delicious treats are offerings to various divinities and buddhas. As well as the tower, my mother shaped a cone called a *tschema* out of *tsampa* mixed with a little butter, sugar and Tibetan beer, and stuck three ears of corn into the top of it. There were other gifts to the gods on the altar: a sheep's head made of dough, seven dishes of water contained in a bowl of freshly sprouting wheat, a dish of Tibetan *chang* beer, fruits and flowers. A butter lamp burned in front of the offerings.

My father took Tibetan New Year's Day off work and my brother and I stayed home from school. Early in the morning, we dressed in our best Tibetan clothes. Tibetans are supposed to go to a river and fetch water for *losar* at the first cock crow, but in Switzerland no one had to walk all the way to a river or a spring; we simply filled one or two jugs with water from the tap. We still had to get up early, though; Mola saw to that. She was up and about at three in the morning to say all the prayers necessary on this special day. I would be lying half awake in my room, hearing her prayers like a far-off stream, punctuated by the quiet beats of the drum and the ring of her prayer bell.

Immediately after we got up, Amala started the day by handing us a cone of *tsampa* decorated with butter. Each of us took a little of it three times over, throwing it in the air and saying, '*Tashi delek pün sum tsok, a ma bak dro ku kham zang, ten dang de wa thob par shok, dü san da tsö la, tra ru ru jel gyu yong wa shok,*' which means, 'May all things be happy, outstanding and flourishing, and may the mother of the house remain happy and healthy. May everyone be lucky at all times, and may everyone see the others again at this time next year.' After this offering to the gods, and the blessing, we were allowed to take a little *tsampa* and put it into our mouths, and then to tuck into the candies and chocolates to our hearts' content.

Once Mola finished her special prayer, which she said only at this time of the year, the whole family joined her in the room where she had made her altar. Each of us placed a *katak* on the altar, a white scarf for good luck. If Tashi or I had invited friends to stay the night, they too put on Tibetan clothing and joined in the cere-mony. Even my Swiss grandmother Ula came to celebrate with us, though she never arrived before nine in the morning. We spent the day eating, drinking, laughing and dancing to Tibetan music. Later we played canasta, the only card game Mola could play; it was her favourite game as long as she won.

On the second day of the New Year festival we visited other Tibetan families and they visited us, and on the third day we took the old prayer flags down and hung new ones between the branches of the trees in our garden. In Tibet, all the villagers walked to a holy place on this day, usually high in the mountains at a pass or a monastery, to hang up the new prayer flags. They carried plenty of provisions with them: *chang*, butter, *tsampa* and tea for the smoke offerings in the mountains, where they spent the day eating, drinking and praying before they fastened the new flags.

Even on regular days Tashi and I sometimes went to school in Tibetan clothing. At home we often ate Indian or Tibetan food, *tsampa*, curry with rice, Indian dhal, or *momos*, Tibetan dumplings. On these occasions we were allowed to eat with our fingers, and so were any friends who were visiting. They all thought this was really cool, and we were proud to show them how to do it properly.

There were no restrictions imposed on our games; we were allowed to live out our fantasies and experience two different cultures to their fullest. My idol was Pippi Longstocking; just like her, I wanted to live in my own Villa Villekulla. I hung a line across my room and threw all my clothes over it, then pulled my mattress off the bed and laid it on the floor. The only thing missing was a horse, so I made myself one out of old sheets sewn together, stuffed and decorated with black spots. I went to school with my hair in braids, making my mother plait them with wire. During classes I bent the wire down straight and neat, but the moment school was over, I curved my braids straight out from my head like Pippi's. Amala sewed me Pippi Longstocking dresses and I crocheted myself a monkey, Mr Nilsson, and sewed him on to my dress.

At the time, my fantasy life seemed perfectly normal, but now I see in it the seeds of my career as an actress, and that my elaborate games of make-believe weren't entirely typical.

I had hardly learned to write before I scribbled the word 'singer' in large letters in my album, in the space reserved for 'What I want to be when I grow up' where my friends wrote 'nurse', 'vet' or 'riding teacher'. Soon afterwards I crossed out 'singer' and replaced it with 'actress'. I felt like an actress before I even started school. Our kindergarten was putting on a play of Cinderella and there was nothing I wanted more than the leading role, because at the end

Cinderella got to kiss the prince, and the prince was bound to be the boy all the girls, including me, liked.

None of the other girls had wanted the part because there were so many lines to learn, but I liked playing the starring role, and I can still remember how I merged into the character; what it felt like to be Cinderella, the girl no one cared about. The play was a great success. My mother was very touched, because she identified with the role. As a young woman she had felt like Cinderella, a poor and modest girl whom nobody took any notice of, who was brought into a new life by the love of a prince. The idols on my walls were always characters from films: Ronja the Robber's Daughter, witches and pirates. Before I fell asleep at night I dreamed of the South Seas and swordfights. I lived in my own dream world. One day my brother Tashi came into my room and found me standing on the ledge of the open window with a broomstick between my legs, about to take flight. He screamed out, 'Mum, Yangzom wants to fly!' Amala came running up and tore me away from the window, horrified. 'I am a witch, I can fly' was apparently the last thing I said before my mother treated me to a very angry scolding.

The only thing that interested me as much as acting was painting and drawing. I could sit for hours drawing from my imagination, inspired by comic characters. My parents were always amazed at how much imagination went into my pictures. My mother could never draw figurative forms, even though she later became an artist herself – an abstract painter. My grandmother draws like a small child. When my brother and I were young, we thought it was great fun to get Mola to draw. 'Draw our family,' we would demand. All she managed was a round face composed of a wobbly circle, two dots and two lines, with arms and legs growing straight out of the head. She didn't draw like that to

233

make us laugh; she simply couldn't do any better. It has nothing to do with her childlike nature, but with the fact that she has no ability for abstraction. For her, everything happens directly, with no diversions through mental constructions, generalizations or artificial filters.

30

News from Tibet

In those years, happiness had a permanent place at our table. Tashi and I had plenty of interests, and our hearts were full of enthusiasm. Sonam was feeling more and more at home in the Western world, while Mola enjoyed the variation between noisy children and the silence of her daily contemplation. Martin climbed the career ladder rung by rung and was appointed Deputy Director of the University of Zurich's Ethnographic Museum. His exhibitions made a great impression on his colleagues and the general public, his books on Buddhism and the history of art and culture in Tibet and other Himalayan states were published and won respect from international experts. Despite the pressure of his work, our *pala* flourished in the bosom of his family. Everything seemed to be in perfect harmony – except for the discordant note of longing that echoed relentlessly for Mola and Amala. That note was Tibet. The two of them yearned for my father, my brother and me to know the country of their birth

Until the 1980s, the Chinese government refused to let most exiled Tibetans visit the land they had left. It was as if their past had vanished behind them. Sonam and Kunsang had no idea what had become of their relatives in Tibet. They had learned years before that both Mola's brothers had been captured by the Chinese while attempting to escape to India. They had to assume they must have died during the brutal years of the Cultural Revolution. The news from Tibet that seeped out to the West via new refugees, a handful of journalists and Tibetan exile organizations did not give them much hope: people spoke of ruined monasteries, vanished monks, farmers forced to relocate and nomads having to live a settled life. The Chinese had systematically bled Tibet of its customs, suppressing both the language and the culture. Chinese was introduced as the new school language, and hundreds of thousands of Han Chinese immigrated to the country. Mola and Sonam feared that if things continued as they were going, all that they would recognize of their homeland would be the mountains, the rivers and the sky. And even they were threatened: excessive logging in the forests had led to erosion and flooding, rivers had been controlled by dams, and the sky was so badly polluted by the fumes of hundreds of Chinese factories that it was no longer the pellucid blue they had known.

In 1978, my mother met a Tibetan monk who told her that after the death of Chairman Mao and the end of the Cultural Revolution in 1976, he had written a letter to his brother in Tibet and received a reply. Sonam had thought it was impossible to contact anyone in Tibet. In the past there had been no public postal system, only government messengers, and she had been told that the Chinese secret service intercepted all letters coming from abroad. 'How did you do it?' she asked the monk. There were no addresses in Tibet, no street names or postcodes.

The monk smiled. 'My brother was also a monk,' he said. 'I wrote his name on the envelope, then underneath it the name of the bridge he lived beside, and the name of the river. I added the name of the village and the name of the monastery. At the very bottom I wrote the words Tibet and PRC, People's Republic of China, in English and Chinese. The answer came a year later. My brother told me which of our relatives are still alive, who has died and how everybody is faring.'

Stunned, my mother returned home and immediately repeated the monk's story to Mola. My grandmother just shook her head. 'All our relatives are dead.'

But Sonam didn't give up. 'Perhaps they're still alive?'

'There's no point, it's too late.'

Sonam wrote a letter the same day, addressing it to Mola's brother Pema Lodroe, whom she remembered vividly from her childhood. As soon as Mola saw her daughter setting the familiar Tibetan characters down on paper, she became interested. She leaned over the letter with my mother, giving her tips for one character or another that wasn't written exactly as it should be. When they had finished, they wrote everything they knew about Pema Lodroe's possible location on the envelope. It was so much information it hardly left space for the little Swiss postage stamp.

For two long years Sonam received no reply. Her initial excitement gave way to anxiety, then disappointment, then gradually she forgot about the letter. Until a remarkable coincidence occurred. One of Mola's nephews was visiting Lhasa, where he met a friend who told him there was an office there full of letters from abroad that had never reached their destinations. Anyone could go to the post office and collect letters addressed to them. Anything not claimed was going to be incinerated.

'You've got relatives who escaped to India,' his friend said to him. 'Maybe there's a letter there from them.'

The nephew shook his head. 'They're all dead. We heard they didn't make it.'

The nephew's friend kept encouraging him, telling him there was a chance that a letter might have come from his relatives after all. So the young man made his way to the office, sorted through a mountain of letters and finally came across the envelope with his father's name on it, though it was barely legible. Mola's brothers, Pema Lodroe and Karma Dorjee, were astounded to hear their sister was alive. Rumours had gone round their village that the group of refugees had frozen to death in the mountains as they tried to escape.

A few weeks later, my mother received a letter covered in unfamiliar stamps. Only at second glance did she see that it had come from China. 'I was just wondering who on earth would write to me from China when I finally realized – it was the longed-for letter from Tibet!' Like most Tibetans in exile, she had repressed the fact that Tibet had officially been part of China since the 1950s.

Sonam called to her mother and opened the letter hastily. It was from Pema Lodroe! Breathlessly, the two women read the Tibetan characters written in a slightly shaky hand. They could hardly believe what the letter said: though Mola's sister, Pema Dolma, had died, her brothers were well and living in Pang, the village below the Pang-ri monastery in which Sonam had spent the idyllic years of her childhood.

Pema Lodroe told them which of their other relatives were alive and which had died. And he wrote about new members of the family as well. When my grandmother had fled in 1959, her older brother Karma Dorjee had had only one child and her younger none, and now, all of a sudden, she had eleven nieces and nephews.

Both Mola and Sonam were overtaken with relief and happiness. 'We have to go to Tibet' was Mola's immediate reaction. Sonam agreed: now that there was a rediscovered family to visit, not merely a dead past to inspect, she was determined that they would return.

The People's Republic of China was still making it extremely difficult for former inhabitants of the country and their children to get visas for its 'Tibet Autonomous Region'. As luck would have it, in 1981 Martin received an offer from a company specializing in study tours who were seeking an expert on Tibet and Buddhism to accompany a group of tourists to the country. He seized the opportunity. He could not find a way for Mola or Amala to accompany him, but he did telephone my mother from Lhasa. He had just walked through the Potala palace. Amala sat at the kitchen table in Switzerland, sobbing into the phone. 'It can't be true! Martin? Are you there? Are you really in Lhasa?'

Martin's tales of his time in Tibet only intensified Sonam and Kunsang's longing for their homeland. But the authorities would not let them back into Tibet. They had to make do with visits to other Himalayan states. As part of his ethnological research, preparation for exhibitions and his development work, Martin travelled frequently to the Himalayas. He continued these travels throughout my childhood, and whenever possible, the whole family accompanied him. For my brother Tashi and me, these were thrilling journeys. In tiny propeller planes, rickety buses, dusty jeeps and in some cases on foot or on horseback we reached some of the most remote places in the world. We cooked over an open fire in an ancient wooden Nepalese farmhouse, stayed with monks in a monastery in Bhutan and went on hour-long treks to pastures high in the mountains. Our adventures were numerous, each more memorable than the last. I was attacked by fleas, bugs and lice in a makeshift hut where I was supposed to keep watch by night with Bhutanese children to protect a field of barley from wild boars and bears. We all fell fast asleep and the wild animals made merry in the fields, while I brought back scars from the lice bites all over my body as souvenirs. My brother and I climbed up a huge tree in

Bhutan, known there as a *leo-leo* tree, and watched with amazement as the local children, without a trace of embarrassment, relieved themselves while hanging from the branches. We spent hours trekking through forests and mountains with our luggage on horse-back, visiting hermits, climbing up to pastures as high as the sky, sucking home-made strawberry and raspberry mush out of cut-off bamboo poles, and making our own bamboo whistles, and rings out of straw and spit.

The most important thing we gained from all these exotic adventures was an early knowledge that the security, cleanliness, peace and order we experienced day by day in Switzerland was not typical. Not everyone was as rich as the Swiss. We had been taught this at school, but it was much more powerful to feel, smell, taste and see how people lived without the things we thought essential. For me, these Asian expeditions had the inestimable advantage of teaching me how to do without luxury, not only on my travels but at home as well. Of course I would rather stay in a nice hotel than a nasty one, but I can accept a hotel room that's too small or a bed that's too hard or a primitive toilet. I learned the value of simplicity, spontaneity and uncomplicated pleasures. And I believe that all the attacks of diarrhoea, stomach upset, fever and insects we fell prey to on our travels made us more robust and less vulnerable to bad food or poor hygienic conditions, very useful indeed for someone who has to travel as much as I do.

31

Paradise Lost

Kunsang and Sonam had lost all hope of ever seeing Tibet again when what seemed like a miracle occurred: the Chinese authorities relaxed the entry restrictions for tourists and exiles. In 1986, the year of the fire tiger in the Tibetan calendar, our entire family boarded a plane bound for Lhasa. My brother Tashi was four at the time and I was six. Was it just coincidence, or perhaps fate, that I was exactly the same age on my journey to Tibet as my mother had been when she had fled? Now she was a thirty-three-year-old woman, returning to her old home for the first time. For my brother and me it was a new adventure, for my father it was an Asian research trip, and for Mola and Sonam it was a longed-for return to their past. It had been almost thirty years since they escaped from Tibet. Mola was now in her mid-sixties. Their anticipation was deep and thrilling. They could hardly wait to set foot on the soil of their homeland.

At first glance, Lhasa looked as we had always imagined the Tibetan holy city. The drive along the dirt road from the airport to the city took half the day, there were only a few basic hotels and little evidence of the Chinese. It seemed as if not much had changed, though there were electricity poles on every corner, electric street lamps, and a few cars driving along the city's rough streets. The most notable change was the thousands of bicycles the Chinese had brought. Before their arrival, bicycles had been virtually unknown in the country.

But after a few days, my parents and Mola started noticing the changes and the destruction the new regime had wreaked: monasteries had been bombed and reduced to piles of rubble or foundation walls, streets in the old town dug up to build a sewage system. The Chinese had torn down many old buildings and were in the process of replacing them with drab concrete boxes in the socialist utilitarian style. Although they did rebuild some of the damaged houses to their former appearance, they had redesigned important sites such as the square outside the Jokhang, stripping this most important Tibetan sacred site of its original atmosphere.

Luckily most places stood in peace and tranquillity. Mass tourism had not yet arrived; there was no pushing and shoving or guards at the gates. My parents often got into conversation with Tibetans, conversations I couldn't understand but which made Amala and Mola so sad that my mother was regularly in tears. I knew only that they were talking about the old days, what difficulties they had been through in the past decades, and what relatives or friends had lost their lives.

For my brother and me, Lhasa was an exciting city. I loved the magnificent Jokhang, the largest Buddhist temple, which stood in the centre of old Lhasa. This almost 4,000-year-old temple is one of Tibet's most important sacred sites. Every Buddhist is supposed to see it at least once in their lifetime. It had been even more majestic before it was looted during the Cultural Revolution, then misused for many years as the headquarters of the Red Guards, Mao's troop of young communist thugs and re-educators.

Still the interior was splendid. I was fascinated by the sea of butter lamps flickering before the giant gilded Buddha statue in the main hall, and by all the frescoes and statues and divinity images before which worshippers bowed low in veneration, reciting the mantra *om mani peme hung*. The long rows of prayer wheels in the courtyard outside the temple were kept in almost constant motion by hundreds of pious Buddhists. Above them rose the gold-shimmering roof and the two golden deer on either side of the rooftop dharma wheel.

After our first visit, my brother and I pleaded until we were allowed to return to the Jokhang. Mola was delighted by our obvious interest in Buddhism. She would have liked nothing more than to spend the whole of our time in Lhasa in the elaborate temple. We didn't tell her that it was not only the sacred atmosphere that fascinated us but also the prospect of lighting countless new butter lamps and setting as many prayer wheels in motion as possible at one time.

We also visited the Potala palace. The Potala was first and foremost the residence of the Dalai Lama and his large staff. It was the seat of Tibetan government, where all ceremonies of state were held; it also housed a school for the religious training of monks and administrators, and was one of Tibet's major pilgrimage destinations because of the tombs of past Dalai Lamas. We children knew that the Dalai Lama had had to flee to India to escape the Chinese and was no longer in residence in Lhasa. We had even met him in person when he had come to Zurich to open one of my father's exhibitions. So we were all the more impressed by the Potala. Everything looked as if he had simply gone into one of the other thousand or so rooms of the palace. The handful of visitors, among them Mola and my mother, threw themselves to the ground in reverence, praying and kneeling in silent contemplation. Amala and Mola were overwhelmed by their good fortune. After all these years, here they were at this most sacred site. My mother would never have dared to hope that she could one day show her husband and children her homeland and even the Potala. At last she could see the Dalai Lama's winter residence with her own eyes, at last she could once again smell, feel and hear Tibet.

But her happiness was shadowed by sorrow and anger. She could not hold back her tears. She cried because she felt that the Dalai Lama's abandoned palace represented the collision between a beautiful dream and bitter reality. The empty throne with one of the Dalai Lama's robes draped carefully across it symbolized a country that had been robbed of its soul. My mother sensed that the Potala was becoming nothing more than a museum, like Versailles or other European palaces, where the past was preserved with no intention of bringing it to life again. She had a visceral sense that she and her escaped compatriots had failed; what was the point of all their protests against the occupation of Tibet? The Potala, the heart of the country, had become a mere tourist attraction. Sonam felt she had not done enough for her homeland. Were she and all her fellow exiles far too preoccupied with themselves and their own problems and too little with the country that was the source of their culture, even their existence?

Yet how much sadder my mother would have been if Lhasa had been as it is now – an almost thoroughly Chinese city composed of dull tower blocks, bright neon advertising, countless tourist hotels and Chinese bars complete with prostitutes. It's a hellish hubbub of roaring, stinking traffic, the streets spilling over with Chinese soldiers, passers-by, tourists and workers.

32

Back to Pang

My family had come to Tibet first and foremost to visit Pang, the village where most of our relatives lived. There were no cross-country taxis or rental cars in Tibet at that time, so my parents had to charter an entire bus to take us there.

As soon as we had left Lhasa, the world began to dance and prance. The road seemed composed entirely of hills and holes and stones. We held on tight to the poles in the bus, grabbed hold of Amala, pressed ourselves against Pala and clung to Mola, bouncing against each other at every turn. We drove alongside rivers that roared so loudly we could hear them over the rattling and clattering of our bus. We drove through broad valleys and across steppes and stone and sand, spotting the dust trails of trucks and columns of yaks ahead of us, leaving behind us our own clouds of dust. The sun was scorching; all the windows were wound down. We wore breathing masks that were soon as grey as our skin, our hair and our clothes.

For my mother, it was a bittersweet journey through a landscape she had last seen a quarter of a century ago. This landscape reminded her of long, excruciating night treks, cold, hunger, physical and emotional exhaustion, and constant fear. She spent the trip staring out of the windows, especially during the last part of the journey. 'Look!' she called out as the bus descended into another valley. 'That's where we walked, I know we did. The river was by our side every day. I was amazed how far a river could flow.'

Mola too was glued to the window. 'There weren't any roads,' she said, more to herself than to us. 'We had to walk across fields or along herdsmen's paths.' She grew more and more quiet as a great sorrow welled up inside her. This had once been her country, the country of her childhood, and now she was driving through it like a tourist.

Pala was busy taking photos to document our trip. Mola soon seemed to lose interest in viewing the sites of their former trek. With stoic calm, she slipped her mala beads through the fingers of her left hand, one after the other, until she had worked her way through the entire chain of 108 beads. 'Om mani peme hung,' she murmured once for every bead, and then she began the next round again. It was hard to tell what she let into her soul through the tiny slits of her eyes. It was only when we stopped at a high pass that she suddenly hurried out of the bus, took a deep breath and gave a loud call of lha gyalo three times over. Loosely translated it means: 'May the gods be victorious!' We children, infected by her high spirits, joined in her shouts: 'Lha gyalo!'

After a few more hours, the driver brought the bus to a screeching, rattling halt. 'We're here,' he announced. As we got ourselves and our luggage off the bus, we saw nothing but a raging river, and all around, towering mountains covered in dense forests of oak, birch, willow and fir. There was no sign of a village.

Amala and Pala were not used to the altitude, nor the thin air and the blistering sun. Their heads ached and they felt nauseous.

246

The altitude had no effect on my brother Tashi and me. Nor was Mola affected by it, even though adjusting to high altitudes is supposed to be harder the older you are.

As the bus rattled off, we heard the roar of the water raging deep below. We bent low to peer over the abyss, with a fearful Amala holding us back. That was when we spotted the rope bridge leading across the river gorge. The ropes were so thin that it took a while for us to catch sight of them. Four skimpy ropes strung across the river, tied together with other ropes to make rungs, with a few loose boards laid across them. And then it dawned on us that Pang was on the other side of the river. We would have to cross the raging waters on this flimsy ropebridge.

Oh, we had heard stories about this bridge, and about the mighty Pang-chu, a tributary of the Tsangpo, the largest river in Tibet. Mola had told us that no one who fell into its roiling waters came out alive. We had always thought she was exaggerating, telling us a gruesome grandmotherly tale. Now we knew she had not exaggerated at all. As we stood on the bank watching the raging water in silence, gripped by fear, Mola shouldered one of our kitbags and set off down the stony path towards the bridge. 'What are you all waiting for?' she called. Our grandmother was in a hurry to get home.

To our amazement, we managed to cross the bridge. The path on the other side was so narrow, there was no room for two people to pass one another. Finally, as we crested the slope, we saw the village. The handful of homes looked almost like old Swiss farmhouses, their stone foundations topped with wood, their sloping roofs weighed down with stones to prevent them from blowing away in storms. The meadows were covered with mallows and fibrous ferns. As soon as the villagers caught sight of us, our relatives came running to greet us – Pema Lodroe,

Karma Dorjee with their wives and some of their children. They held good-luck scarves and shouted and waved as we made our way down the slope; they'd been expecting us for some time. They laughed and cried and chattered; embraced us and tugged at our clothes and pinched our cheeks. They acted as though they had always known us.

They led us to their house where a skinny cow – the shadow of a Swiss cow – stood in the front yard. We were taken straight inside; the rest of my family was sitting in anticipation around a fire that crackled invitingly. The only other light in the room was a dingy petroleum lamp. Evening was drawing in, the Tibetan mountains already casting their cold shadows over the fading summer's light. The women of the house added branches to the fire, unconcerned that they protruded from the stone hearth. Smoke spiralled towards the ceiling, only partly disappearing through a black hole. The rest filled the kitchen. The hearth had round openings from which the flames licked when there were no pans on them. Large tin pails filled with water stood by the hearth; there was no running water in the house. On the table was a ball of butter, into which someone had pressed a hole with their thumb so that it resembled a buttery apple. This butter was put into a *dongmo* – a hollow bamboo tube with a lid and a built-in stirrer. It acted as a kind of Tibetan mixer, and made butter tea.

The children leaped about between the grown-ups, everyone talking at the same time, laughing and joking at our unfamiliar faces. A toddler they called *kyag schora*, 'pants-shitter', crawled between our legs. He wore trousers with a long slit in the seat through which he could relieve himself whenever he felt the need. The dogs would lick the floor clean. Everything seemed primitive and unpredictable, noisy and strange, and yet, because I knew this was my family, comfortable and exciting. Though Tashi, Pala and

I could barely understand the dialect they spoke, Mola and Amala were happy to translate for us.

In the midst of this jolly and relaxed atmosphere, my great-uncle Pema Lodroe darkened the mood. He had some very sad news for Mola that weighed so heavily on his heart that he didn't want to put it off any longer. With a trembling voice, he told us that the Chinese had forced him to destroy Trishul Rinpoche's *daru*, the hand drum, and his bell, which Mola had entrusted to him before her escape, along with the holy scriptures and other sacred objects he possessed. During the Cultural Revolution people were forbidden to own religious objects.

How ruthlessly the Chinese occupiers had outlawed even the tiniest details of Tibetan life, and how meticulously they had worked to destroy out culture! It made Mola and Amala even sadder that my great-uncle feared they might reproach him for the loss.

There were few signs in Pang of the much-heralded 'blessings of the modern age' that the Chinese claimed they had brought to Tibet. The villagers had no toilets, no running water, no baths. They managed perfectly well without. Tibetans don't wash their entire bodies in one go. It was enough for them to go occasionally down to the river and wash their legs, upper bodies and hair. They rarely brushed their teeth or changed their clothes, nor did they remove marks and stains from their clothing. Their skin was tanned like old leather and their clothes were stiff with dirt, their shoes worn, their hands calloused. They didn't smell unpleasant, though. Somehow, although they sweated, they never smelt of sweat.

It all seemed like a wonderful dream to me. They were like my heroine Pippi Longstocking! She didn't wash either, and was ignorant of tidying and cleaning; she did whatever she wanted, just like my relatives in Pang. The Tibetans in my family didn't feel they were missing out on anything. They were happy with their simple way of life, with their days spent outside in the sun and the wind.

Amala imposed her own rules on my brother and me. Tashi and I had to go down to the river with her, where she piled dried driftwood between three large stones, lit a fire and heated a large pan of water, with which she washed us. Accompanied by the laughter of the village children hiding in the bushes, she soaped us down and rubbed us until our light brown skin was red from cold and friction. The villagers found that even funnier.

We spent our afternoons walking through meadows abloom with edelweiss and gentians, rare plants back home in Switzerland that mustn't be touched. We jumped from the stones by my family's little barley field, climbed cliffs and played everywhere with our cousins and the local children.

One morning I watched a goat being slaughtered. It was lying outside the house with its legs tied together. One of my female cousins slit its belly open with a knife, as quickly and routinely as if she were opening a parcel. I watched in horror, then turned and ran away. My relatives laughed. My reaction was better when I lay beneath the udder of the family cow, which Amala milked right into my mouth and over my face. I loved the fresh hot milk. When I tried to milk the cow myself, I couldn't get a single drop out of her.

I did not like the way the villagers solved the toilet issue. The outhouse reeked to high heaven and was aswarm with flies. The toilets inside were no more than a couple of holes in the ground. The holes were too large for us, and Amala had to hold us over them so that we didn't fall in. I preferred to heed the call of nature behind a bush or a tree, even though the pigs came running every time, almost knocking me over in their greed to get at my deposits. It seemed rather odd to me, but it was all part of the wild, free life we were to live here all summer long.

Amala had decided to go up to Pang-ri, where she had spent the first six years of her life. Pala was to go with her. My brother and I had to stay in the valley; the path was too steep, they told us, and the walk was too long. Mola had her own reasons for staying behind in Pang. 'What do I want up there?' she asked, knowing that nothing remained of the monastery but a few foundations.

While my parents went up to Pang-ri with a cousin and a monk who wanted to make a smoke offering in the ruins of the monastery, Mola looked after my brother and me. That was hardly difficult. Tashi and I didn't need much supervision, we were in paradise. I had made friends with Pema, one of my numerous 'sisters'. That was what I called all the girls of my age in the family, even though they were really cousins or second cousins. Pema is two years younger than I am, so she was four at the time. Her mother said she had been born when the birds were eating the ears of barley, so it must have been autumn.

Pema was smaller than me, and she was darker-skinned and dirtier, but just as cheeky. She was the oldest child in the family, which meant she got the blame for everything that happened at home – and plenty happened. Yak's milk got spilt, tsampa was knocked over, a pile of firewood collapsed, a hen got into the kitchen, the family's only tube of toothpaste was suddenly filled with a paste made of flour, water and saliva instead of its original contents, because Pema had eaten the white paste, thinking it was a special treat. Her parents couldn't afford to waste anything; they had little enough food as it was. The family was extremely poor, living on nettle soup, tsampa and butter tea.

The two of us ran around the village and the surrounding slopes.

We made chewing gum out of tree resin, chased after the dogs and teased the black pigs. One of them was particularly intelligent: whenever it thought no one was looking, it ran up to a certain cow and began to suckle at its udder, until my aunt chased it away again with shouts and screams.

33

Ruins of Childhood

With the monk and a cousin to show them the way, my parents set off along a narrow path across rocky slopes and through thorny undergrowth, arriving in a sparse wood of oaks, birches and evergreens. Long threads of climbing plants hung from tangled branches, a bird of prey screeched, a pheasant croaked, and was that a hoopoe?

On this path, Amala told the others, a giant bear once appeared in front of her father as she, Tsering and the old neighbour were taking a walk. Tsering had thrown himself to the ground with his face down, holding his hands protectively over his head, remaining motionless as if he were dead. The bear paused in surprise and came closer, sniffing curiously. The old neighbour hit it on the back with her flask of tea, screaming and thrashing out at the beast with the now broken jug. The bear reared upright in amazement, gave a threatening growl and lumbered off.

Pang is some 10,000 feet above sea level, and the Pang-ri monastery was about 3,000 feet higher. In Switzerland, the peak of the Matterhorn is at a similar elevation. The small group climbed through the undergrowth, which grew higher and higher the sparser the trees became. Once they ascended beyond tree level, Sonam knew she had arrived not only in Pang-ri, but also in her childhood.

They made slow progress along the trail, which was overgrown with tough, high grass and dry thorns. It seemed no one had walked this way in a long time. When my mother beheld the monastery ruins, she was flushed with excitement. She stumbled over a pile of rubble and ran to and fro between walls that had collapsed to chest height and were almost entirely overgrown with juniper – the sad remains of the monastery. A few steps away stood more former walls, all that was left of my grandparents' old home. 'This was our kitchen,' said Sonam, pointing at a square of walls full of stinging nettles, 'and here was the fireplace.' They did indeed find a pile of bricks, some still visibly blackened by soot, even though the last fire had burned there a quarter of a century ago.

It was all much smaller and more modest than Sonam had remembered: the rock from which the spring emerged where she had fetched water every day, the *stupa* slightly below the monastery, the remaining *sangbum*, one of the original two ovens in which the smoke offerings had burned. Though the rugged ridges of the Tibetan Alps were the same, the rest of the landscape was different from that of her childhood. Much of the deep forest had given way to scarred, rocky slopes or weed-choked valleys. The Chinese had chopped down the once never-ending wealth of trees, transporting them back to a motherland greedy for construction material and fuel. They did not replant the forest.

My mother wept to see how much destruction had been wrought. During the Cultural Revolution in the 1960s, Red Guards and Chinese soldiers, along with terrified Tibetans, razed some

6,000 Buddhist monasteries to the ground – a tragic fate that Pang-ri had not been spared. The villagers down in Pang had told us that a father and two of his sons had even broken into the *stupa* outside the monastery to steal relics and valuable holy objects intended to honour the remains of the lama laid to rest there. These robbers, the villagers said, all died prematurely of terrible diseases.

There was nothing for my mother and father to do but make a smoke offering and recite a few prayers. Soon Martin warned that they ought to head back to the village again. They had a two-hour trek ahead of them, and the sun was already low over the ridges on the other side of the valley. The idea of spending a night up there was not inviting for my mother either, to say nothing of the thought of the bears that still lived here, and the rare snow leopards.

One day, not long after we'd arrived, we were sitting in our family's kitchen when a woman suddenly appeared in the door of the house, her face stained by tears. Mola didn't recognize her at first, but then her face trembled and tears rolled down her cheeks too. The two old women fell into each other's arms. It was Puko Ani-la, the nun who had been one of Mola's closest friends from her time at Ape Rinpoche's hermitage. Puko Ani-la was still alive! Mola had heard so many terrible things about the rampages of the Red Guard during the Cultural Revolution, about murders and killings, abductions, torture, prisons and re-education, that she hadn't dared hope she'd see her friend again. And here she was standing before her. Puko Ani-la looked as if she were Mola's older sister: her face was more deeply furrowed and wrinkled than that of my grandmother, her back was more bent, her gait more halting, her hands spotted with age.

It was several days before Puko Ani-la could talk about what she and her family had been through during the Cultural Revolution. The Chinese had forced her to let her hair grow long and taken away everything she possessed. Her aristocratic parents had been brutally tortured by Chinese soldiers. Overcome by desperation and shame, they had jumped into the river and committed suicide. Her family had lost many members, doubly exposed to terrible persecution as an aristocratic and also a religious clan. Tears flowed freely in the valley of Pang as Puko Ani-la repeatedly faltered in telling her story, and my mother and Mola wept along with her.

A few days later, Puko Ani-la quietly asked to speak to Kunsang where the other relatives could not hear them. Hesitating and unsure of herself, she told her old friend that she wanted to sell Kunsang her dzi stone – she had next to nothing left to live on. The dzi, a magical Tibetan stone, was the only thing she had managed to hide from the Chinese. Folk tales tell that such stones come rolling directly down a mountain. If you see one you have to throw a hat over it quickly or it will keep on rolling. These stones usually bear black and white or black and brown patterns: the more 'eyes', as the Tibetans call the white etchings in the dark base material, and the smoother and silkier the stone's surface, the more valuable it is. These stones are said to protect people against bad luck and illness, and they are often the most valuable things a Tibetan will possess. The Tibetans regard the way the dzis get their eyes and their shape as a great miracle.

Mola paid Puko Ani-la the sum she wanted and at first refused to accept the stone, but Puko Ani-la insisted, not wanting to take charity. Choking back her tears, Mola accepted the valuable stone. Since then my mother has worn it around her neck, not as mere jewellery but also as a reminder of the long, sad story it represents.

For Sonam, this stone is more valuable than any gem; it has become her talisman, less because of the miraculous powers attributed to it than because of the fates and the family history that it embodies.

34

Summer in Tibet

With our new-found relatives, we went on all kinds of trips in the region around Pang. We visited a holy site where a footprint, allegedly belonging to Padmasambhava, was visible in a cave. There we heard the sound of drums and cymbals, as if from a great distance. They were not played by living people, our relatives told us. Only my sceptical father and mother heard nothing at all. We also went to the sacred lake Basum Tso, which Mola had circled four times with the sick Sonam on her back on the instructions of the rinpoche. This lake, at the foot of the mountain Namlha Karpo, meaning 'white sky god', had been visited by many legendary figures, including Gesar, the Tibetan national hero – a brave ruler from pre-Buddhist times. As we walked around the lake, local farmers showed us several objects sacred to Gesar, including a 400-foot-tall stone, which they said was the same height as the mythical ruler, a tree said to be Gesar's *bla zhing*, or 'soul tree', a stone with a hoofprint from his horse and even one with a print from Gesar's own foot.

These unspectacular local sacred sites had survived the iconoclasm of the Chinese Cultural Revolution better than most temples or Buddha statues because the vandals didn't understand that such apparently commonplace memorial sites were of particular religious significance for the Tibetans. Many of these testaments to ancient times may well no longer be in place today, as shrewd businessmen have removed them and offered them up for sale. Over the past thirty years, thousands of objects have made their way from Tibet to the West and more recently to the People's Republic of China, to be sold as art. They are not art, but sacred religious objects that ought to be treated with great respect and shouldn't be traded as commonplace goods.

In the evening we camped on a deserted bank of the holy lake, where we heard musk deer bleating and roaring during the night. We climbed to high pastures, slept at an altitude of 16,000 feet in yak-skin tents on the frozen ground, picked mushrooms and visited monasteries where monks showed us their cells and their photos of the Dalai Lama. 'You must be very careful,' Sonam couldn't help saying. 'Those pictures are banned. If they catch you . . .'

But the monks reassured us. 'I don't care,' the old abbot told us. 'I've been in prison before. If I have to go back again I'll go back. I don't want to escape to India. I'm staying in Tibet; my place is here. I'm waiting for the Dalai Lama to return.'

The monastery where he and the other monks lived was old and in need of repair. The walls were crumbling, the roof was crooked, glass was missing from the windows and the doors were rotting from their hinges.

'We won't betray the Dalai Lama,' the abbot said, 'so they don't give us any money to renovate, and nobody has anything to donate. Other monks collaborate with the Chinese and their monasteries are bright and shiny because they get money. We don't want that.'

That summer in Tibet was a very important and exciting time

for my brother and me, as well as for the adults. For the first time we saw the culture we had been told so much about and heard the language we were exhorted to learn. Tibet was no longer a dreamland for us, but tangible reality, a country we had seen, felt, smelled and walked upon.

When all too soon the time came for us to leave, we had great difficulty finding a vehicle to take us back to Lhasa. It had room for only one of Mola's brothers, Pema Lodroe, to accompany us. Her other brother, Karma Dorjee, wanted to follow us in another vehicle to say his farewells at the airport, but he didn't turn up, making us all terribly worried. There was no telephone line to Pang at that time, so we waited in vain for him in Lhasa and in the end had to leave without saying goodbye. It was almost unbearable for Mola. Was she never to see Karma Dorjee again? She had not said goodbye to him.

This omission weighed so heavily on her soul that she returned to Tibet a year later, this time alone. Karma Dorjee was awaiting her when she arrived. He was terminally ill. The two of them said their final farewells, and not long afterwards he drew his last breath. Mola said many prayers for a good reincarnation for her brother, thanking the gods every day that they had enabled her to see him one last time in this life.

After these two visits, Mola and Sonam never lost contact with their family in Pang, sending them money every year. At that time Mola had begun receiving a small pension in Switzerland, though she was puzzled as to where the money came from. When she got her first payment, Martin had to explain in great detail how the money had found its way to her. Mola had never heard of anyone getting money without working.

'The people who work give money for the old people who can't work any more,' Martin told her. At that time Swiss pension payments were not simply credited to an account, but delivered by the postman. Mola always placed the money on the altar in her room for a few days as an offering to the gods, thanking in her prayers the people who had worked to earn it. Then she marched off to the post office and sent money to our relatives in Tibet and friends in India. It was only then that my Tibetan family were able to buy shoes and socks and clothing for losar. My cousin Pema in Pang got her very first dress of her own. She was so proud of it that she didn't put it on until the next losar festival, keeping it safely under her pillow until then.

Now, twenty years on, my family in Pang have a cow that provides them with fresh milk, along with a shower with a solar cell to heat the water. The money for these investments came from Frau Steiner, Sonam's Swiss benefactor from her time in India. When Sonam came to Switzerland, the two of them met up and stayed in contact until Frau Steiner's death. My mother visited her on numerous occasions, sometimes going shopping or cooking for her to return some of the kindness she had received as a child, which was still benefiting her Tibetan family.

When Frau Steiner donated the solar shower for Sonam's family in Pang shortly before she died, she had no idea what her gift would set in motion. With their shower, my relatives set up a small business. Almost all the neighbours and even people from surrounding villages now pay three yuan each to use the only shower in the area. This is a great benefit to my family's customers as well, who previously had to travel much farther to the public showers, which were owned by unpopular Chinese. The villagers were much happier to give their money to my family. The only person who has never used the shower is my aunt. Although she lives in the house with the shower, this new-fangled invention is incompatible with her world. She walks into the shower, fully clothed of course, to admire the lovely smooth tiles, the taps and the showerhead, but then she walks out again. She would never undress entirely, even if no one could see her. Even my uncle, now a convinced shower-user, can't persuade his wife. For my aunt, nudity, and therefore showering, is simply indecent.

35

The Berne Years

When my brother and I got older and more sophisticated, my parents wanted to move back to the city, to Zurich. They had to spend more and more time taking us there anyway, to the theatre, sports events, parties and museums. Through us, my *amala* had plenty of contact with other women and families in the village of Münchwilen, where we lived, but my father worked in Zurich and hadn't really put down roots in the countryside.

Martin had been looking for houses in and around Zurich for some time, but it proved difficult to find anything appropriate. At the same time, he was growing more and more unhappy with the way his beloved museum was being run, and he longed to change jobs. He had wanted to work in the Swiss development sector for some years, and when he was offered a job with a church-run charity in his home town of Berne – although he had long since formally renounced his membership of the church – he accepted immediately. The job was part-time, so he could continue to work at the museum in Zurich for the rest of the time.

In the same period, Martin's father was diagnosed with severe cancer and died not long afterwards. So we moved into the now vacant Brauen family villa, a handsome house with large windows looking out like curious eyes at its equally beautiful neighbours. In front of the house was a flagpole, from which a large Tibetan flag was soon billowing. Mola hung little prayer flags from the wrought-iron bars of the balcony so that the winds of Berne might scatter the prayers printed on them. Before votes and referenda, I hung bed sheets spray-painted with slogans from the façade below my window, making sure the entire neighbourhood knew which way the Brauen family would be voting.

The move to Berne began a new chapter in our lives. Although the city is the capital of Switzerland, the huge clocks welcoming visitors on the many medieval church towers seem to tick more slowly there than elsewhere in the country. The locals are even calmer and more placid than the average Swiss, and they have their own character. My mother noticed this too, first thinking the Berners were cold and dismissive until she realized that people simply took longer than in Zurich to warm up to new arrivals.

Never attached to any particular residence, Mola had nothing against moving to Berne, although she thought it was a shame that fewer Tibetans lived there than in the east of Switzerland. From then on, she took the train to the two annual meetings of her religious friends, which were always held in the Buddhist monastery in Rikon near Tösstal in eastern Switzerland.

Tashi and I went to a regular school in Berne, but because we were Buddhists, we were excused from Christian religion classes. We were more than happy about that, as it meant we could go home two hours earlier than the other students. But our parents only had us excluded from religious education at school under condition that we learned to read and write Tibetan from our grandmother during those two free hours. It was a pleasure for Mola to teach us, and we looked forward to the end of her lessons, when we were either given a five-franc coin or allowed to choose candies she kept in her wardrobe.

The only thing I was really passionate about was the stage. I joined a tap-dancing class and in the summer I went to acrobatics courses in a real circus tent and learned to walk a tightrope, juggle and ride a unicycle. At the end of every season, the children surprised their parents with entire shows, which I absolutely loved. Except, that is, for the year when I was only allowed to do magic tricks because I had fallen from the tightrope and broken my arm.

In Berne, Amala had more time and began knitting sweaters in riots of wild colour. My *pala* was very impressed and encouraged her to try out these colour combinations on canvas. She didn't take him seriously; she had never even picked up a paintbrush before. Once again, coincidence, or fate, intervened. A neighbour suggested the two of them attend a painting course together at the local adult education college. My mother agreed on impulse but didn't enjoy the course because the teacher couldn't deal with her inability to paint from nature. Later, she took a course at the Berne Art School with Fausto Sergej Sommer, a teacher who opened up a personal path to painting for her, showed her many artistic techniques and helped her on her way to becoming an independent artist.

Martin not only gave Sonam the first encouragement to discover her artistic side, he also pointed her in the direction of contemporary Western art and classical music. To begin with, violin music sounded awful to Amala's ears; she hated the high notes and had no sense of the harmonies. But gradually she grew to like it. Today she loves Mozart and Beethoven, their music moving her to tears just as the works of the expressionist painter Franz Marc and Mark Rothko do.

When Sonam first arrived in the West, it was not only the big wide world of art that was new to her, but also everything she found around her: in stores, on plates and in refrigerators. In the early years, it took all her mental energy simply to adapt. Gradually she began to realize that the Westerners she had previously thought so educated and civilized did all sorts of things that appalled her. She was horrified to see how many wars they waged, how they were destroying the world by overexploiting nature and polluting the environment, how they spent money on weapons rather than feeding the starving millions. She recognized that though much of the unfamiliar food she came across in the West not only tasted wonderful, was easy to cook and looked good, it also contained all kinds of unhealthy preservatives, colourings and other chemical additives. When my brother and I were small, she bought us bright orange soda, only to discover on reading the label carefully that the drink consisted of water, sugar, colouring and artificial flavourings. That was the last bottle she ever bought. She got very upset that products like that weren't banned for damaging people's health. Cola, sweets, Spanish hothouse tomatoes and battery-laid eggs were all banned from her shopping basket. Her Buddhist conscience helped her make many of her decisions at the supermarket. Although she did cook meat dishes, and ate them too, she was not prepared to buy meat from animals that had been kept under tortuous mass farming conditions and fattened up with chemical additives.

Mola no longer ate any meat. She had eaten meat her whole life long but had never been happy about it, and had always prayed to fend off the bad karma it brought upon her. Like most other Tibetans, she had always believed she had to eat meat to stay healthy, but in Switzerland she heard that it was not all that good for you, and that it was much better to eat vegetables, tofu, fruit, milk and bread. She was delighted to switch to a vegetarian diet.

This one decision made her happier than anything else the West had offered her, and she has stuck to it to this day. If there is the slightest bit of meat gravy on a vegetable dish, she won't eat it. When Sonam and Martin told her that many farmers in the West use chemical pesticides on their fruit and vegetables, killing insects and other small animals, she began to buy organic products. Despite all her efforts, she couldn't persuade Sonam to become a vegetarian as well. Amala doesn't want to go without meat entirely, and especially not without fish, which Mola and most Tibetans reject completely.

Sonam did most of her shopping in organic food stores or bought directly from farmers, making us one of the first organic families in Berne, although she did buy other products occasionally if she considered them unobjectionable. It was at this time that she returned to the old Tibetan staple food *tsampa*. This roasted barley flour was not available anywhere in Switzerland, so she started making it herself. She and Mola roasted organically grown barley, then ground it. Tashi and I loved the batter she made out of *tsampa*, water and butter, milk or yoghurt, and our friends loved nothing more than rolling the nutty, sticky and wonderfully sweet mixture into balls and eating huge amounts of them.

When a Berne department store organized a Tibetan week, Martin convinced Sonam to present her *tsampa* there. She and Kunsang began to roast organic barley in the garden and grind it in the basement, while Tashi and I packed the flour in pretty paper bags for which Martin had designed and copied labels. Sonam transported it all to the store. On the first day, however, she didn't sell a single bag, because nobody knew what *tsampa* was, and she realized she would have to offer instructions and free samples. The next day her stall was equipped with sugar, milk, butter and yoghurt and encircled by dozens of customers, who not only asked her about *tsampa*, but also wanted to know about the situation in Tibet, the Dalai Lama and Buddhism – everything is interconnected, indeed. By the evening, Sonam had sold all thirty bags and could only give the customers one answer to their question of where else they could get it: 'Nowhere.'

Their interest prompted her to look more closely at *tsampa*. She found out from friends, acquaintances and via the internet that it is not only eaten in her home country, but is also known under other names in different parts of the world that have never come into contact with Tibet. The indigenous people of the Canary Islands, for example, know this roasted flour under the name of *gofio*, the inhabitants of the Ecuadorian highlands call it *machica*, and in Lapland it is known as *talkkuna*. The farmers on the high plains of Eritrea and Ethiopia in East Africa are also familiar with the method of making a tasty basis for their cold-stirred porridge out of roasted and ground barley. That proved to Sonam that *tsampa* is a global food, but one that was unknown in her new home of Switzerland.

Sonam continued roasting and grinding. She signed a delivery contract with the largest organic store in Berne, but soon had to admit that she would never be able to meet the increasing demand. So she looked for a trustworthy manufacturer who could make *tsampa* exactly as she wanted, and for a supplier of the best organic barley. She also organized an organic distribution service to deliver the product to stores around Switzerland. Later came another distribution service in the north of Stuttgart, which delivers to Germany and Austria. From then on, she concentrated on spreading the word, travelling to food events and organic trade fairs, handing samples to numerous retailers, wholesalers and customers, having a website put together, and taking care of quality control for the production. In this way, a cottage industry in a Bernese villa grew into a company that supplies to organic food stores across half of Europe, still earning my mother a supplementary income from licensing fees – every bag boasts the label 'Sonam's Tsampa'. My *amala* guarantees with her name the quality of a product that is slow food and fast food in one: primal, natural and delicious, but also fast and easy to cook. It seems to me like a small triumph of good over the globalized food trade we so often see as evil. It introduces people to a product that helps them not only to eat a healthy diet but also to find out about people in Tibet. How amazing that my mother, the daughter of a nun from the Tibetan highlands, who only a couple of decades ago didn't even know there was such a thing as a post office that takes letters from one place to any other place in the world, now runs a European distribution company via a Skype account from her kitchen table in New York.

36

All the World's a Stage

The years passed, and I grew up like any other Swiss teenager. My gelled hair got higher and higher, my skirts got shorter, my eyelids darker and my jeans tighter. The waistband of my trousers soon slipped so low that you could see half my backside, but that was the fashion. Mola thought it was indecent, telling me off every time she saw me, but she had no influence over me when it came to that kind of thing; my parents were in charge of bringing me up. Amala never banned me from wearing make-up or short skirts even if she didn't like the way I looked. 'I don't like it,' she said on more than one occasion, 'but it's your business. As long as I don't have to walk around like you, you can dress however you like.'

I wanted to be an actress or an artist, so I applied to the Berne School of Design. To my delight, they actually offered me a place. I loved drawing, spending hours with pencil and paper. My parents had always thought I would one day do something to do with art, but they never pushed me in any particular direction, leaving it up to me what I wanted to be.

The first year at the School of Design didn't suit me. Although I learned artistic techniques from screen-printing to painting, the teachers were too conservative for my taste, boring and uninspired, and I had no chance to give my imagination free rein. Just to be on the safe side, I also put my name down for the entry exam for the Berne Drama School. I had wanted to go there for a long time, but I was still too young, and my parents weren't sure whether I had any talent for acting. I was surprised and thrilled when I won a place to study drama there.

I left art school and started at drama school. At only seventeen, I was the baby of the class, a role I enjoyed because I liked being with older people, but I often felt I wasn't fully equipped for everything the school demanded of me. I was a teenager who had to grow up very quickly.

I liked the practical aspects of the training best. It was fun exploring other forms of expression than theatre. We had a very experimental teacher who introduced us to the idea of performance art, took us to exhibitions and taught us about Far Eastern ideas. We were even encouraged to come up with our own pieces of performance art. Mine consisted of fifty or so large snails that I placed all over my naked body, so close together that they looked like a dress. But they wouldn't stay in one place and moved all over my body, which was a wonderful feeling. In the background I played a tape of train sounds, and train tracks I had filmed out of a carriage window rushed by on a screen.

Mola and Amala helped me to collect and feed all the snails. It wasn't an easy job, as they kept escaping from their provisional cage, and we had a task on our hands collecting them all up again. My family didn't understand what I wanted to do with the snails, but that didn't matter. Amala joined in because she knew drama school was important to me and because she always enjoyed my odd ideas. Mola fed the snails with dandelion leaves because she was worried they might be hungry and thirsty.

We took classic acting classes, voice training individually and in groups, acrobatics, speaking classes, dancing, fencing, qigong, shiatsu massage, gymnastics and singing. The schedule was so packed that we were usually in school from nine in the morning until nine at night. We needed a lot of self-discipline, often spending even Saturdays and Sundays there. We ate at school; all our relationships and parties took place there. Sometimes I had the feeling that the only reason I went home was to sleep.

I often questioned why I wanted to be an actress. Why was I here? What did I want to tell people? It took me years to find what I was looking for. I had to take my feelings back a generation, look to my Tibetan side. I could use the pain and anger I felt about China in my roles. I realized that I had found my motivation in the stories of my mother, my grandmother, and their people.

After graduation I set out on a long audition tour, which took me around half of Germany and Switzerland. Nobody offered me a job, but in any case I was beginning to find it more and more difficult to imagine being tied to a theatre. And after nine years at school and one year at art college, immediately followed by four years of drama school, I'd had enough of the permanent pressure of institutions. I wanted to work more freely, to travel and experience different things so that I could fill my acting with new content and emotions.

With all this in mind, I created a play along with two friends from drama school. We called it *Everest 96 – The Summit*, and each of us tailored a role to ourselves. I played the part of a Tibetan journalist reporting critically on extreme climbing on the roof of the world after a catastrophe on Mount Everest. The others played climbers who described the accident from their own perspective.

The play had a lot to do with my origins, with my mother and grandmother's experiences as refugees, and it ended in a deliberate mélange of fiction and reality until the audience could no longer tell the difference.

Directly after this I was hired for my first play at Aachen's Municipal Theatre. That meant an exciting three months of looking behind the scenes of the theatre business. I had a part in a successful staging of Goethe's *Torquato Tasso*, playing Eleonore von Este. The director, Gabriele Gysi, had deliberately cast me for the role because I didn't look the part. But by the end of the engagement, I knew this was not the route for me to take, at least not in the next few years. I couldn't imagine working at the same theatre for a long period of time.

During my time in Aachen I made up my mind to try and get into movies rather than the stage. I made my first short film and began working on Swiss and German film and television productions. I also took on modelling jobs in between and had a few appearances in TV ads. Life was full. I had met an actor called Vincent and we were living together in his flat in Geneva. Vincent was a native of Geneva, and therefore French-speaking. He spoke hardly any German and no English. I was determined to learn perfect French, and took private lessons, getting better and better at the language. I've never spent so much time on trains before or since. I was endlessly commuting between Geneva, Berne and Zurich. But something was missing. Whilst I knew that I had got to a point where acting and modelling could fulfill my financial needs, I realized that they couldn't fulfill me spiritually, as they say in the West. I knew there had to be something else in my life, a freedom I longed for deep in my heart.

37

An Activist Education

I had begun to be actively involved in the campaign to free Tibet
in 1999, when I was still a student at drama school. Jiang Zemin,
president of the People's Republic of China, came to visit Berne. I
was already well aware of the political issues surrounding Tibet;
even as children, Tashi and I had participated with Amala, Mola
and sometimes Pala in various demonstrations for Tibetan independence. Our mother had taken us to vigils, solidarity bazaars,
benefit concerts and all the other events for a free Tibet.

The announcement of Jiang Zemin's visit transformed Berne into
a fortress; the Swiss government was afraid of embarrassing itself in
front of the Chinese statesman if the police couldn't keep the protests
under control. Soldiers occupied the square outside the Federal Palace
housing the Swiss government and parliament. The government rolled
out the red carpet for the official guest, flags were raised, and the
police and press took up their positions. The atmosphere was tense
– Tibetans had registered a demonstration, but it had been banned.
Meanwhile, Amala and a number of other Tibetan and Swiss activists
climbed on to the roof of the Vatter organic supermarket building.

The supermarket owner had opened the attic door for them and showed them the way. My mother had a good relationship with the Vatter family, being not just a regular customer but also the supplier of their tsampa.

Up on the roof, at a dizzying height, with a marvellous view of the old heart of Berne and its church towers, Sonam and the other activists pumped gas into balloons, attaching them to long white sheets with the word DIALOGUE written on them in large letters. They were not advocating violence or aggression, nor even independence for Tibet, merely calling for the Chinese to take action towards solving the Tibetan question.

As soon as the police discovered Amala and her helpers, they wanted to remove them from the rooftop. But the Swiss president at the time, Ruth Dreifuss, was waiting outside the Federal Palace for her guest to arrive and forbade the police from intervening. She was afraid someone might fall off the roof. She knew from past experience that we Tibetans don't use violence, but fight for a free Tibet by peaceful means only. The activists released all their brightly coloured balloons and the wind blew them directly towards the Federal Palace for all to see. The wind god was merciful! Our protest caused quite a stir: Jiang Zemin refused to walk along the red carpet from his luxury hotel as planned, a distance of just over 200 yards, instead taking a limousine and arriving late. Then he stormed angrily into the elegant old building, not without noticing my brother Tashi, his class from school and many of his friends, who greeted him with a chorus of whistles and boos from the edge of the square outside. During the event the Chinese guest insulted the Swiss president, saying she did not have the Swiss people under control and had lost an important friend.

Jiang Zemin was staying in a hotel situated high above the River Aare on the edge of the old part of town. The hotel has a wonderful view of the Bernese Alps. It also looks over a football pitch that lies beside the river. My father had organized a Tibetan flag as large as the entire pitch to cover the grass, and many helpers to spread it out. The police had given official permission for the flag, but the city authorities got cold feet and ordered its removal before the state guest arrived. My father didn't let them talk him into that. Instead he borrowed large yellow scaffolding tarpaulins from a friend in the construction business and used them to cover up the flag so that it could be revealed again at an opportune moment. To protest against the authorities' actions, he asked an artist to paint a huge stamp saying 'OFFICIAL COVER-UP' on the middle of the yellow sheeting. It wasn't long before the police arrived, covered up this message too and made sure neither the stamp nor the flag was visible. There was one thing they couldn't remove, though: the advertising strips at the side of the pitch reading: 'Tibetans want Dialogue with China'.

Back then, I felt the whole campaign had been monitored and kept in check by a police state, but I was soon to find out that Switzerland was far removed from that; a real police state is very different. As I now know, there is hardly any country in which protest campaigns against such a high-ranking state guest as the Chinese president would be allowed to take place and dealt with so mildly as in Switzerland; none of us was punished for violating the ban. My mother could hardly believe she could express her opinion so openly even though she was not Swiss born. She had never dared to imagine such freedom.

For me, this protest in Berne not only revealed the arrogance of the Chinese government and brought me into closer contact with pro-Tibetan activists; it also proved that we Tibetans can attract attention for our cause with imaginative campaigns even in a media-saturated world. Before then, every year on 10 March, the anniversary of the

Dalai Lama's escape after the failed uprising of 1959, some of Switzerland's 3,000 Tibetans would gather outside the Chinese embassy chanting 'We want freedom' and 'China out of Tibet'. The same pro-Tibetan journalists turned up every year, their reports taking up only a couple of lines in the next day's newspapers; there was little to write about and not much to photograph. The real news was that perhaps 400 people had gone home relieved at having done something good, but still feeling frustrated that it wouldn't change anything. This was precisely the conflict under discussion among Tibetan activists in Switzerland: how far should we go to shake people into action? What is non-violent resistance? Is there any point in taking to the streets in Switzerland? What does it do to help the Tibetans in Tibet?

After I finished drama school, I wanted to get more involved on behalf of my second homeland, so I was happy when a Tibetan activist asked me if I'd like to stand for president of the Tibetan Youth Association in Europe. After a long talk I agreed to take on the post, on condition that I could have a co-president to help me, so that I could carry on working as an actress at the same time. The Tibetan Youth Association gave me what was missing in my life as an actress: identification with a cause I was pursuing not for personal reasons, for my career or my bank balance, but for others: for my people, my family and my country. We met regularly, usually in Zurich, to talk about what we could do to keep the subject of Tibet on the political agenda. Sadly, the media and the public tend to forget all too quickly that our country has been occupied by a foreign power since 1959, and they need reminding of our cause.

As president, I wanted to come up with new forms of campaigning, but the older Tibetans and parents of the other members kept a watchful eye on us, making sure that not too much changed. Many of the members came from different walks of life from me. As bankers, trainee lawyers or social workers, they took a more cautious approach to activism. Tibetans tend to be rather reserved, and suddenly they were confronted with me, a young woman who had not been a member of their association before and was now suddenly its president, wanting to shift its focus to high-profile political actions.

The same conflict divides our ranks as divides older Tibetan exiles: one group favours freedom for Tibet and fights for complete independence from China, the other campaigns for Tibetan autonomy within the People's Republic of China, something the Chinese government formally granted long ago but has never put into practice. I call the first group idealists and the second realists, but China's official policy condemns and combats both as separatists. The Tibetan Youth Association in Europe is a branch of the international Tibetan Youth Congress (TYC) in Dharamsala, and therefore calls for complete freedom for Tibet in line with the parent organization's statutes. Of course I was all for that too, but I always explained to my fellow campaigners that true autonomy, genuine cultural self-determination, would be a huge step towards freedom for the Tibetans. That was my personal opinion; as president, I was supposed to campaign for complete independence from China. My speeches didn't always fully conform with the TYC statutes, often hinting that striving for genuine autonomy for Tibet was a realistic political option. I don't believe that we can turn the clock back, that the millions of Chinese settlers will give up their new lives in Tibet and that the People's Republic will abandon its province. I think we have to find a solution that enables the Tibetans and Chinese to live together in such a way that both groups are guaranteed their respective rights and freedoms. Part of this must be a change in the Chinese attitude towards Tibet. The Chinese people know far too little about our culture and history, having for decades been fed a constant diet of misinformation and negative propaganda.

The excessively long discussions on the issue of whether to campaign for complete independence or simply for autonomy for Tibet seemed a waste of time to me. I thought we young Tibetans ought to be more daring. The generation before us had made a start, but it had not yet been very successful. Now it was our turn. One thing that remained just as important for me was preserving the Tibetan language and culture, even though I could see for myself how difficult that was in exile. Travelling to Tibet was now impossible again; I had little contact with Tibetans in Switzerland outside of the association, and no one else I knew spoke Tibetan.

It was in this context that I first understood the term 'mother tongue'. The language a mother speaks to her children is the language that finds its way into a child's heart. I am very grateful to Amala that she spoke only Tibetan to Tashi and me in our early childhood; it was the only way to plant in us the seeds of the Tibetan culture, despite our exile. This culture will always be a part of us. Regardless of the fact that we don't know the Tibetan national anthem by heart, have many gaps in our language and can't read or write Tibetan perfectly, the essence of the culture is firmly anchored in our hearts.

At times I have had the painful experience of not being perceived as a real Tibetan by some of my compatriots, because I have a Swiss father. Shouldn't we half-Tibetans and the non-Tibetan partners of Tibetans be integrated into Tibetan society as well, not least because there will be more and more mixed marriages in the future? Non-Tibetan partners often work very hard for the country, which benefits all Tibetans.

In my new role as president, I threw myself into action. I organized a happening in Geneva, outside my front door – which happened to be next to the chamber of commerce. A Swiss-Chinese friendship meeting was due to be held there, and I came up with the idea that every Tibetan should turn up with a white sheet and lie down on the ground in front of the building, covered with the sheet. Then we'd wait and see whether the Chinese would step over Tibetan corpses, in a figurative sense, to get to their meeting. We didn't register the happening with the police because they would never have allowed it, but we did inform a few journalists in advance. Shortly before the Chinese guests arrived, 200 of us met up nearby and lay down on the road outside the chamber of commerce. The Chinese were initially taken aback when they climbed out of their cars, but they stepped over us without batting an eyelid, right in front of the photographers. The photographers got their pictures, the journalists got their stories, and Tibet was in the public eye in Switzerland. Meanwhile, my father and a few other Swiss activists staged a kind of guerrilla action inside the conference building, unsettling the Chinese guests by handing them business cards printed not with their names but pointing out the predicament of Tibet.

During my time as president, I met the Dalai Lama several times – not only in my official capacity but also as Martin Brauen's daughter. Pala had stayed in contact with His Holiness over the years, keeping him informed about his exhibitions and publications. The Dalai Lama esteems my father's work very highly; he has written forewords for his books and attended several of his exhibitions in Zurich.

When I met His Holiness face to face for the first time, I was overwhelmed. I stood beside my parents in the thick of the crowds at the exhibition opening, where my father greeted the Dalai Lama as an old acquaintance and my *amala* bowed low. When the Dalai Lama's gaze turned to me, a wave of heat flooded through me. He gave off a palpable feeling of serenity, joy and goodness. He placed his hand on my cheek, and I felt his warmth, then he smiled, almost laughing, and moved on to greet others who also wanted to feel his touch.

'We have known each other for many years now,' he said to my father in his speech at the exhibition opening. 'You are not only a personal friend of mine, you also are seriously concerned about Tibetan culture and spirituality and have worked on the subject for many years . . . That is very, very important. That is very helpful at this critical time. As a person who bears responsibility for the preservation of Tibetan culture and spirituality and for the entire nation of old Tibet, for this unique cultural heritage that is now at risk of disappearing, as this person I assess your contribution as very large. I would like to give you my heartfelt thanks.'

38

A Moscow Media Storm

Not long after first meeting the Dalai Lama, I went to Strasbourg with a delegation from the Tibetan Youth Association to inform His Holiness about our largest action so far, which we had planned for the upcoming award of the Olympic Games to Beijing in 2008. The International Olympic Committee (IOC) were holding a conference in Moscow where the decision was to be announced, and we wanted to stage a demonstration against it. Frank Bodin, a Swiss advertising executive who does a great deal for Tibet, designed a poster for us free of charge, showing a stone wall with five bullet holes in it arranged like the Olympic rings. Beneath it was the legend 'The Games of Beijing with Tibet'. The Dalai Lama liked our idea, warned us to maintain non-violence, as we intended, and wished us the best of success.

It was a huge campaign. I'm still amazed at everything we managed to achieve, given that all of us had to earn a living alongside our political work. After a long organizational phase, we landed in Moscow and sent out press statements inviting journalists, photographers and camera crews to the scene of our demonstration.

The next day we launched into action, meeting up on the square opposite the Moscow World Trade Centre, where the IOC conference was to be held. A friend and I unfurled the poster and the journalists began filming and taking photos. Within seconds, a man in plain clothing ran up to us and tried to grab our poster, but I kept hold of it, calling out to another Tibetan to help me hold it up again.

The man rushed to my aid and the poster with the five bullet holes and our message were visible again, albeit only for a moment. There must have been a group of police waiting just around the corner, for they instantly surrounded us, blocking the photographers' view. The police began leading my fellow campaigners away, but I raised my voice to the journalists, wanting them to report not only the arrests but also the motives behind our protest. I explained why we didn't want the Olympic Games in Beijing and told them about the repression of Tibetans in their own country. I had prepared a much longer statement, but there wasn't time to read it out.

Two officers grabbed hold of my arms and pulled me away from the journalists. I screamed, tore myself loose and ran around the press people to evade arrest. 'What's your name?' one journalist shouted at me, and I called it out. Then I was lifted off the ground, my feet kicking in mid-air; I was so overwrought, tense, tired and frightened that tears rushed to my eyes. That was the moment when the photographers clicked their shutters and shot the pictures that went around the world only hours later. I was shoved into a police van and the whole event was over, only five minutes after it had begun.

The police put all of us – not just our small group of three Tibetans and one Swiss man, but also an uninvolved Russian-American interpreter, a Swiss journalist and a Tibetan from India – into custody cells. We were held there all day and into the night, being interrogated and having to submit to demeaning searches. We were refused food and drink. After the interrogations, when we were back in the cells, we noticed that the police officers hadn't locked them, so we sneaked out into the corridor and fetched our mobile phones from the bags they had taken from us and deposited there. The telephones had been ringing non-stop; we had given many of the journalists our numbers, and they wanted to know what had happened to us.

We crept quickly back into our cells. My first call was to my parents in Switzerland. My father knew what had happened; the reports of our arrest had already gone around the world via news agencies and the internet. Pala reacted calmly. He had already called the Swiss Foreign Office, who had assured him that they would do everything they could to get us out of jail. Hearing this news lifted a weight off my shoulders. Then we gave telephone interviews to journalists from around the world. At some point the police saw that we had phones in our cells, but they didn't care. They had no idea what they were supposed to do with us, so they left us in peace.

Finally the guards took us to another room above the jail, where a lawyer, the brother of the Russian-American interpreter, met with us. He had a thick law book with him, which he constantly flicked through. Another two or three hours passed before we were led one at a time into a room where officers in strange uniforms with huge caps sat at a long table. It was like something from a cheap Cold War spy thriller. These old men decorated with ribbons of medals gave us fierce looks and told the lawyer we had to sign a paper saying that we would come to our trial the next day. Then they set us free, something none of us had been expecting. When we turned up in court the next day, the judge established that the police had made many procedural errors. She sent all the files back to the police and the case was closed, at least as far as the courts were concerned.

In the meantime, the Swiss press had found out the identity of the crying girl being dragged away by Russian police officers: not only the president of the Tibetan Youth Association, but also a young actress. The media machinery cranked up to full gear. The pictures of me were already on the television news. When our plane landed in Zurich, the gate was crowded not only with my parents and many Tibetans holding white good-luck scarves, but also with a large number of journalists. I spent the next few weeks giving interviews, attending photo shoots, appearing on talk shows and reading the results of all this in magazines and watching it on screen. It was the first time I had experienced first-hand how the media machinery works. It was clear to me that though the journalists were interested in Tibet and the Moscow protest, the fact that I was an actress as well as an activist gave them an angle for their stories – something I was determined to make use of in future protests.

39

A Pilgrimage to India

Although I was living with my boyfriend Vincent in Geneva, I often went home to Berne to visit my family. My parents, my brother, Mola and I would sit around the big kitchen table or on the sofa next to it, the doors to the garden open, and talk and drink tea. The kitchen has always been the heart of our home, the place where we have argued, cried, danced, and discussed our everyday problems. On one such occasion, Mola announced that she wanted to go on a pilgrimage to India.

'I don't know how much longer I'll be able to travel,' she said, 'and I want to go back to the big pilgrimage sites and to the Dalai Lama in Dharamsala.'

In our eyes, Mola had become a cosy pensioner, someone who took the family dog out for walks, helped Sonam in the kitchen, carried out her daily prayers and offerings, chatted to the neighbours in her broken Swiss German and sunbathed on the balcony outside her room. Now she wanted to go to India with a small group of friends her age and younger, other Tibetan exiles in Switzerland and followers of the Nyingma school of Buddhism.

She seemed to have already made most of the preparations for her trip; all she needed now was Martin's help to book her flights. I listened to what she had to say and registered my parents' concerned comments about whether it wouldn't be too much for her and her companions. But then a thought struck me and all of a sudden I heard myself say: 'Mola, I'll come with you!'

Everyone stared at me – it was unexpected for them, and for me. 'You want to go to India?'

'Yes,' I said, as if I'd been planning it for years. 'I want to see all those places too, and I want to make a film about them.'

I had been thinking for a year or so that it would be great to make a film of my own, and I had already made a couple of videos on borrowed cameras. This would be the perfect opportunity to make a proper documentary. There was very little filmed material about Tibetan pilgrimages in India, and I wanted to introduce people in the West to popular Tibetan Buddhism, the faith of the ordinary people as opposed to the monks trained in the monasteries, whose lives had been portrayed in a number of films. Mola and her friends may well be the last generation that is not only familiar with this traditional grass-roots Buddhism, with all its rites and rituals, but also practises it with every fibre of their being.

Inspired by this idea, I got on the train to Geneva. A couple of hours later I was explaining my plans to Vincent. Before his amazed eyes, I covered the kitchen table with a map of India I had bought at the station. 'We're going to make a film,' I told him. He looked at me as if I was crazy. 'We haven't got any money,' he objected, but I was well prepared for that. 'So let's get some. You sit down and write a proposal so we can get funding.'

Three months later, Vincent and I were on the plane with Mola and her group of pilgrims en route to India. Vincent was still studying the instruction manual for our new camera, which we had bought with public cultural funding from various Swiss cantons and a donation from the Tibetan Youth Association. He would be the cameraman, and I the editor, director and translator. It was an exhausting job, as I had to translate not only between English and Tibetan for Mola and her group, but also between Tibetan and French for Vincent, and from English to French and back; while Mola translated the Amdo dialect spoken by one of her group into the Tibetan I could understand. It was a Babylonian mishmash of languages.

Our journey began in Dharamsala, where we participated in a *tsok* ceremony, a sacrificial and cleansing practice in Vajrayana Buddhism enabled by the donations of the Buddhist pilgrims from Switzerland. His Holiness the Dalai Lama was also present. The members of our pilgrimage group were allowed to sit in the temple, a privilege not usually granted to lay worshippers unless they make generous donations. In Buddhism it is not only the spiritual level of a person but also their willingness to donate that matters. Mola was so modest that she couldn't bring herself to sit in the temple, where women are not usually allowed. Instead she crouched down outside with the other lay worshippers and nuns, although she had given just as much money as all the others.

The highlight of the journey was our audience with the Dalai Lama, held especially for our group. As one might expect, it was a great privilege for everyone to be in a room with His Holiness, the 'precious master', the 'jewel that fulfils all wishes'. The pilgrims in our group only ever referred to him by these honorifics; the Mongolian official title, Dalai Lama, would have seemed too disrespectful and unceremonious to them, as it would to all Tibetan Buddhists.

Our next stop was Tso Pema, in Rewalsar, where we visited the caves of Padmasambhava. We also went to the cave of the great yogi Mahasiddha Tilopa, which was overgrown with hanging plants. Stories say that the yogi, considered to be the founder of the Kagyupa school of Tibetan Buddhism, spent his days in the cave on the banks of the river, meditating and living on fish he caught himself. As it would not have been very good Buddhist practice to kill so many fish, the local guides, who revered him, had a different explanation: Mahasiddha Tilopa didn't kill fish, they told us, he only caught them and sent their souls straight to buddha heaven before he ate their lifeless flesh.

We also went to Bodh Gaya, the essential destination for all Buddhist pilgrims. It is under a giant tree there that Buddha is said to have attained enlightenment. Pilgrims call this site the 'seat of the diamond'. We took part in a twelve-day bum-tsok ceremony to remove the obstacles on the paths of the pilgrims' lives. As I sat alongside them, I had the feeling that after meeting the Dalai Lama in person, our group felt there were no more obstacles in their paths. Mola was in a permanent state of bliss. She could hardly believe she was travelling to all these places she had visited forty years ago on her first Indian pilgrimage, poverty-stricken and under great hardship. This time she came as an old woman, wealthy by Indian standards, with enough money in her pocket not only to pay for train and bus tickets and comfortable hotel beds, but also to distribute generous donations to all the pious men and women she met in the monasteries and holy Buddhist sites. According to her, this form of charity would make a decisive improvement to her karma.

Two years after my pilgrimage with Mola, my parents returned to India with her. Unfortunately I couldn't go along this time because I had a role in a film. Pala had a private audience with the Dalai Lama in Dharamsala to talk about an upcoming exhibition. There they met

Sonam's cousin Pema, the girl from Pang with whom I had played in the fields and meadows on our visit to Tibet. Pema had had a very difficult time getting to India. Like Mola and Amala she had crossed the Himalayas illegally, but her journey had been even more arduous and fraught with danger. She was now living in Dharamsala, in a school for Tibetans. The dreadful details of her story offered my parents new proof that many Tibetans, in despair over the conditions in their country, were still setting out on the life-threatening journey to India. Several members of Pema's group had not survived the trip.

Along with Mola and Sonam, Pema was allowed to take part in Martin's audience with the Dalai Lama. The moment she entered His Holiness' audience room, she burst into tears. For we Tibetans, the Dalai Lama is such a highly venerated person, and thus so enrapturing, that most people can hardly believe it when they face him in person. He took Pema in his arms, held her and spoke soothing words to her.

When Pema had first arrived in India, she found it hard to believe that the Dalai Lama was a living person. In Tibet she had thought he lived in statues, but wasn't someone of flesh and blood. Her parents hadn't corrected her mistake. It would have been too dangerous to tell children about the Dalai Lama, as they might let this knowledge slip to the wrong person, such as an overzealous Chinese teacher. To be in his presence was overwhelming for her. Sonam also felt His Holiness' great warmth, and was so moved by the scene that tears came to her eyes as well.

In Dharamsala, Mola and Amala enjoyed being close to the Dalai Lama and finding themselves among so many Tibetans. His Holiness gave them strength and the sense that they had returned to their homeland. But Amala was an observant person, who thought a great deal about what she saw. In Dharamsala she came across rich Tibetans who exploited their Indian servants and employees. She disliked the child labour she saw in the hotels and restaurants belonging to Tibetans, who sent their own children to private schools. She couldn't believe that these Nepalese and Indian children had to work from dawn to dusk while their masters lived in luxury.

This is one of the inherent contradictions in Buddhism. Buddhists are supposed to be kind and compassionate and support their fellow human beings, but often this sympathy for all living beings is not put into practice but instead is made the basis of one's own contemplation. Buddhists often maintain that it is important to empathize with other people's suffering through meditation, helping them more through prayer than with monetary donations or food. The reasoning behind it, a monk explained to me, is that the latter would benefit the sufferers' bodies but not their minds. My mother and I are often troubled by ideas like this, and the problems they cause.

40

Around the World

My unedited documentary about the Tibetan pilgrims was languishing on my hard drive. As soon as I had returned to Europe, I was offered jobs on the other side of the camera. I was pleased that I had enough work; I had to earn a living, and I had lost the impetus for my political work for Tibet the way I had been approaching it. I no longer wanted to be actively involved in politics and Tibetan organizations, feeling that I couldn't put across or push through my opinions and ideas. Also, I wanted to see the world. There was no more obvious step for me than to go to Berlin, where Germany's largest film and TV studios are. At the beginning of the new century, after decades of stagnation, Berlin had become the new hub of European film. A few good friends of mine were already living there.

In Berlin I lived alone for the first time in my life. My relationship with Vincent had ended. He didn't want to leave Geneva, or if so only for France or Brussels. There seemed no option for us but to part. I have always admired people with strong roots, people who know where their home is and feel at one with themselves there, but that is not the case for me. I commute between cultures. At that time, I didn't feel genuinely at home anywhere, which had the advantage that I could settle in any place there were opportunities for me. And that place was to be Berlin. But it wasn't easy. Although I had always loved being alone, retreating to my room to think my own thoughts, read and watch films, it was something else knowing there was no Amala cooking and cleaning downstairs in the kitchen, no Pala hammering away at his computer keyboard next door, no Mola murmuring over her smoke offerings one floor above. The view from my window was no longer of the luscious garden of my childhood, but of a Berlin backyard, the only green consisting of a few pots of stunted flowers on the other tenants' windowsills. I had to learn to deal with the fact that no one was there to monitor when I got up, where I went, when I got home again and how I was feeling.

But that was how I had wanted it, and that was how it had to be. I threw myself into my work. Sometimes I felt I was missing the ability to let go, to find the emptiness my grandmother was so good at feeling. In dark moments of rejection, difficulty and loneliness, I couldn't always translate my Buddhist principles into my life. I didn't want to feel envy, jealousy, longing for a particular situation or for something as worldly as an offer of a role in a film, but sometimes I couldn't help feeling those emotions.

In difficult phases, some Buddhists seek solace in a monastery, going on a retreat, as Western Buddhists like to say, but that was out of the question for me. I could not afford this luxurious variety of Buddhist practice, but more importantly, I thought it was too simple a solution to find peace in sublime self-contemplation far removed from all my real-life problems. The challenge I was facing was that of bringing my life as an actress, a Berliner and a job-seeker into harmony with my Buddhist side. I wanted to be calmer, more balanced in the face of all the demands the film business made on me, but still get on in the world.

At times I couldn't help thinking of the Berlin bear, the symbol of the city that crops up everywhere you go. I was familiar with bears from my home town of Berne, which also has a bear in its coat of arms. I thought of the peace and the strength that bears possess. I imagined a bear's combination of courage and composure, a very Buddhist characteristic. I resolved to strive for bearlike qualities in myself. What I didn't know then was that I was soon to move to another place connected with bears. When I realized that the state of California had a bear on its flag, I didn't see it as a coincidence, but as karma.

After Berlin, there was only one logical next step in my acting career, and that was to go to Los Angeles. Hollywood was the city of my dreams. I wanted to try to get my foot in the door of the world's greatest illusion factory. I found a place to live there with Ronny and Rebecca Novick, a filmmaker and a writer. The two of them were practising Buddhists who had done a great deal for the Tibetan cause. They took me in without even knowing me, and gave me a room of my own. They had five dogs in their house, all of them rescued from the street, which they nursed and brought back to health. Through the Novicks, I came into contact with other Tibetans living in LA. They took me along to the temple where they worshipped, which was called Thubten Dhargye Ling, Tibetan for 'park of flourishing teachings'.

Thubten Dhargye Ling was in a very different setting to any Buddhist temple I had seen before. It was situated in the industrial port town of Long Beach, just south of Los Angeles, and housed in a nondescript two-storey former residential and office building, along with the Tibetan cultural centre and the monks' apartments.

The façade was painted in the familiar style of Tibetan temples. After you took off your shoes in an anteroom and entered the temple, you were in another world, filled with the scent of butter lamps, incense, fruit and flowers, which were placed as offerings on the altar. Outside sounds were dampened by carpets and cushions. Whenever I had the chance, I would immerse myself for a couple of hours in this peaceful oasis, and listen to the teachings of Geshe Tsultim Gyeltsen, a wise and experienced Tibetan monk who had fled to India in 1959 just like Mola and Amala. A Khampa from eastern Tibet like Mola, he was thirty-five when he went into exile. As a respected Buddhist scholar, he would have been unlikely to have survived the Chinese purges after the failed Tibetan uprising.

Sadly, Geshe-la, as everyone called the founder and guru of the Long Beach temple, died recently at the age of eighty-five. Three hours and three days before his death, he began a light meditation from which he intended to pass into his next life. During this time he was still alive but he no longer moved, spoke or ate and drank. Directly after his death, Buddhists said that an extraordinarily clear and beautiful double rainbow stretched over Long Beach, from the houses and the industrial plants and the port to the beach on the Pacific Ocean – a rare phenomenon in such a dry place that many of the locals admired in amazement. Thousands of people took photos of this celestial appearance; it was even pictured and described in the next day's Los Angeles Times. Geshe-la's memory will always be important to me; he was a valuable support for me, especially during my early days in Los Angeles.

My hostess Rebecca Novick had launched a radio show about Tibet, which broadcast news, interviews and documentaries in the LA area and was available worldwide on the internet. The Tibet Connection has since grown into more than a radio show, providing an up-to-date internet platform on all issues surrounding Tibet, the Chinese-Tibetan conflict and campaigns for an autonomous or free Tibet. Because Rebecca liked my voice, and because I am committed to the cause, I started work as the show's anchorwoman, presenting the one-hour programme recorded once a month. For me, The Tibet Connection provides a hub for international networking among Tibetans. We may not have a common free country, but we do have a worldwide free communication system.

I had a new man in my life. During a trip to Berlin, I had met and fallen in love with an actor called Guido, not even knowing he had lived in Los Angeles for years and still had an apartment there. We set up home together in Los Angeles. Guido's apartment was too small for two people, so we found a wooden bungalow to rent, right next to the big Hollywood studios. The bungalows – so small they would have been garden sheds in Switzerland – had once been accommodation for the actors working in the surrounding studios.

Apart from the odd helicopter hovering overhead looking for criminals, life in Hollywood had an air of calm, not unlike living in a small town. I would spend lazy summer evenings sitting in the rocking chair on our small porch chatting to the neighbours, who were mostly Spanish speaking. The waitress in the diner around the corner knew just what I liked for breakfast. Even the silent Asian man in the liquor store on the corner occasionally nodded his head when I entered the shop, and I gave all my empties to the old woman who wandered the streets with a shopping cart, collecting up cans and bottles for the deposits. I spent most of my time on the freeway, driving from one casting to the next. I earned a living with commercial jobs; it seemed I had the right look for advertising. In LA I can pass for many different nationalities, Asian, Russian, Latina or Italian, and that got me a lot of work. If I braid my hair they can take me for a Namibian, and with the right make-up I can play a

Japanese woman. It was only in Germany that I was always Asian and nothing else. In Asia it was the precise opposite: there, I could only ever play Europeans and never Tibetan, Chinese or Japanese parts.

Finally I met an agent in LA who liked my work, but I had to do two things before he would put me on his books: get rid of my indefinable accent and get hold of an artist visa. I took classes from a speech coach and went to a lawyer specializing in immigration issues. But when I returned to LA after a couple of weeks, filming in Europe, I found that the agent had emigrated to Korea without even sending me an email. That's the way it is in Los Angeles; you mustn't take it personally. No one ever gets rejections or negative news, because nobody takes the time to send them out. There is only either success or silence, everything moves forward and no one ever looks back. Knowing this now, I take nothing for granted any more; I have learned to move through my world with my full concentration. This attitude has changed my view of Europe. A lot of things are easier for me there now because they are simpler than in America. Next to LA, Berlin seems like a cosy village with a secure social network.

41

Uprising in Lhasa

I sat frozen in front of the TV, tears streaming down my cheeks, my fingers twitching frantically across the remote control, hastily zapping from one news channel to the next. The pictures were all the same: police officers with helmets and shields wielding their sticks over angry young protesters, mass formations of soldiers marching through the streets, military trucks bringing the next delivery of recruits. I saw Tibetans throwing stones at Chinese stores, I saw cars going up in flames, men in civilian clothing beating up other civilians. I saw monks lying motionless on the street, and more police and soldiers. It looked as if war had broken out on the streets of Lhasa.

The largest Tibetan uprising since 1959 began on 10 March 2008, when monks from the Sera monastery on the outskirts of Lhasa tried to commemorate the forty-ninth anniversary of the crushed uprising with a peaceful demonstration, once again calling for independence for Tibet. The Chinese security forces didn't intervene until monks from other monasteries joined in the demonstrations and the protest spread to central Lhasa. Young people took to the streets, looting stores owned by Han Chinese, setting cars alight and defending themselves with violence against the police. When the first pictures of the uprising went around the world, the Chinese security forces took a tough stand. Shots were fired at monks and Tibetan civilians, killing at least eighty people, most of them Buddhist monks. Only the Chinese authorities know the exact number of deaths; they imposed a news blackout on Tibet. Western journalists were not allowed in, and those who were already there had to leave the country immediately. As a result, the flood of pictures soon subsided, leaving me even more perplexed in front of the television, which was permanently switched on, as it was in the homes of almost all Tibetan exiles during this time.

I spent hours on the telephone to my mother and father and Tibetan friends in Switzerland. Everyone was trying to get hold of their relatives in Tibet, but nobody could get through. No one knew whether the network was overloaded or the Chinese authorities had turned off the phone lines. Anyone who did manage to speak to someone in Tibet learned only that this person was still alive but was given no other information; no Tibetan would dare to speak openly on the telephone. Everyone knows that phone calls are tapped and regularly cut off when the wrong subjects are mentioned. All too often Tibetans who have made calls to the West receive visits from the police. As in all dictatorships, any contact with foreigners is treated as suspected espionage. The only difference in this case is that the international community doesn't classify the People's Republic of China as a dictatorship, even though there are no elections and no self-determination for the various nationalities, no right to freedom of expression, no free press, no unmonitored contact with the rest of the world and no independent justice system. I could continue, but it would have little impact. China is a huge and powerful economy, a trading partner and consumer of raw materials valued by all the other countries. Any small state that restricted its citizens' rights so strongly would be ostracized by the international community, yet the rest of the world courts China's favour and in 2008 allowed it to present itself as a legitimate host of the Olympic Games – allegedly a huge worldwide celebration of peace – only months after the brutal events in Tibet.

In a state of despair, with reports on the violent suppression of the uprising coming in from helpless, angry people, I went to the *Tibet Connection* studio to record a show. All this brought up a lot of questions for me. Was it a good thing that the Tibetans had finally stood up to their Chinese oppressors and turned to violence? Did it make any sense to destroy Chinese businesses, some of which belonged to little people trying for a chance at fortune in Lhasa? Was there a point to throwing stones at soldiers from the world's largest army? I could understand these outbreaks of violence, but I couldn't condone them – because they so often affected the wrong people, because they did nothing to change the situation, and because they led to a deterioration of everyday life for all Tibetans, who have since experienced an even stricter and tougher police state.

On the other hand, I had to acknowledge that the Tibetan freedom fighters were heroes, perfectly aware of the consequences of their actions. Were they acting out of total desperation because they could see no other future? It was the first time since the Tibetan uprisings in the late 1980s that the world had seen pictures of the Chinese occupiers' oppression. The despairing insurgents wanted to make themselves heard, and their actions did achieve that; the world's eyes were at last trained on Tibet. My country has been occupied for more than sixty years, but the world's politicians have taken no action. They know about the arrests for no reason, the re-education camps, the violence and the torture, but they close their eyes to it.

During the 2008 uprising, many Tibetans paid with their lives for worldwide media attention.

'We've created international awareness of Tibet,' Sonam said, 'but in Tibet we haven't changed anything; we can't achieve the slightest thing in Tibet.'

A few months later, I found myself on a large stage in front of the Brandenburg Gate in Berlin along with many other Tibetans and German friends of Tibet. Next to me stood the Dalai Lama, speaking words of reconciliation towards China on behalf of the 25,000 people in the audience. As ever, he won the spectators' hearts, consoling them and filling them with enthusiasm for the Tibetans' longing for genuine autonomy – but he was preaching to the converted. Many people don't even know where Tibet is, or think there is no need to concern themselves with this conflict that has been smouldering for over half a century.

On the day after our rally at the Brandenburg Gate the newspapers talked disparagingly about how the Berliners' 'spontaneously practised hobby Buddhism', and about a 'B-list religion for underemployed actors'. This criticism is justified to some extent, and I often wonder what makes people indulge in the kind of naïve enthusiasm for Tibet that is limited to waving flags and attending events of this type. But what else can they do if they condemn the Chinese authorities' treatment of my people? Ought they to stay at home instead? Should they throw stones at the Chinese embassy? I believe a demonstration is a better option, at least it shows the politicians that the cause matters to people outside of Tibet.

My mother found her own outlet for her frustration. In her studio, she put all her feelings of helplessness and impotence into her paintings. She chose the Beijing 'bird's nest' stadium designed by Swiss architects as the subject of one of her pictures. Mola spent a lot of time in front of her altar in Berne during this time, praying for the welfare of her fellow Tibetans and all other human beings. Yet as long as our politicians continue to kowtow to the Chinese, we in the West can do nothing more than occasionally demonstrating and informing people about the fate of Tibet. I am determined never to stop standing up for human rights and far-reaching autonomy in Tibet, so that my people do not face the same destiny as the Native Americans or the Australian Aborigines, leading a tragic life as dying races of insignificant and landless folklore performers.

I have no illusions about the fact that we have to be patient when it comes to freedom for all Tibetans. My mother's generation and perhaps even my own may well not experience a genuinely autonomous Tibet. Nevertheless, we have to be aware that Tibet's fate is closely tied to China's incredible economic power. When we demand that our politicians intervene in a region occupied by a state that will soon be the world's most important economic force, we have to bear in mind that there is hardly any product today not bearing the stamp 'Made in China'.

In deference to China, American presidents had not met publicly with the Dalai Lama. President George W. Bush broke the tradition in 2007, when he attended a ceremony in which Congress presented His Holiness with its highest civilian honour, the Congressional Gold Medal. Yet President Obama, when he finally met with the Dalai Lama in February 2010, took pains to avoid the perception that this was a meeting between heads of state, by holding it in the White House Map Room rather than the Oval Office. Even so, China was 'strongly dissatisfied' that the two men had met, and called for the US to make amends. It accused Mr Obama of 'seriously damaging' ties between the two countries, and lodged a formal complaint with the US ambassador to China.

After the meeting with Obama, the Dalai Lama told the press

that he was happy with the visit. He even playfully tossed some snow at reporters. He continues to desire to return to China to advocate greater cultural and religious freedoms for the Tibetan people. He says again and again that he wants only genuine autonomy for Tibet, not independence.

42

Diaspora

My family lives the life of many Tibetan exiles: scattered across the globe, our hearts tied to a homeland that some of us have barely or never seen but love nevertheless, each in our own way. If Tibet were free, I would go there to visit my relatives, but I would never want to live there. Although it is a part of me, it is far removed from the values and ideas with which I grew up. I'm an actress; I want to live where there is a film industry. I want to be part of the pulse of a thriving city; my entire socialization has anchored me in the West.

My mother Sonam is quite different. If Tibet were free, she would return immediately and help to build up the country, perhaps not for ever but for a while at least. She would have a second home there. My parents could never imagine living separately in two different countries, let alone two continents.

And Mola? Even though my grandmother is now over ninety years old, she wouldn't hesitate for one moment to pack up her few belongings and move back to her homeland to live with her relatives in the village where she raised little Sonam and gave birth to her youngest daughter. Her greatest wish is to die in Tibet, accompanied by a lama who can carry out all the important rituals so that nothing stands in the way of a good reincarnation. My greatest pain is that I can do nothing to help Mola fulfil her dream. And that's why I have written this book, in an attempt to prevent the culture, traditions and true story of Mola and Amala's country from being forgotten.

Tibetan culture is upheld today not only by Tibetans living in Tibet, but also by the younger generation who were born or grew up in the diaspora. Many young people have been trained in the Buddhist nunneries and monasteries of India and Nepal to teach in Asia, or have emigrated to Europe or the USA. More and more people in the West are interested in Buddhism.

Many years ago, friends of my parents in Switzerland sent their two sons, both of whom had been recognized as incarnations of deceased lamas, to India. One of the boys couldn't cope with living there. He left his monastery, returned to Europe and is now married and lives in Germany. His brother has since become a guru himself. I can hardly believe that the boy who chased around the front gardens of Münchwilen with me and mowed our lawn, which his parents objected to because he might kill insects, is now a high lama. He lives in a Tibetan monastery in the south of India, and spends several months of every year travelling, giving teachings, keeping in touch with other Asian, European and American rinpoches and building global networks for his monastery. He speaks not only fluent Tibetan, Hindi, and Chinese, but also English, German and of course Swiss German. My one-time playmate is so much more modern than I am. Even though I can make confident use of mobile phones, the internet and email, he has as many email clients, VoIP accounts and video streams on his telephone as other people have keys jangling on their key rings. His laptop and telephone connect him to the entire world, he listens to the latest soul music on his iPod, and when he is meditating in the temple he sets his phone to vibration mode so that it doesn't disturb the other worshippers when it rings – even in the temple, he always wants to know who's calling.

This monk is a wonderful Buddhist, a magnificent person, a clever problem-solver, but he is nothing like the Tibetan Buddhists of Mola's era, for whom contemplation, emptiness and spirituality take pride of place. He represents a modern interpretation of Buddhism, which I admire but which shows me that the old Tibet that my grandmother resurrects every day in her practice will soon cease to exist. This Tibet is disappearing not only because the Chinese have occupied our country, but because the people who knew it will soon no longer be alive. Yet Tibetans have to change, and they will change, like all the other people on our planet. If only the process were guided by Tibetans themselves and not by a foreign power that wants to force its own, very different form of development upon them. Unfortunately, whenever a Tibetan still living in Tibet fights for freedom, they risk their lives or face imprisonment.

Exile changes individuals, and Tibetans are no exception, not even the gurus they so idolize. Some of them lose touch with their faith when they are suddenly worshipped and waited on hand and foot by European or American Buddhists. Sometimes they abandon the core of their beliefs – having no ties to worldly things – and devote themselves to the lives of comfort that their Western fans enable, wearing expensive watches and staying in luxury hotels. The Dalai Lama is a shining example to all those who have not succumbed to this trend. Despite his numerous contacts with stars and politicians, despite his travels around the globe, he still has his feet firmly on the ground. He comes across as a simple monk, in all his modesty, directness and lack of possessions, in his one hundred per cent devotion to his religion, his people – and to every individual he meets.

Epilogue

In 2008 my *pala* became Chief Curator at the Rubin Museum of Art in New York, organizing wonderful exhibitions of the art and culture of Tibet and the Himalayan nations. Pala would never call himself a Buddhist, but to us he is one; he has few ties to worldly things and he personifies the Buddhist virtues of modesty, calm, honesty, harmony and charity. He supports those who are less well off, both socially and economically, and has spent many years working for an aid organization for the Third World.

Since my parents have been living in New York, that city has become a new base for our family. We all meet for the Christmas holidays at their Chelsea apartment. I fly from LA; Mola and Tashi come from Switzerland. My brother was a teacher in Zurich for four years, in an area with many immigrant children, who were very fond of him. He would spend his free Saturdays at basketball training with the kids, helping children from around the world to integrate into Swiss life. He has since become an artist. He still lives in Zurich but he often visits Berne, staying with Mola in our family's old Swiss home.

Our family gathering is a wonderful reunion. Sonam bubbles over with her impressions of New York. She finds the city fascinating, enjoying its cultural diversity and its many inspirations. My *amala* is now fifty-six, but at times she looks like a little girl, impish, curious and alert. She wears her hair in a makeshift bun; her black curls constantly threaten to explode from all the creative tension in her head. My mother is an artist, creating abstract paintings and installations that reflect the world's problems; thoughts and new forms and colours are permanently brewing in her head. I can see all that just by looking at her.

She didn't find it easy to adapt to her new home. My mother tends to stick to routines and habits, quite unlike my father. She had problems dealing with the dirt and the summer heat of New York City, but most of all with the noise. The city emits a constant background buzz of air-conditioning, subway trains, street sounds and sirens, a buzz that never stops entirely, even at night. In the beginning she greatly missed silence – the absolute silence of her early life in Pang, which she also experienced in Switzerland whenever she retreated to the mountains for a few days' peace.

She is happier now. She has gradually learned that she can blend in with her new surroundings just as a chameleon adapts to the colours around it. But she is still appalled by the sights she sees every day in New York, by the many beggars and homeless people, the hopeless figures at the subway entrances, the people clothed in rags pushing trolleys piled high with cans and deposit bottles, which is their only way of raising cash, and in stark contrast by the wealth and the waste she comes across at every turn in Manhattan. She finds the obvious power of money in New York and especially the behaviour of super-rich men very disturbing. She can hardly believe that so much injustice goes unameliorated, often even unnoticed, in this wealthy country.

The longer she lives in the USA, the more she discovers things she would never have thought possible: that no other country in the world has such a high percentage of prison inmates, that the percentage of black and Hispanic prisoners is astronomically higher than their actual share of the population, that almost forty million Americans live below the poverty line and have either limited access to health care or none at all. The most shocking thing for her is that many US states still enact the death penalty. She found a studio where she could work all these perceptions and reactions into her art.

New York reminds my *amala* more and more of her time as a stone-breaker in northern India. Back then, she and Mola experienced how dependent they were on the people who employed them: they got work when it suited their employers; when the employers didn't pay their wages, they had no choice but to put up with it. Having got to know a different world in Switzerland, she experiences the ruthless capitalism of mid-twentieth-century India once again in New York City, where the links between power and money are demonstrated every hour.

Mola copes much better with the complexities of the modern world. On her first visit to New York, she gazed with an expressionless face at the towering façades of the skyscrapers lining the streets, something she had never seen in her life – until she discovered a familiar sign on the roof of a building, for the Swiss bank UBS. My grandmother still has such sharp eyes! Her response to the mass of clashing neon billboards on Times Square was: 'My neck hurts from all this looking up. The houses are so high that I have to hold my head too far back to see their ends.' When we took her up one of the skyscrapers, she simply looked down at the ground and said she felt dizzy. 'Isn't it incredible that people can live up here?' she asked, not expecting an answer.

Even in New York, Mola's favourite activity is sitting on her bed, slipping her 108 prayer beads through her wrinkled fingers, murmuring prayers to the scent of burning incense. The only difference from her practice in Berne is that the offerings she uses for her prayers go not to the sparrows, but to the northern cardinals. My *mola* loves the bright red birds in my parents' tiny New York garden. And she is no longer alone with her contemplation; my *amala* has begun reciting the old prayers from her childhood again. Line by line the long-forgotten verses have come back to her, and from time to time she murmurs them to herself quietly. She does this not because a new faith has awoken within her, but because these prayers soothe her mind, because she recognizes herself in them and feels a bit closer to her roots.

These roots have given Mola an inner peace and strength her whole life long. In Berne, she has an altar in her room with a Buddha statue and pictures of the Dalai Lama and her rinpoche, along with small statues of Tibetan deities and a dish of dried leaves from Tibet, from the banks of the holy lake Basum Tso. She would never have bought any of these items herself; she doesn't approve of hoarding possessions. Nearly everything on her altar came to her as a gift from someone, or as something she found. Some are the remains of objects that are no longer of any use to others. Despite this, for her the altar makes the house a holy site, around which she can walk to perform *kora*, which she does every day, acknowledging the neighbours who stop to chat with her, probably taking her routine for a sprightly pensioner's daily walk. In New York, Mola has her altar next to her bed, albeit in a very compact form: a photo of the Dalai Lama, a picture of Dudjom Rinpoche and a small Buddha statue. She therefore performs *kora* around the block of my parents' Chelsea apartment.

When I see my grandmother walking the streets of Chelsea, a

311

nun with closely cropped snow-white hair, wearing her reddish-orange *chupa*, a silent smile on her face, performing her *kora* amongst all the busy, rushing people of Manhattan, I instinctively think of the Four Noble Truths of Buddhism. Life is suffering; that is the first truth. The origin of suffering is attachment, the second truth tells us. Attachment and thus suffering can be overcome by a virtuous life and meditation is the third truth. And the fourth tells us how to live a virtuous life, which includes the 'noble eightfold path', the path that Mola has taken all through her life and that leads her ever closer to her destination.

It is my greatest wish that I too find it within me to walk the path of my own strength.

Acknowledgements

I would like to thank my grandmother Kunsang Wangmo, my mother Sonam Dolma Brauen and my father Martin Brauen for standing by me in researching my family history with all their great knowledge, resourceful help and deep love. Without you, there would be no book. My heartfelt thanks also go to Lukas Lessing for his support.

Thank you to my agent Lianne Kolf and Isabel Schickinger. I will always be grateful to Guido Föhrweißer, who believed in me and was always there for me. *Merci* to my brother Tashi, my grandmother Ula Brauen, Tamdin, Heike Fademrecht, Martina Harrer, Nina Hauser, Lexy Rapsomanikis, Gerold Wunstel, Garo Kuyumcuovic, Dominique Schilling, Georg Georgi, Barbara Ryter, Andreas Messerli, Yangchen Lhamo Tagsar, Jampa Tagsar, Kavie Barnes, Hansjörg Sahli and my German publishing house Heyne Verlag, who enabled us to publish our story; Ulrich Genzler, Heike Plauert, Claudia Limmer, Sabine Hellebrand and Johann Lankes, thanks for your hard work. A big thank you to my British and American publishing houses Harvill Secker and St Martin's Press, and the editors there who worked on the book: Rebecca Carter, Lindsay Sagnette and Daniela Rapp. Thanks also to editor Ann Patty who played such a crucial part in the process. And a special thank you to the four young men who have been keeping an eye on my *mola* since my parents moved to New York: Kaspar 'Wüdu' Sutter, Christoph 'Stobal' Frey, Christian Schneider and Pierre Strauss.

Last but not least, I would like to express my gratitude to all those who work for freedom and autonomy for Tibet and the preservation of the Tibetan culture. Without them, the homeland of my *mola* and my *amala* and thereby my country too would be a blank spot on the map and the fate of my people would be absolutely unknown.

Timeline

1911 End of the Qing Dynasty in China. The country becomes a republic and Chinese troops leave Tibet.

1913 Thubten Gyatso, the 13th Dalai Lama, returns from exile in Sikkim and declares Tibetan independence on 14 February; however, he fails to make efforts towards international recognition for the country.

1914 In the Shimla Convention, representatives of Britain, China and Tibet draw up the borders between the then British India, Tibet and China. They establish Chinese suzerainty over Tibet, with China controlling foreign affairs and Tibetan autonomy on domestic issues, yet the Chinese never ratify the agreement.

1917 The Tibetan army recaptures the majority of the province of Kham, previously occupied by the Chinese.

1924 The 9th Panchen Lama Thubten Chökyi Nyima flees to Inner Mongolia after a dispute with the 13th Dalai Lama, coming under Chinese influence.

1935 Birth of Tenzin Gyatso, the 14th Dalai Lama, *kundun*, or 'teacher of wisdom'.

1949 Foundation of the People's Republic of China under the leadership of Mao Zedong, who immediately exerts Chinese claims over Tibet.

1950 Chinese invasion of eastern Tibet. The fifteen-year-old 14th Dalai Lama is enthroned prematurely in view of the threat from China.

1951 On 23 May, representatives of Tibet and China sign the Seventeen-Point Agreement for the Peaceful Liberation of Tibet in Peking, in which the Chinese promise the Tibetans political autonomy and freedom of religion in return for control of foreign trade, foreign policy and defence. Tibet thus formally becomes part of the People's Republic of China. On 24 October, the Dalai Lama also agrees to the treaty, under duress from Chinese troops occupying the entire country, to avoid 'the complete destruction of Tibet'. To this day the Chinese government has yet to fulfil the most important point, Tibetan autonomy on domestic policy.

1954 The 14th Dalai Lama travels to Peking at Mao's invitation, and is elected there as a 'deputy chairman of the Standing Committee of the National People's Congress' in the hope of gaining an influence over Tibetan policy. His aim is peaceful co-existence between the two nations.

1956 Armed Tibetan rebels fight against the increasingly brutal Chinese occupation in the eastern Tibetan provinces of Kham and Amdo. China increases its military presence in response.

1959 On 10 March, a Tibetan uprising against the Chinese occupation breaks out in Lhasa, costing tens of thousands of Tibetan lives. The People's Liberation Army fires at the Dalai Lama's summer residence, the Norbulingka, prompting the Dalai Lama to flee to India with his loyal supporters on 17 March.

1964   The Panchen Lama accuses China of genocide of the Tibetans and is thereupon arrested by the Chinese.

1965   Formal foundation of the Tibet Autonomous Region (TAR) as part of the People's Republic of China; however it does not include the entire territory of Tibet. Large areas of eastern Tibet remain in the Chinese provinces of Sichuan and Qinghai, small parts in Yunnan and Gansu.

1967–76 During the Cultural Revolution Chinese soldiers, Red Guards and agitated civilians destroy almost 6,000 Buddhist temples and monasteries. Hundreds of thousands of Tibetans die or disappear.

1976   Following Mao Zedong's death on 9 September, the man presumably responsible for more than forty million deaths, the political pressure lessens across the whole of the People's Republic of China.

1979–86 A further wave of liberalization in Tibet under the Chinese reformer and head of state Deng Xiaoping. Religious freedoms are reintroduced, monasteries are renovated and monks begin to be trained again.

1987–89 Demonstrations for Tibetan independence in Lhasa are brutally suppressed by the Chinese military.

1989   The 14th Dalai Lama receives the Nobel Peace Prize, with the world's media focusing on oppressed Tibet for the first time.

1995   The 14th Dalai Lama recognizes the six-year-old Gedhun Choekyi Nyima as 11th Panchen Lama. The Chinese, however, appoint the six-year-old Gyaincain Norbu as 11th Panchen Lama. Strongly influenced by the Chinese, he still holds this office to this day, unacknowledged by the Dalai Lama and most other Tibetans. Gedhun Choekyi Nyima is abducted and has never been seen since.

319

2001 Moscow protest by the Tibetan Youth Association against the awarding of the Olympic Games to Beijing.

2007 The newly built Beijing–Lhasa railway line starts operating, encouraging mass immigration of Han Chinese to Tibet.

2008 Non-violent demonstrations by Tibetan monks marking the 49th anniversary of the 1959 Tibetan uprising lead to violent clashes between Tibetan youths and Chinese security forces on the streets of Lhasa, crushed with great brutality by Chinese police and military.

2008 The 29th Summer Olympics take place in Beijing, regardless of international protests against China's occupation of Tibet.

2009 The 14th Dalai Lama declares his struggle for Tibetan independence a failure. The Tibetans cancel their celebrations of the Losar New Year festival for the first time in human memory, against express Chinese orders to celebrate the most important festival of the year as usual.

2009 On the occasion of the 50th anniversary of the 1959 Tibetan uprising, the Chinese security authorities increase the pressure on Tibet, particularly on monks, dissenters and sympathisers with the Dalai Lama, with the aim of smothering unrest around the country. The Chinese declare the date of the Tibetan defeat a national holiday, the 'Day of Liberation from Slavery'. Once again, they close the Tibetan borders to journalists and foreign travellers. The first death sentences are passed against Tibetans involved in the demonstrations of spring 2008. At the time of publication, hundreds of similar cases were pending.

2010 A shocking earthquake strikes Tibet. There are estimates of more than 400 dead and 10,000 wounded, mostly farmers and nomads in the province of Qinghai, where the 14th Dalai Lama was born. The Chinese authorities promise immediate aid, less out of concern for Tibetans than fear of political riots. Tibet also has landslides and floods, some of them a direct consequence of the reckless Chinese policy of felling Tibetan forests and exploiting natural resources. A more insidious cause is climate change. Experts claim that heavy showers and storms are connected with the major increase of the air pollution over China.

Addresses

Tibetan Youth Association in Europe (TYAE)

The largest Tibetan youth organization in Europe runs campaigns on political issues and organizes events on Tibetan culture.

Binzstraße 15

CH-8045 Zurich

Switzerland

Phone: +41 (0)79 5068512

www.vtje.org

International Campaign for Tibet (ICT)

For more than twenty years, over 100,000 supporters have been speaking with one voice, heard all around the world. Offices in Washington DC, Amsterdam, Brussels and Berlin, field teams in Dharamsala (India) and Kathmandu (Nepal).

1825 Jefferson Place NW

Washington DC 20036

USA

Phone: +1 202 7851515
www.savetibet.org

Students for a Free Tibet (SFT)

Student organization of Tibetans and non-Tibetans running international campaigns for freedom in Tibet.

602 East 14th Street, 2nd Floor
New York
NY 10009
USA
Phone: +1 212 3580071
www.studentsforafreetibet.org

International Tibet Support Network (ITSN)

ITSN is a global coalition of Tibet-related non-governmental organizations.

c/o Tibet Society UK
Unit 9, 139 Fonthill Road
London N4 3HF
United Kingdom
www.tibetnetwork.org

The Tibet Connection

Radio station and internet database for up-to-date information on Tibet.

www.thetibetconnection.org

The Tibet Office (USA)

The official agency of H.H. the Dalai Lama and the Tibetan Administration in Exile to the Americas.

241 East 32nd Street

New York, 10016

Phone: +1 212 2135010

www.tibetoffice.org

The Tibet Office (UK)

The Office of Tibet in London is an official agency of His Holiness the Dalai Lama.

1 Culworth Street

London NW8 7AF

Phone: +44 (0)20 77225378

www.tibet.com

The New York Rubin Museum of Art

The New York Rubin Museum of Art, where my father is Chief Curator, is world-renowned in its field, showing art from Tibet and the Himalayan nations.

150 W 17th Street

New York

NY 10011

USA

Phone: +1 212 6205000

www.rmanyc.org

Family websites:

My personal site: www.yangzombrauen.com

My mother Sonam's *tsampa* company: www.tsampa.ch

My mother Sonam's art: www.sonam.net